Philip Mulvey is a specialist in soil and water chemistry with over forty years' experience in soil science, land repair, and groundwater. He is founder of the leading Australian environmental geo-science group EESI Group; was co-founder of 3D-Ag, a sustainable farm systems consultancy; and CEO of Carbon Count, the world's first commercially available online soil carbon project management software. Phil is part consultant, part researcher and part entrepreneur. He has made it his personal mission to restore 10 per cent of the world's degraded land in his lifetime.

Freya Mulvey is a commercial lawyer and environmental enthusiast. In 2017 she won the National Civil Justice Award for championing the rights of Timorese seaweed farmers in the Montara class action. Freya is Phil's youngest daughter.

GROUND BREAKING

Soil Security and Climate Change

PHILIP MULVEY & FREYA MULVEY

KERR
Melbourne, Victoria

First published 2023
Kerr Publishing Pty Ltd
Melbourne, Victoria
ABN 64 124 219 638

© 2023 Philip Mulvey and Freya Mulvey

This book is copyright. Apart from fair dealing for the purpose of private study, research, criticism or review, or under Copyright Agency Ltd rules of recording, no part may be reproduced by any means.
The moral right of the author has been asserted.

Opinions expressed in this book are those of the authors and are not the views of any past or present employers or affiliated organisations.

ISBN 978-1-875703-56-2
ISBN 978-1-875703-57-9 (eBook)

BIC Category:	RNU EARTH SCIENCES/Environmental Management/Sustainability
BISAC Category 1:	SCI019000 SCIENCE/Earth Science/General
BISAC Category 2:	TEC003000 TECHNOLOGY & ENGINEERING/Agriculture/General
BISAC Category 3:	NAT036000 NATURE/Weather

Cover photograph: J M Hacker
Cover and book design: Paul Taylder of Xigrafix Media & Design
Typeset in Adobe Caslon Pro 11/15pt

National Library of Australia PrePublication Data Service:

 A catalogue record for this book is available from the National Library of Australia

*For Allison and the grand-babies,
and all future grandchildren the world over*

Contents

Prologue	1
Introduction	5
Chapter 1 — Soil Security	15
Chapter 2 — The Science	33
Chapter 3 — Climate Change	73
Chapter 4 — Should We Have Known?	97
Chapter 5 — Agricultural Practices' Impact on Soil	127
Chapter 6 — The Emergence of Regenerative Agriculture	141
Chapter 7 — Carbon Sequestration in Soil	151
Chapter 8 — Australia in Focus	163
Chapter 9 — Environmental Law in Australia	169
Chapter 10 — Economic Imperative	181
Chapter 11 — Acid Sulfate Soils	187
Chapter 12 — A Solution	193
Chapter 13 — Land Management for Climate Change	219
Appendix	223
Acknowledgements	227
Endnotes	229
Acronyms and Abbreviations	243

Of Attica:

The land was the best in the world, and was therefore able in those days to support a vast army, raised from the surrounding people. Even the remnant of Attica which now exists may compare with any region in the world for the variety and excellence of its fruits and the suitableness of its pastures to every sort of animal … but in those days the country was fair as now and yielded far more abundant produce … Many great deluges have taken place in the 9000 years … since the time of which I am speaking … and during all this time and through so many changes, there has never been any considerable accumulation of the soil coming down from the mountains, as in other places, but the earth has fallen away all round and sunk out of sight. The consequence is, that in comparison of what then was, there are remaining only the bones of the wasted body … all the richer and softer parts of the soil having fallen away, and the mere skeleton of the land being left … Its mountains were high hills covered in soil, and the plains … were full of rich earth, and there was an abundance of wood in the mountains … Moreover, the land reaped the benefit of the annual rainfall, not as now losing the water which flows off the bare earth into the sea, but, having an abundant supply in all places, and receiving it into herself and treasuring it up in the close clay soil, it let off into the hollows the streams which it absorbed from the heights, providing everywhere abundant fountains and rivers … such was the natural state of the country, which was cultivated, as we may well believe, by true husbandmen, who made husbandry their business, and were lovers of honour, and of a noble nature, and had a soil the best in the world, and abundance of water, and in the heaven above an excellently attempered climate.

Plato, *Critias* dialog, 360 BCE

Prologue

In 1859 thirteen wild European rabbits were imported into south-east Australia and released for sport shooting. Their number exploded, and within decades they had spread across most of the continent, devastating crops and native vegetation, eroding soils and hurting economies from the family farm to the colonies' accounts.

To mitigate the rabbits' destructive scourge and slow their spread, in the first years of the 20th century Western Australia built the world's longest fence. Between 1901 and 1907, the 3256 km or 2023 mile rabbit-proof fence was installed. It was built to help control the rabbits in the south-west of the state, where native vegetation was cleared for the planting of crops, fields of golden wheat especially, sown in winter and harvested in spring or summer. Eventually, 130 000 km^2, an area the size of England or Alabama, was cropland. Whereas large portions of the eastern side, though grazed, remained native vegetation.

After fascinating studies by Murdoch University, led by the late T J Lyons, on rainfall differences either side of the fence in the 1990s, an international academic consortium was formed to study this unusual climate phenomenon. In 2005 the world's largest experiment in climate change and desertification began on the two sides of the fence. The landscape offers striking evidence of the negative impacts of agricultural practices on soil and climate. It became known as 'the Bunny Fence

Experiment', the only regional scale, paired-climate experiment in the world; where a treatment is applied to part of the landscape and not to the equivalent adjacent landscape.

In 2005, 2006 and 2007, led by Undaysankar Nair of the University of Alabama, an international team worked in the field from the late growing season to after harvest to measure east and west of the fence. They released balloons carrying radiosonde instruments which measured altitude, pressure, wind speed and direction, temperature, solid particles, and water-vapor droplet size. They flew two specialised Flinders University aircraft at 10 to 20 m above the canopy, measuring energy flux and fine and ultrafine aerosols. Soil sensors were stuck in the ground, ground stations set up, NASA satellite images studied, and mainframe computers crunched data.

The resulting picture was stark, though expressed in the careful language of the lead scientist. All observations 'suggest that the anthropogenic land use change … may be altering the regional climate'. It was known, and a matter of concern to WA farmers, meteorologists, agricultural experts and government, that since substantive vegetation clearance, rainfall had fallen by 20 per cent in cropland areas. Clouds that formed on the eastern side stopped abruptly and dramatically at The Bunny Fence because the dark vegetation created more turbulent air, compared to agricultural areas, making cloud formation from the condensation of water droplets high in the atmosphere more likely. The study also found extensive removal of native vegetation with deep roots led to a rise in the water table and in turn, increased salinity at the surface. As well as greater fine and ultrafine aerosols in the agricultural areas, making agricultural areas more conducive to the formation of willy-willy's or dust devils. Changes all directly attributed to land use management practices.

There was curiously little reaction in the Australian media, but the *New York Times* saw the implications, reporting Lyons' hopes that the research would help scientists 'understand the relationships between the land surface and atmosphere and to provide ideas for sustainable agricultural practices'.

Government funded work (including the international bodies) seemed to cease in 2007. Caution thrown to the wind.

The findings alone are compelling but they are also corroborated by history. Historical mismanagement of soil and the land has led to desertification and after prolonged decline, the decimation of our bread baskets—eventually the collapse of civilisations. The evidence is clear, making changes in agricultural practice imperative and urgent.

The climate change discussion is saturated but the debate has just begun.

In 1978, when asked by President Jimmy Carter on what the government should do about climate change, scientist Charles Keeling said that 'the problem was far too complicated for people to understand, so focus on greenhouse emissions'.

And so began a self-fulfilling prophecy in which, when examining climate change, we largely failed to consider much else.

The report released following the first World Climate Conference in 1979 records in relation to climate and the future: 'The causes of climate variations are becoming better understood, but uncertainty exists about many of them and their relative importance. Nevertheless, we can say with some confidence that the burning of fossil fuels, deforestation, and changes of land use have increased the amount of carbon dioxide in the atmosphere by about 15 per cent during the last century and it is at present increasing by about 0.4 per cent per year. It is likely that an increase will continue in the future. Carbon dioxide plays a fundamental role in determining the temperature of the earth's atmosphere, and it appears plausible that an increased amount of carbon dioxide in the atmosphere can contribute to a gradual warming of the lower atmosphere, especially at high latitudes. Patterns of change would be likely to affect the distribution of temperature, rainfall and other meteorological parameters, but the details of the changes are still poorly understood.'

Notwithstanding that the details of climate science and their relative importance remained poorly understood, by 1990 the emerging acute focus on GHGs was cemented at the Second World Climate Conference, which led to the negotiation of the United Nations

Framework Convention on Climate Change. Finalised in 1992, the objective was 'stabilizaiton of greenhouse gas concentrations in the atmosphere at a level that would prevent dangerous anthropogenic interference with the climate system'.

Then in 1997 the Kyoto Protocol was adopted based on the scientific consensus that global warming is occurring and that human-made CO_2 emissions are driving it. The narrow focus of climate change discussions continues to this day.

Interestingly, all the while simultaneous global conventions were occurring to combat desertification. Following severe drought in the late 1960s in the Sudano-Sahelian region, the United Nations General Assembly in 1974 passed a resolution to convene the first UN Conference on Desertification in 1977. Conferences dedicated to combating desertification have occurred at various intermissions ever since.

The connection between the two problems, desertification and climate change, remains less well known and understood. The true problem is heat. Discussing what regulates heat opens up the climate change debate. Only by investigating the root problem will we begin to understand the nuances of the individual and collectively complex relationships between terrestrial and atmospheric processes and their effects on local and regional climate.

In this book, drawing upon the work of a range of expert scientists, we contribute to this debate. Concurring with the findings of the Bunny Fence Experiment, we too conclude that the evidence demonstrates that landscape changes principally from agricultural practices, are a major cause of climate change. The state of our land changes how heat is absorbed, processed and emitted, and consequently how heat effects atmospheric processes. We do not ignore the contribution to climate change by CO_2 emissions but growing evidence is accruing that suggests that land use change may be more important. The need for changes in how we manage the land is clear, essential and urgent. We must secure our soil, return the small water cycle and reverse anthropogenic climate change. The long-term survival of humanity depends on it.

Introduction

This book aims to broaden the discussion around what remains the most pressing problem of our time: what is causing climate change?

The answer is heat. What causes and contributes to generating excess heat is at the heart of solving our human-made climate catastrophe. Excess heat starts with land use change and its impact on soil security. Securing our soils is crucial to preserving the clean water we drink, the food we eat and the air we breathe. It is integral to preserving our biodiversity and the ecological sustainability of our environment, as well as regulating our climate. Soil security and climate change are the defining emergencies of our time, and the two are intimately connected, in Australia and globally.

We demonstrate that our landscape practices are as important to climate change as atmospheric processes, of which greenhouse gases (GHGs) are only one. The key to carbon dioxide's (CO_2) strong influence on climate is its ability to absorb heat emitted from our planet's surface, preventing it from escaping out to space. CO_2 and the other GHGs do not in and of themselves generate heat. While GHGs are an important component of climate change, their outsized influence is responsive, not causative.

Australia's former Chief Scientist Dr Alan Finkel stated that 'The first step in developing a solution is to identify the problem'.[1] He explains that preceding the climate change debate is the problem posited by Joseph Fourier in the 19th century, 'What is regulating the earth's temperature?' Fourier was the scientist who in 1824 identified that the atmosphere was keeping the Earth's surface warm like the windows of a greenhouse. In 1896 Swedish chemist Svante Arrhenius developed Fourier's argument, essentially what is now known as the enhanced greenhouse effect.

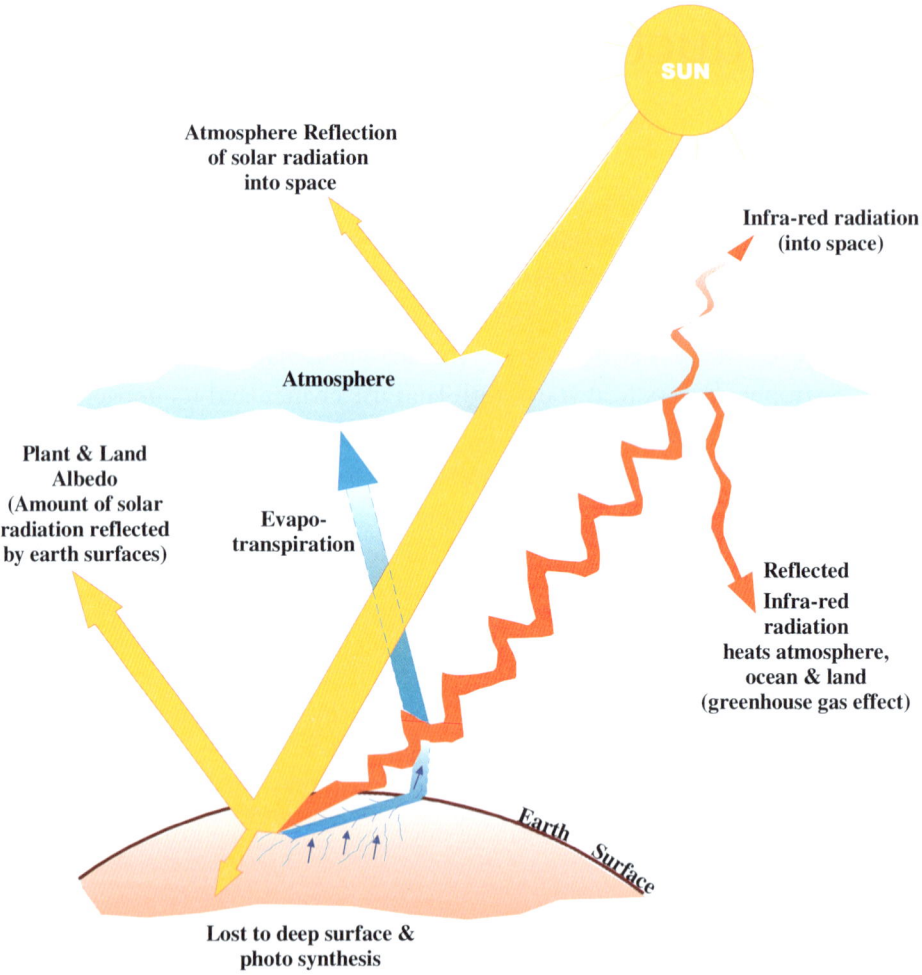

Figure I-1. Fate of solar radiation on Earth and the greenhouse effect

The sun shines through our atmosphere warming the Earth's surface (as shown in Figure I-1). Heat emitted from the sun is solar radiation. When solar radiation, the sun's energy, reaches Earth, some of it is absorbed by the atmosphere, land and ocean, and the rest is reflected back into space as infrared radiation. Arrhenius found that rather than infrared radiation escaping back into space, some was being trapped by GHGs and re-emitted in all directions. That is, GHGs are partly transparent to incoming solar radiation and only reflect a portion of the outgoing infrared radiation back as it is exiting the atmosphere. Some of the re-emitted infrared radiation does escape to space, but the rest further heats the earth's atmosphere, or is absorbed by the land, and the majority, over 90 per cent, is adsorbed by the oceans.[2]

The greenhouse effect is a natural physical process. It is necessary for human survival; without it the Earth's average surface temperature would be too cool. The problem arises when excess heat is absorbed by the land, oceans and atmosphere. Excess heat to the atmosphere is in part due to the enhanced greenhouse effect, when emissions from human activity contribute more heat-absorbing gases to the atmosphere. Increased concentrations of GHGs in the atmosphere in the last 50 years is not natural and contributes to additional warming of the Earth's surface. However, while what is regulating the earth's atmosphere is multifaceted, principally it is a two-step process: a heat source and a blanket.

In concentrating on GHGs, which act as the blanket, investigation and understanding of the heat source has largely been forgotten. The ultimate heat source is the sun's energy which is foremost absorbed by the land. GHGs are not the heat source, but the blanket that only traps outgoing infra-red radiation. The heat source for GHGs to reflect then, is what the land does with solar radiation. Increasing the size of either the way the land processes solar radiation to create infrared radiation or the volume of GHGs in the atmosphere, increases global atmospheric heat. Increasing the size of both accelerates the heat rise having a compounding effect.

Greater investigation and concerted effort directed to addressing the first element of the process, the heat source, and what alters the heat source, is critical to mitigating anthropogenic climate change. While carbon neutrality or decarbonisation are helpful in reducing the blanketing process, and thereby the acceleration of anthropogenic climate change, reaching net zero emissions will not reverse anthropogenic climate change if the source of the infrared radiation is not also reduced. Reducing CO_2 and other GHG emissions alone will simply not be enough. What seems to be missed so often, by scientists and lay people alike, is that the key factor of anthropogenic climate change arises as a result of the increased heat of the Earth's surface caused by our land-management practices.[3] The state of our land changes how heat is absorbed, processed and emitted, and consequently how heat effects atmospheric processes. Poor land management is the cause of excess heat, and GHGs trap and hold that heat.

Sitting beneath it all, is soil. Soil plays a critical role in regulating the earth's temperature. Soil is vital for life, from the smallest organisms to the planetary climate system. Soil is what holds life as we know it together. Soil organic matter is 50 per cent carbon. Carbon today is often misunderstood and wrongly demonised; it is a primary component of all known life on Earth. By gluing soil together, organic matter provides a home for micro-organisms, feeds both micro-and macro-organisms, stores nutrients, resists pH change, and as we set out below, performs many other critical functions. On the macro scale, aerated organic-matter-rich soils protected by vegetation, propagate rainfall into the interior of continents. Soil provides the structure that underpins landscape resilience, and sick soil is a key and under-recognised aspect of climate change.

Through science the key role soil, land and landscape play in regulating our climate is increasingly being recognised in practices such as conservation agriculture, regenerative agriculture and natural-sequence farming. These land-management practices have demonstrated that it is possible to restore degraded land and in so doing restore the small water cycle (when water which evaporates over land returns to the same land in the form of precipitation; locally derived rain). However, the connection between soil as a key environmental function and climate change is less well known and understood.

Soil provides the structure that underpins landscape resilience, but the health of the soil beneath our feet is not obvious, and this lack of awareness results in management practices which degrade soil. Degraded soil drastically increases infrared radiation, a primary driver of climate change. Soil health also has a critical impact on precipitation, as degrading soil health diminishes the small water cycle. Climate change is initially and almost primarily controlled by loss of precipitation from continents. As such, global temperature rise is an inadequate measurement of climate change. We will suggest measurement of precipitation loss predates agreed measurable global temperature increase by at least 20 to 30 years.

Crucially, the complexity of the climate system and the limitation of computing power means caution should be exercised in overreliance on current modelling methods. Nevertheless, given the critical role of science in shaping how we understand climate change and our policy responses, modelling global temperature rise is necessary to explain the range within which an outcome may occur, as well as evaluating impacts of proposed solutions. Even so, we argue that because precipitation is a better precursor of climate change, climate model projections of precipitation must be carried out that account for soil and vegetation season variability, and all associated sensitivity analysis.[4]

Soil and precipitation, especially the small water cycle are interconnected aspects of landscape management. For example, much of southern and central Australia has experienced a reduction in rainfall of as much as 30 per cent in the last 50 years, along with a decrease in rainfall predictability. However, it is not generally recognised that this rainfall loss is directly attributable to degraded soil from agricultural practices.

In Figure I-2, the boundary of the Rabbit Proof Fence in Western Australia stands out and demonstrates the effect of consequent land management practices: on the right the cloud build up over native vegetation is obvious and, on the left there are no clouds over the less

Figure I-2. Aerial view of clouds forming preferentially over native vegetation. J M Hacker in Esaul N, Lyons T J, *Agricultural and Forest Meteorology* 114 (2002) 3–13. Source J M Hacker

vegetated agricultural ground. However, in order to understand that the climatic events captured in the photograph are not a coincidence, first we explain the basic science which underpins the landscape and atmospheric processes at play.

Agricultural mismanagement of soil has historically marked the collapse of civilisations, including the river-dependent people of Mesopotamia through to the rain-fed upland people of ancient Greco-Roman civilisations, to the irrigation-dependent New World of the native American Ancestral Puebloans.

Although soil is the foundation of life, in Australia it is not regulated as an environmental function—in the way that water, air, flora and fauna are. Furthermore, in state government planning acts, agriculture is not subject to the same scrutiny as urban development. Each farm is seen as its own entity and not part of an integrated landscape. The aggregated impact of farms on landscape are not considered in any planning regulation. We contend that the accumulated impact of this neglect is a key factor underpinning continental climate change.

Immediate action is required to develop sustainable solutions for soil security, not just to moderate but to reverse anthropogenic climate change. Soil security is about more than soil health and soil quality, it extends to a qualitative framework of allied soil aspects. For obvious reasons, how we practise agriculture is a key influence on our environment. Landscape resilience, soil and ecosystem health are collectively the components of Natural Capital. Mining soil organic matter and generating bare ground, outcomes of historical and in many instances current agricultural practice, run down our Natural Capital. The running down of Natural Capital has had a huge impact on the productivity and health of our country. Financial Capital is the financial capacity of the farmer to economically run the farm for optimum sustainable return. Currently, and historically, most farms have run down Natural Capital to bolster Financial Capital, which is a false economy and perpetuates a cycle of poor land management.

Maintaining farm profitability, improving Natural Capital while retaining Financial Capital, is key to any proposed solution. Addressing our soil security issue, at a very simplistic level, mandates that we sequester organic matter in soil, create air turbulence by eco-corridors and mitigate and prevent bare ground. As stated above, regenerative agriculture and natural sequence farming demonstrate the success of land remediation, and consequently are a critical part of the solution to anthropogenic climate change.

None of this makes for easy reading. The fact that our agricultural practice is a cause of anthropogenic climate change is disturbing. No one person or policy or event is to blame. The problem is not like previous problems with the environment; it is not a limited number of point sources of pollution which our regulations are equipped to deal with. It is hundreds of incremental, cumulative and diffuse impact sources. It is not what a few did or do, but what many thousands do that impacts the soil, and as a result our climate. The fact that climate change and loss of soil security are interlinked requires not only an understanding of the science and culture of the landscape but a whole new approach to the future.

A whole new regulatory system and a new profession is required to address diffuse sources of activity that have adverse environmental impacts. To succeed, this new approach must involve the whole nation, at every level (individuals, councils, government, media, scientists, peak bodies—everybody). We must design and back a funded landscape management policy framework for a positive way forward. Lore, science, regulation and collective community action is critical every step of the way.

Climate action failure will impact the world far worse than Covid and all other pandemics combined. Famine, heat waves, drought, displacement, migration, extreme climatic events, and wars will follow. But the increased severity of climate-related disasters is preventable. Below we explain how. We step you through the science, policy and regulation around soil security and landscape management, and conclude with recommendations as to how we can better mitigate climate change.

It is not going to be easy and there is no quick fix but reversing anthropogenic climate change is possible. By understanding and managing soil security, we can break new ground in the fight against the collapse of our own civilisation.

The Catalyst

The extreme meteorological events of 2020–21 provide an indication of what climate change offers from now on. At the time of writing, the last six months have seen floods ravage the east coast of Australia, Winter Storm Uri cripple Texas and off-season Cyclone Seroja-Odette, resulting from a rare and spectacular Fujiwhara effect, claiming lives across south-east Indonesia and East Timor. Extreme events continue to test the character of humanity.

Phil Mulvey and I—father/daughter, scientist/lawyer, and baby boomer/millennial—don't always agree, but both of us are frustrated by the misinformation and the misunderstanding that constitute the climate debate in the early 2020s.

The catalyst for writing this book arose when, in all that was necessarily the focus of media attention in 2020, one key event garnered little acknowledgment: the review into Australia's national environmental law, the *Environment Protection and Biodiversity Conservation Act 1999* (EPBC Act). The review is critically important because the EPBC Act underpins the health of our nation's environment. And unbelievably soil is given no consideration in the Act—plants live in it, off it and can't live without it—it has a reciprocal relationship with water—soil is quite simply a crucial part of the answer to securing Australia's long-term economic and environmental future.

For decades my dad's energies have been directed toward nurturing and repairing degraded land. Foremost a soil scientist, he is also a business owner who has been in the landscape remediation/repair business for over 40 years. For most of my childhood the business operated from the same properties on which our family lived. I learned a lot through osmosis and directly from Phil. I am by no means a scientist; Phil explains the science and is lead author. My role in this is as catalyst and contextual narrator. However, it is my understanding of soil science, and my frustration at the lack of coverage linking soil security to climate change, and policy directed to that end, that brought us here in mid-2020.

The year had started with Australia's worst recorded bushfire season Black Summer, COVID was sweeping the world and, about the time I really registered the EPBC Act Review, the West Coast of the US was burning. I had been saying to Phil for some time that in order to make the kind of change he hoped to see in land regeneration and landscape management, he needed to write policy position papers and provide submissions on legislative reform.

So, it was time I put my money where my mouth was. Phil and I worked together to formulate a submission on the interim report on the EPBC Act. In our submission we argued that without including provisions on soil the Act would not achieve its principal objectives: environment protection and biodiversity conservation.

Nothing came of it.

The final review did not provide any commentary on this point, but the momentum to more substantively express ourselves was born. Critical to our conviction was not necessarily the merit of our conclusion but the strength of the scientific method. Applying rigorous scepticism to test and verify assumptions—and to generate robust debate.

Subsequently, the 2020 Royal Commission into National Natural Disaster Arrangements and the State of the Climate 2020 reports were released. Both paint a dire picture of our future and speak more of climate adaptation than mitigation. In yet more evidence of our deteriorating climate, 2020 was declared the second hottest year on record (behind 2016), being almost 1° C above average. Such grave and fatalistic—unnecessarily disempowering—reporting only served to spur Phil and I on. Like a growing number of others in the scientific community, Phil's work was revealing a different and more hopeful solution.

There is much hope. That is why it was important for us to write this book.

Chapter 1

Soil Security

Temperature regulation, desertification and the small water cycle

'Soil security' is a term applied to the premise that terrestrial life is ultimately dependent upon soil for its survival. It would not be wrong to say the ancestral roots for modern science stem from human's efforts to understand the importance of soil security. The word 'chemistry' is derived from the ancient Greek word '*Khemia*', used to describe Egypt, and is based on the Egyptian word '*Khami*' describing the healthy fertile black soil of the Nile basin, Egyptian land. Soil and chemistry were initially interlinked with landscape health and people's wellbeing. In many traditional cultures soil, land and behaviour are seen as one continuum necessary for existence.

The term soil security as we have applied it, is similarly all-inclusive. To assist in developing a common language, we adopt Bennet *et al's* definition of soil security: 'the Soil Security concept incudes consideration of other allied soil facets, including societal connections, education, policy, legislation, current land use, the requirement for conservation, condition, and the economic and natural value of our soils. Soil Security does not simply identify discrete soils, rather it aims to quantify additional pressures which could result in soil becoming unsustainable or insecure. Quantification provides a framework for realizing the potential for improved productivity, function, and ecosystem services. In this way, Soil Security is much more than soil health, or soil quality.'[5]

Through landscape management practices, soil is vulnerable to changes in land use, vegetative cover, plants and their dead matter. In turn, these practices impact atmospheric processes including, among other things, the small water cycle, changes in weather and climate change.

As well as climate change, poor soil security underpins many of our modern 'existential' crises, including water and food security, human health, and environment and biodiversity loss. Despite soil being an essential and precious part of life, as well as a non-renewable resource and a major asset underpinning our agricultural productivity, we have not carefully managed or cared for it. The absence of soil security has increased the duration and severity of our droughts, with resultant bushfires and floods of increased intensity, for example the February 2019 Townsville floods.

It is well understood that Australia's soils are comparatively old and infertile, and yet we continue to exacerbate soil degradation through our actions. Soil degradation includes acidification, salination, erosion and loss of soil carbon, ultimately leading to desertification. How we degrade our soils will be discussed in detail later, but principally includes predominant farming practices and land clearing, including land banking properties. Bare ground is blasphemy to soil security.

A number of scientists worldwide, including hydrologists, meteorologists and soil scientists, believe the greatest anthropogenic impact on climate change is not CO_2 emissions, but the land use changes we have made, in particular how we practise agriculture.[6]

Soil security is crucial to landscape health and climate. Soil security is dependent on suitable organic matter to achieve an aerated soil which is a direct measure of soil resilience and health. A key feature of achieving appropriate organic carbon levels is with plant cover. Carbon is a key component of soil organic matter and a lack of carbon in soil is a precursor to reduced soil security, resulting in significant land degradation and all the consequences of this: habitat fragmentation; invasive species; compacted, impenetrable soils leading to increased runoff; salination; increase in sensible heat; a poor local water cycle, and so on. In addition, the lack of carbon in soil is also the key component in rainfall loss across Australia, resulting in prolonged droughts leading to catastrophic fires, increase in frosts, as well as increased intensity of floods.

Though it is well known that soil organic matter is important for many soil functions and as the primary indicator for soil health, its impact on regional climate is not well known. The impact of degrading soil security as the root cause of degraded landscapes remains unrecognised. Similarly, while the regenerative farming movement has to an extent recognised the emergence of soil security as a systems crisis, the movement is still nascent and not yet capable of having wide impact. So, it is imperative that steps to secure the health of our soils are accelerated.

'Soil security' was a phrase coined by Alex McBratney from Sydney University,[7] and it is time Australia again took the lead in pioneering further change in landscape management worldwide. In Australia, the need to respond to the soil security crisis was aptly described by a number of eminent Australian scientists in a 2019 paper titled 'Soil Security for Australia', which concluded: 'This soil security concept is motivated by sustainable development and is driven by the need to: secure food and fiber production that is not only productive, but profitable; preserve our biodiversity; and contribute to our water and climate sustainability. All of these drivers are critical to human health and the health of our nation and planet.'[8]

The escalation of environmental challenges heightens the urgency for responsive action. It is critical that soil security is recognised, communicated and discussed broadly. Now is the time for a major co-operative effort. Hopefully this effort will be applied through evidence-based, bipartisan policy-making and will include reframing the EPBC Act to include soil as an additional environmental function worthy of protection, as we do for air and water.

A choice between the economy and soil security is not required.

Solutions are already being discussed which using market forces benefit both. These include moving from homogenous commodities such as corn, wheat, beef and soybeans; to working through contracts, local markets, and other avenues to produce commodities that more directly supply consumer demand. Changes can be encouraged through social licensing of projects to ensure the approval and ongoing acceptance of the local community; as well as incentives and subsidies to drive change to secure the future prosperity of Australia. Making these changes is not an option: connection to soil and knowing and valuing soil as one of Australia's greatest assets, is essential.

The Aboriginal custodianship of Australia is currently thought to be more than 65 000 years old. At our existing rate of soil mining our custodianship will be lucky to go another 100 years.

After the Great Depression and the Dust Bowl years of the 1930s, President Roosevelt said, 'the nation that destroys its soil destroys itself', thereby creating an essential platform for the development of the US. Since then, American soil scientists from each generation have produced books—for example W C Lowdermilk 1953, D Hillel 1992 and D Montgomery 2012—setting out the proof that most civilisations have collapsed through agricultural mismanagement of soil. It is time we paid heed to what is now a truism.

Understanding the soil security crisis

Desertification, the outcome of poor landscape management, has been demonstrated by the collapse of numerous civilisations.[9] Desertification is a type of land degradation occurring mainly in medium to low latitudes, in which soil organic matter is lost due to natural processes or induced directly as a result of human agronomic practices. In 1986 it was predicted desertification is likely to decimate all the bread baskets of the world within 50 years.[10] Knowing this makes changes in agricultural practise in Australia urgent.

Soil organic matter improves soil infiltration, and reduces runoff, rain-drop erosion and dispersion of soils. It also minimises sensible heat, reduces diurnal temperature variation, increases available moisture to plants, reduces albedo from the soil (which burns the underside of plants), reduces bulk density by fluffing the soil up, overcomes some impacts of sodicity (sodium salts cause certain soil to rapidly erode) and salinity, adsorbs many toxins, protects and anchors plants, filters groundwater and, with vegetative cover, creates the small water cycle, which minimises the impact of drought. That is, aerated, organic-matter-rich soils, are critically important as the foundation of many crucial environmental and atmospheric processes.

The consequences when organic matter in soil approaches zero is demonstrated by examining what happened in the Middle East, the home of Western agriculture. Agriculture appeared on the Iranian Plateau about 12 000 years ago. While the regional climate has not significantly changed, the vegetation cover has, to the extent that most of the area is now desert. This process started with the reduction of vegetative cover as a result of agriculture, leading to a loss of soil organic matter. First, commencing in Mesopotamia, a period of about 7000 years of agriculture and forestry during which timber was removed for fuel, construction and iron forges. As the land lost its productivity, the centre of the civilisation moved northward. About 2000 years before the present, under Roman occupation of the lands formerly farmed by the Natufian Culture, agriculture intensified primarily in Israel and Lebanon.

When the forest and woodlands were removed from the Levant, biotic pumping stopped. Biotic pumping is a process by which vegetation, particularly forest cover, spreads rainfall from the coast to the interior of continents. Initially without forests, and then loss of woodland cover, the spread of rain inland reduced, consequently the land was replaced by savannah. Removal of trees within the first 600 kilometres of the coast resulted in the loss of agricultural production further inland and ultimately the creation of arid vegetation.

Finally, the process of desertification was completed in recent regional wars, in particular the Gulf Wars and the 30 or so years of consequent civil unrest, which included the burning of marshlands, concentrated bombing and the intense uncontrolled use of 4x4 vehicles across the dunes.[11] Grass-cover and soil organic matter in this area was further reduced and vegetative regrowth prevented, creating classic drifting sand-dune deserts.

Consequences of desertification include elevated sensible heat levels—heat that you can feel—which leads to the loss of the small water cycle. Essentially, sensible heat is the energy moving from one system to another that results in changes in the temperature. In 2019 in Kuwait, in the region of southern Mesopotamia, the resultant massive build-up of sensible heat caused record breaking extreme temperatures of 68° C. Now most of the area is devoid of all vegetation and the soil contains almost no organic matter, causing massive drift from sand dunes, a major problem for Kuwait since the first Gulf War.

Similarly, over the past two centuries in Australia, the natural ecology has been subject to considerable modification, largely due to land use and management practices. We estimate, vegetative cover before 1788 had dropped from nearly 100 per cent in an average season, to a continental average of below 30 per cent in the early 1980s. Since the 1980s due to the introduction of greater conservation agricultural practices vegetation cover has increased by about 6 per cent, mostly in the northern arid and semi-arid parts of Australia,[12] but in the southern arable portion vegetation has continued to decline. Contamination, urban encroachment and damage caused by the mining sector are also significant causes of degraded land, but the greatest cause is agriculture.

It appears likely that before colonialisation by Europeans, all aspects of the Australian landscape were actively managed by the Aborigines in a proto-agricultural manner,[13] with nearly complete vegetative cover in all but severe droughts.[14] Depending on where you are in Australia and relying on written records of explorers in the mid-19th century, organic carbon levels in soil from areas under agriculture production of 10 to 20 years were possibly around 2 to 4 per cent and as high as 10 per cent.[15] Unwittingly, our agricultural practices have mined organic matter from our soils so that currently soil organic carbon in the eastern wheat belt is typically below 0.8 per cent, whereas in the western wheat belt in the clay areas it is around 0.4 per cent, and on the sand country organic carbon can be as low as 0.1 per cent.[16]

Sensible and latent heat

Greater than 95 per cent of incoming radiation from the sun is converted to one of two types of heat: latent heat and sensible heat. Latent heat is used in the phase change of materials from one state to another: solid to liquid and liquid to gas; for example, snow melt and water from lakes to clouds. Sensible heat is the heat that is removed from or added to a system in which there is no change of state, just a change in temperature.

This distinction is best illustrated through an experiment.

- Step 1: put a thermometer calibrated to 600° C in a large pot of water and heat the pot. The temperature of the water increases to 100° C and then stops and remains at 100° C while there is water in the pot. No matter how high the heating knob is set, while the water is boiling, the water temperature will not exceed 100° C.
- Step 2: place the empty pot on the stove and set the heating knob to medium. The temperature rises rapidly past 100° C and soon the thermometer will read above 550° C and the base of the pot may become red. Turn the knob to off and allow the pot to cool.

In *Step 1*, once the water reaches 100° C, the water temperature does not change because the energy is being converted to latent heat as a result of changing the state of the water from liquid to gas. In *Step 2*, as energy is added it is converted to sensible heat and causes a temperature rise in the pot. Sensible heat increasingly agitates the atoms of a material in one state (gets hotter), which, when energy application ceases to be applied (gets cooler) releases infrared radiation as the material returns to the former level of rest. In the same way, in the case of land, when the radiant energy of the sun causes the land temperature to rise it is called 'sensible heat'.

This experiment demonstrates why having land with vegetative cover is so crucial. Plants store water and help to trap water in the soil by providing the substrate for organic matter. The sensible heat is small, latent heat dominates when the land is fully vegetated. Furthermore, by facilitating infiltration and water recovery through plant roots, organic matter increases plant available water, known by farmers as PAW, as a proportion of the total moisture content of the soil, promoting further increases in latent heat.

In the case of soil security there is complete vegetative cover — a lush meadow, rich pasture or open forest — and incoming solar radiation that is not reflected is converted to greater than 75 per cent latent heat and less than 20 per cent sensible heat. Changing the lush meadow to a bare paddock will cause the ratio to flip between the two heats, to 20 per cent latent and 75 per cent sensible heat (the remaining 5 per cent is lost into deep earth and to photosynthesis—Figure I-1 on page 6). This is presented graphically in Figure 1.2, using data first published in 2007 in Slovakia by Michal Kravcík, et al.[17] Kravcík was among the earliest to realise rainfall patterns are key to climate change.

This heat exchange response also occurs in Australia and the Middle East and wherever agriculture is practised. Work reported in March 2021 in Adelaide Australia found, using an air temperature gun, that on a 35°C-day, the temperature above grass was 25°C, above bitumen 35 to 40°C, bare ground 50 to 60°C and artificial grass 50 to 60°C.[18] Vegetation clearly reduces sensible heat and promotes latent heat; conversely an absence of vegetation and soil organic matter increases sensible heat, no matter what the surface.

At night, the sensible heat should be radiated back to space as infrared radiation but GHGs, acting like a blanket, reflect a portion of the infrared radiation back to Earth, thereby increasing the night-time temperature, probably accumulating to a higher temperature the next day. Without vegetative cover, this will result in 75 per cent sensible heat (rather than 20 per cent) of sensible heat being radiated back into the atmosphere at night, resulting in more heat being entrapped by GHGs and increased heat returning to the earth: a damaging cycle.

Our greatest defence against this process is to reduce sensible heat

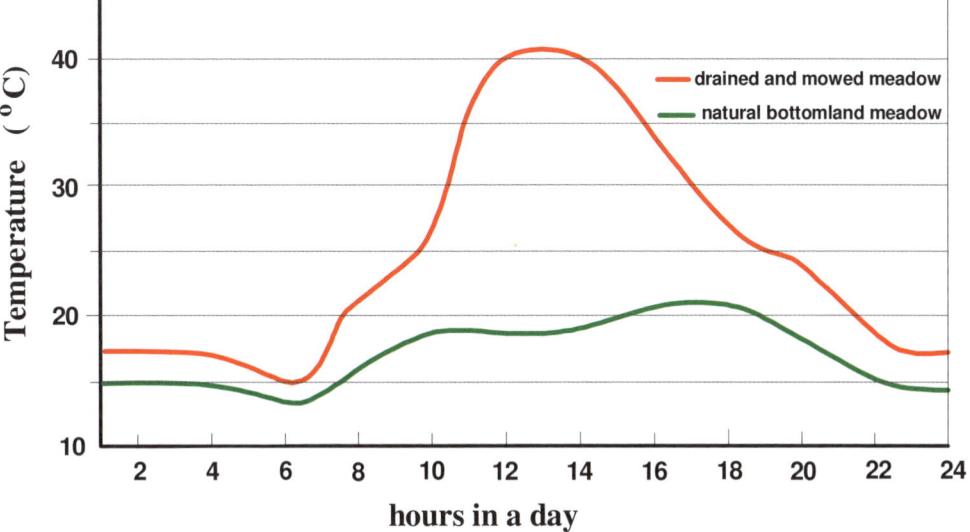

Figure 1-1. Diurnal temperature variation in natural and cleared meadows in Slovakia. Adapted from Michal Kravcík M *et al* 2007 *Water for the Recovery of the Climate—A New Water Paradigm*, Municipalia.s. and TORY Consulting a.s.2007.[230]

by securing our soils through increased vegetative cover. This heat exchange process is crucial to understanding that soil has a greater impact on regulating the earth's climate than carbon emissions and is key to reducing anthropogenic climate change.

Personal experience testifies to this; before you get into bed, the sheets under the blanket are the same temperature as the room. Twenty minutes after you get in, the temperature between the sheets will have increased, and if more bodies are added, more sensible heat, it will increase further until it becomes uncomfortably hot. Increasing the heat source, sensible heat, is more effective in raising the temperature than increasing the thickness of the blanket. It is a two-step process; a heat source and a blanket. Increasing the size of either, increases the sensible heat. Increasing the size of both accelerates the entrapped heat over increasing just one, that is a compounding effect.

From this example, albeit an analogy, it is clear that increasing sensible heat has at least as great an impact to the entrapped heat of the atmosphere as do GHGs. In concentrating on GHGs, which act as a blanket, investigation and understanding of the heat source has been largely overlooked.

The mining of organic matter from the soil by agriculture has had, and continues to have, a profound impact on the ratio of sensible heat to latent heat used in evaporation. Sensible heat heats the earth and via infra red radiation the atmosphere. This drastically reduces, if it does not eliminate, the small water cycle, resulting in a significant impact on the precipitation and temperature regulation of the Earth. The associated reduction of precipitation and increase in sensible heat accelerates desertification by not only the obvious impacts of less rain and higher temperatures, but by the complete destruction of the soil as organic matter diminishes. The net effect is reduced infiltration inputs, by some estimates as high as 40 to 70 per cent from pre-agriculture levels and even as high as 90 per cent.[19]

This heat exchange also occurs in pastoral-tropical and subtropical regions but the situation is more complicated. In subtropic and semi-arid pastoral regions of the world altered weather patterns have in some instances resulted in increased rainfall which in Northern Australia are associated with the increased presence of woody weeds due to the abandonment of traditional burning practices.

From this discussion, we must conclude that changing agricultural practices will be easier, more immediate and have a greater impact than reducing GHGs in the atmosphere through zero emisisons. Reducing emissions is an essential part of climate change mitigation, as is removing excess of the principal greenhouse gas, CO_2, from air—but these are not the most essential mitigatory actions we must be taking.

Removing CO_2 from air should occur, but it is limited to four sinks: oceans, trees, geological storage and soil. So far, excluding oceans, all have proven to be slow, temporary, unsuccessful or even subject to reversal, for example by bushfires.

The important take away is that a significant reduction in vegetative cover is typically followed by, extreme climatic events including heat waves, increased droughts, floods and bushfires. Reversing this, through an increase of soil moisture and vegetative cover, can be achieved in as little as five years. Noting, however, that if a farm is to remain profitable while the change is made, this time could be closer to 10 years. Nevertheless, changing agriculture practises will be a more efficient and effective climate mitigation action than removing or reducing greenhouse gas emissions.

Identifying soil security

As is apparent in Figure 1-2 and Figure 1-3 on page 26 a reduction in diverse vegetative cover and the consequent reduction in organic matter is the beginning of the desertification process. The Bunny Fence Experiment offers striking evidence of the negative impacts of agricultural practices on soil security, and thereby climate. As shown in Figure 1-2 east of the wheatbelt in South West Western Australia (SWWA) is comparatively uncleared pastoral land and between the coast and west of the wheat belt is urban areas, more intensive farming and a mix of parks and forests.

Between 1950 and 1980 rainfall on the western side of the fence declined by up to 20 per cent and has continued to decline.[20] It is the critical winter rain that has declined. Figure 1-3 shows the regional reduction of rain in the 50 years from 1925-1975 compared with the 25 years from 1976-2000. On the eastern side of the rabbit proof fence, rainfall did not significantly decline up to 1999. The contrast is clearly shown in Figure 1-3. A further decrease has occurred in the last 20 years on both sides of the fence as impacts from reduction of biotic pumping and intense grazing of the pastoral zone occurred.

The Bunny Fence Experiment examined the role of land cover change on the preferential formation of clouds in the region.[21] Meteorologists, Nair *et al*, reasoned that the evidence from the Bunny Fence Experiment demonstrates: 'This study identifies some of the processes through which landscape influences weather and climate. It suggests that the impact of land cover changes on atmospheric processes should be a consideration for land management policies in the regions around the globe where significant land clearing for agriculture purposes is occurring.'[22]

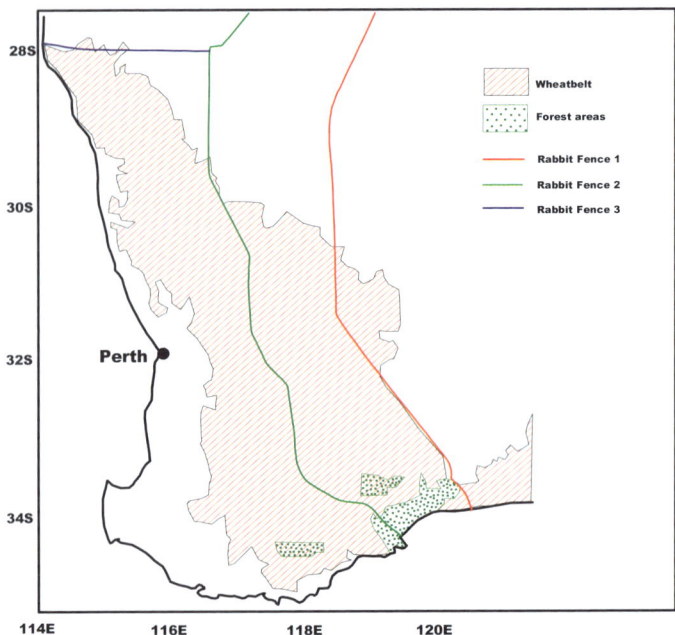

Figure 1-2. South Western West Australia (SWWA) showing the wheat belt of the Rabbit Proof fences. Forest areas east of the wheat belt not shown.[231]

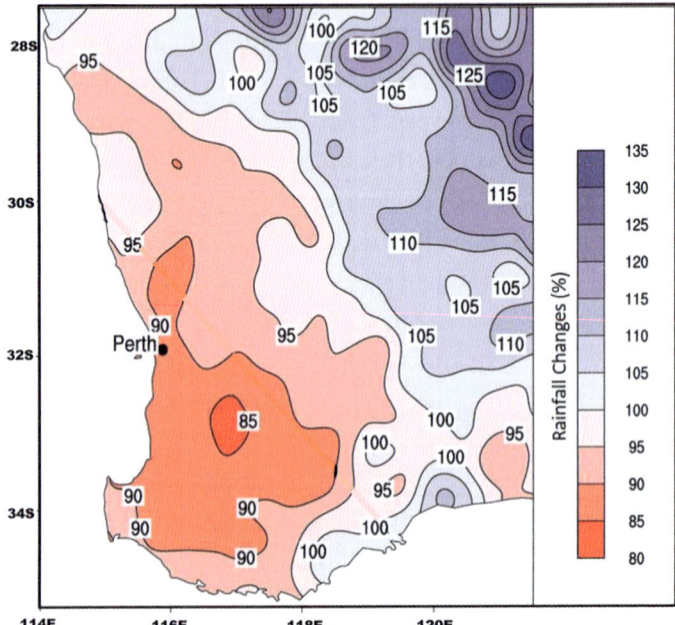

Figure 1-3. SWWA Rainfall Change as Percentage for the average May–October rainfall of 1976–2001 compared to that of the same period of 1925–1975. IOCI, Climate variability and change in SWWA, 2002

Critically, the Bunny Fence Experiment demonstrates the importance of the preservation of the small water cycle. Outcomes from a preliminary review of scientific papers readily available on the Bunny Fence Experiment include:

- The convective boundary layer (that part of the atmosphere impacted by heating of the Earth) is influenced by surface heat and soil moisture (assuming transpiration equates to soil moisture)
- A sharp boundary between agricultural land and non-agricultural land (natural) that has surface heat difference, soil moisture differences, and vegetative height and variability differences, will increase temperature differences and turbulence in air masses, promoting cloud formation, and in particular turbulent cloud formation, which has a greater chance of producing rain
- More rain falls over the natural vegetation than the comparable agricultural areas except during late winter and early spring
- More clouds form over the natural vegetation areas during summer, starting in the early morning right at the boundary. Meaning, on a plain, a boundary of different vegetation height can create clouds
- Due to latent heat, more clouds form over crops in late winter to spring than natural vegetation. However, a change in boundary layer does not mean more rain will fall over equivalent agricultural areas
- Generally, proof of this at continent scales over long time frames is difficult, the exception being the Bunny Fence Experiment.

From about 1996 academia has known of the significant impact past and current agricultural practice has had, and is having, on climate change in the wheat belt of Western Australia. Yet in 2016 the WA Department of Agriculture in a departmental report on climate change makes no mention of land use change impacting climate or the Bunny Fence project, focusing as usual on the majority position that climate change is caused by CO_2 emissions.[23] Numerous other observations and modelling studies around the world have reached the same conclusions.[24]

Almost two decades ago American meteorologist Roger Pielke Sr wrote about the influence of vegetation and soil on the prediction of cumulus convective rainfall.[25] In his 2001 paper 'Influence of the spatial distribution of vegetation and soils on the prediction of cumulus convection rainfall' Pielke referred to over 30 studies,[26] some as early as 1975, which determined that alteration of vegetation and soil moisture by human activities had a significant effect on large-scale climate. He noted that:

- clearing of vegetation by human activity significantly reduces rainfall
- surface moisture and heat fluxes influence rain
- tropical deforestation results in less rainfall in the winter hemisphere continents
- regional climate is very dependent on soil moisture content, and this significantly affects summer rainfall in drought and flood years in both the USA and Australia, and reduced rainfall at the end of the monsoon in SE Asia
- spatial structure of surface heating, as influenced by the landscape, can produce regions of cumulonimbus clouds—thunderstorms

This led him to conclude that 'in the context of climate, landscape processes have been shown to be as much a part of the climate system as are atmospheric processes.'

Pielke is a well-respected meteorologist and his contribution to climate change science has been important. He was part of the international research team engaged in the Bunny Fence Experiment, which provided compelling evidence that landscape processes are important. His position that the climate change debate must be based on more than carbon emissions and fossil fuels, more than limited atmospheric processes, has led to him being mislabelled a climate denier. Discrediting his work, and generally reducing the science to a one-cause hypothesis is setting us back from achieving the goal of stopping anthropogenic climate change.

Pielke was merely proving in his research what has long been known. Charles Keeling's advice to President Carter on what should be done about climate change, to focus on GHG emissions, has been to our detriment. GHG emissions, though important, may not be the major cause of anthropogenic climate change.

Later in 2007, funded by NASA, Pielke led a research team which presented work on the agriculture sector's impact on climate. The conclusion was that 'land use change may have a greater effect on the climate system than the radiative effect of doubled CO_2'.[27] That work should have generated greater debate. Inexplicably, particularly as these numerous studies involve many research institutions from many countries, the findings are not widely known or have been overlooked.[i] Hopefully Pielke's valuable contribution to climate science will yet stand the test of time.

Landscape practices are potentially easier to change than removing CO_2 from the atmosphere, but this is not being considered in the mitigation of climate change. Landscape practices are also absent from assumptions and sensitivity analysis underpinning climate change modelling. Our societies over reliance on erroneous or misleading climate modelling is contributing to misinformation about climate change.

The Intergovernmental Panel on Climate Change (IPCC) in its AR5 report *Climate Change 2014: Impacts, Adaptation, and Vulnerability* recorded a significant increase in the total anthropogenic GHG emissions when including emissions from land use, land use change and forestry.[28] More recently, the IPCC in its recent (2020) special report on climate change, desertification, land degradation, sustainable land management, food security, and greenhouse gas fluxes in terrestrial ecosystems (the SRCCL IPCC Report), does acknowledge the role the landscape plays in climate: 'Land surface characteristics such as albedo and emissivity determine the amount of solar and long-wave radiation absorbed by land and reflected or emitted to the atmosphere. Surface roughness influences

---

[i] Particularly the Bunny Fence Experiment and similar work by the Rain for Climate Institute based out of Slovakia, which included the late Major General Michael Jefferies, former National Australian Soils Advocate, as a member.

turbulent exchanges of momentum, energy, water and biogeochemical tracers. Land ecosystems modulate the atmospheric composition through emissions and removals of many GHGs and precursors of Short Lived Climate Forcers, including biogenic volatile organic compounds and mineral dust. Atmospheric aerosols formed from these precursors affect regional climate by altering the amounts of precipitation and radiation reaching land surfaces through their role in cloud physics.'[29]

This is a comprehensive summary, but its focus remains on GHGs. It does not consider land surface characteristics which determine the infrared radiation that is emitted to the atmosphere for GHGs to reflect back and blanket. It is curious that the IPCC can draw the above conclusions and yet seemingly not incorporate such land surface characteristics into the data or information informing its work. The assumption that the most significant contributor to climate change is GHGs, led principally by emissions of CO_2, is a significant limitation, and is most pronounced in climate modelling.

An example of the excessive reliance on models and the failure to predict variability occurred in 2011 when a reduction in atmospheric CO_2 occurred. This decrease occurred because carbon sequestration during wet years increases enormously and, due to a La Nina year in the Southern Hemisphere, there was heavy rain through 2010 and 2011. This resulted in extensive rapid vegetation growth across the Channel Country in Queensland, extending into the Northern Territory and South Australia, usually semi-arid pastoral areas.

Semi-arid systems cover 45 per cent of the surface of Earth. The mean annual terrestrial sequestration of carbon into either vegetation or soil-organic-matter from the atmosphere is 2.6 PgC (Pentagrams of Carbon).[ii] The 2010–11 La Nina resulted in increased rainfall in South America, Southern Africa and Australia, immensely increasing terrestrial sequestration to 4.1 PgC, Australian semi-arid and desert regions accounted for approximately 1 PgC a year, a huge impact.[30]

---

ii   Petagrams of carbon: 1 petagram = 1 billion tonnes = 10^{12} kg

Importantly, as at 2014, all Earth system models that contributed to the IPCC via the Coupled Model Intercomparison Project Phase, assumed that the semi-arid carbon uptake and precipitation sensitivity that was modelled will remain stable for the model period 1990 to 2090. Prior to 2014, carbon uptake and precipitation sensitivity were unknown and were therefore not modelled. The impact of changing vegetative cover and the balance between latent heat and sensible heat had never been considered with one exception, a modelling study by Professor McAlpine, University of Queensland in 2010.

Contrasting this poor modelling with Australia's actual annual emissions for the year ending March 2019 were 540 Megatonnes of CO_2 equivalent, which is 147 Megatonnes of carbon, which is approximately 14.3 per cent of the sequestration occurring naturally in vegetation during a wet year in Australia. This does not include the carbon in the soil. The Channel Country was again flooded in late 2019 to 2021, which means these events should not be considered exceptional. Now that this previously ignored factor in global carbon sequestration has been discovered, there are a number of studies to determine carbon pool turnover rates in the semi-arid biomes of Australia as drivers of global carbon cycles, including inter-annual variability.

It is now acknowledged semi-arid regions are potentially more important for carbon cycling than equatorial forests due to carbon sequestration leading to substantial inter-annual variability of CO_2 in the air.[31] In 2020 a paper was released that confirms vast areas of managed land have a huge impact on inter-annual variability of carbon and that the climate models either do not consider this or significantly under estimate managed land's contributions to carbon fluxes.[32] They state that managed land represents 70 per cent of Earth's terrestrial surface. Land has a larger role in controlling atmospheric CO_2 variations than previously realised. Amazingly, in acknowledging this impact of managed land on inter-annual variability of atmospheric CO_2, no-one to our knowledge has studied the impacts of reversing bare ground as a percentage of managed land. Nor the impacts of increasing infrared emissions on global temperature rise.[33]

Though the impact of managed land is starting to be recognised as one of the main causes of inter-annual variability on CO_2 in air, the greater impact of landscape change continues not to be considered as a main factor of climate change. We can see the bushfires and the results of drought and feel the heat of the sun, but the health of the soil beneath our feet is not so obvious.

Chapter 2

The Science

How does soil influence our climate?

We have argued that agriculture is having a more significant impact on our climate than GHGs, and identified key ecosystem components that have a significant impact on the health of our landscapes such as soil organic matter, vegetation cover, and sensible and latent heat. Any variations to those components affect climatic processes, including the small water cycle and desertification. To understand these concepts better, it is necessary to investigate the science.

Soil influences surface heat and soil moisture. The volume of moisture in the land and within plants on the land is key to influencing the small water cycle, and the impacts of solar radiation and the consequent latent and sensible heat energy exchange. For instance, when water from the landscape is lost, latent heat is lost and the small water cycle stops. As such, heat conversion is critical to regulating Earth's surface temperature and consequently our climate.

The SRCCL IPCC Report synthesises the current state of scientific knowledge on climate change, desertification, land degradation, sustainable land management, food security and GHG fluxes in terrestrial ecosystems. Currently, the IPCC's 2020 Special Report on land use change and forestry is their only report in which land is the central focus, but it does document similar emerging science: 'Land ecosystems play a key role in the climate system, due to their large carbon pools and carbon exchange fluxes with the atmosphere'. Land use, the total of arrangements, activities and inputs applied to a parcel of land (such as agriculture, grazing, timber extraction, conservation or city dwelling), and land management (sum of land use practices that take place within broader land use categories) considerably alter terrestrial ecosystems and play a key role in the global climate system.

This new recognition marks a shift in the IPCC's historical focus on GHG emissions from industry, power, transport and construction.

Nevertheless, further explanation is required as to why landscape is so important, potentially the most important factor in climate change.

The small water cycle

Most people are familiar with the hydrologic cycle or water cycle, but it's worth recapping as a basis for further explanation of its importance to climate change. The water cycle starts when incoming solar radiation heats the sea, causing water to evaporate and form clouds, as shown in Figure 2-1. At the same time, over the land a greater proportion of solar radiation is converted to sensible heat making the land hotter than the sea, causing the air to rise, resulting in wind, usually bearing moisture-laden clouds, to blow from the sea to the land. This cloud-laden wind is forced up by hills and mountains, frequently resulting in precipitation which runs off via rivers to return to the sea, thereby completing the hydrological cycle.

Less well known is the small water cycle, which is a closed circulation in which water evaporated from land falls in the form of precipitation over the same terrestrial environment, as shown in Figure 2-2. The small water cycle includes winter mists, fog, light rain and summer thunderstorms. See Figure 2-3.

The small water cycle causes between 30 per cent to 90 per cent of precipitation on land, and circulates water into the interior of continents several hundred kilometres and beyond from the coast in a

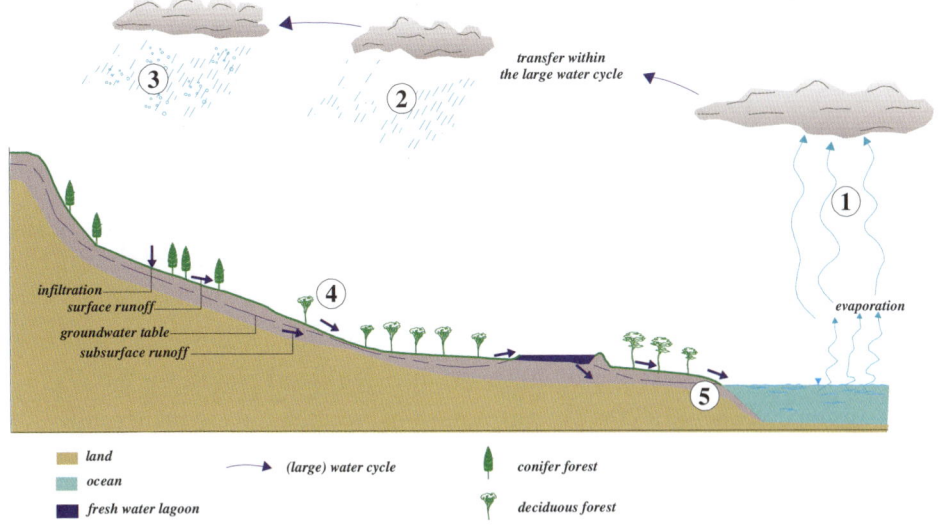

1. Evaporation of water from oceans
2. Clouds pushed over land due to sea breeze, adiabatic and seasonal (trade) winds
3. Air rises over hills, raindrops coalesce and become too heavy and fall as precipitation
4. Precipitation flows downhill in rivers, streams and groundwater
5. Surface water and groundwater flow back into ocean

Figure 2-1. The large water cycle. Adapted from: Michal Kravcík M *et al* 2007 Water for the Recovery of the Climate—A New Water Paradigm, Municipalia.s. and TORY Consulting a.s.2007.

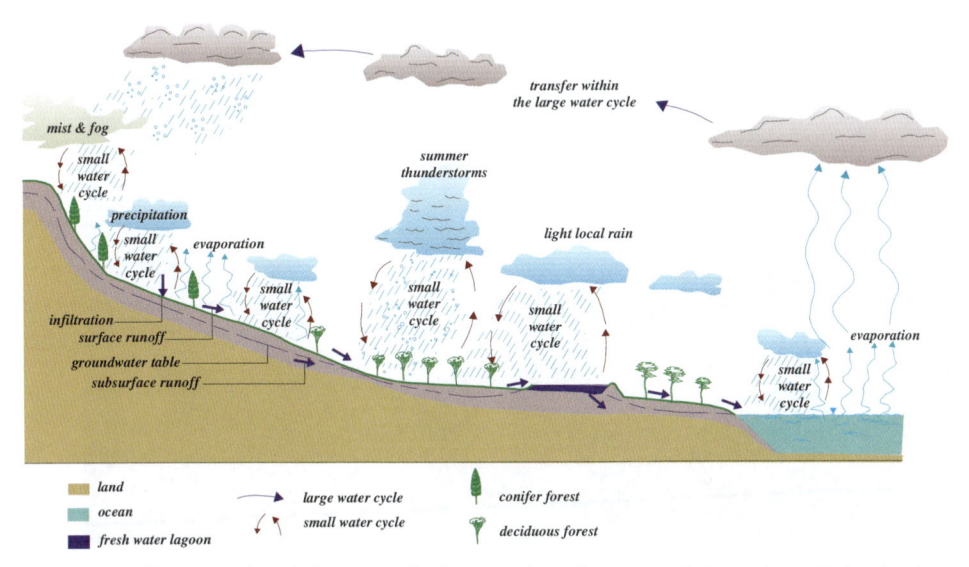

The difference in height between the large and small water cycle is not intended to imply that one is higher in altitude than the other but to make it easier diagrammatically to show the two water cycles together.

Figure 2-2. The small water cycle. Adapted from: Michal Kravcík M *et al* 2007 Water for the Recovery of the Climate—A New Water Paradigm, Municipalia.s. and TORY Consulting a.s.2007.

process called 'biotic pump'.[34] When forests particularly extend inland, the large amount of evapotranspiration can create tropical rainforest conditions up to several thousand kilometres inland.[35]

The small water cycle not only operates locally where atmospheric water is sourced from local evaporation but it also influences large continental basins and thereby regional climate associated with oceanic climate. Under extensive forests or saturated flood plains, the small water cycle becomes the process of moving precipitation inland beyond about 600 kilometres from the coast. Nearly all the precipitation in the Amazon (up to 2500 km inland) and Congo basins is provided by the small water cycle, with oceanic-sourced water effectively only topping up river water runoff at about 10 to 15 per cent of the total precipitation.[36]

Figure 2-3. Summer thunderstorm building up from local evapotranspiration, Mittagong NSW, December 2020

The Science

C - diagram of the circulation of water on land

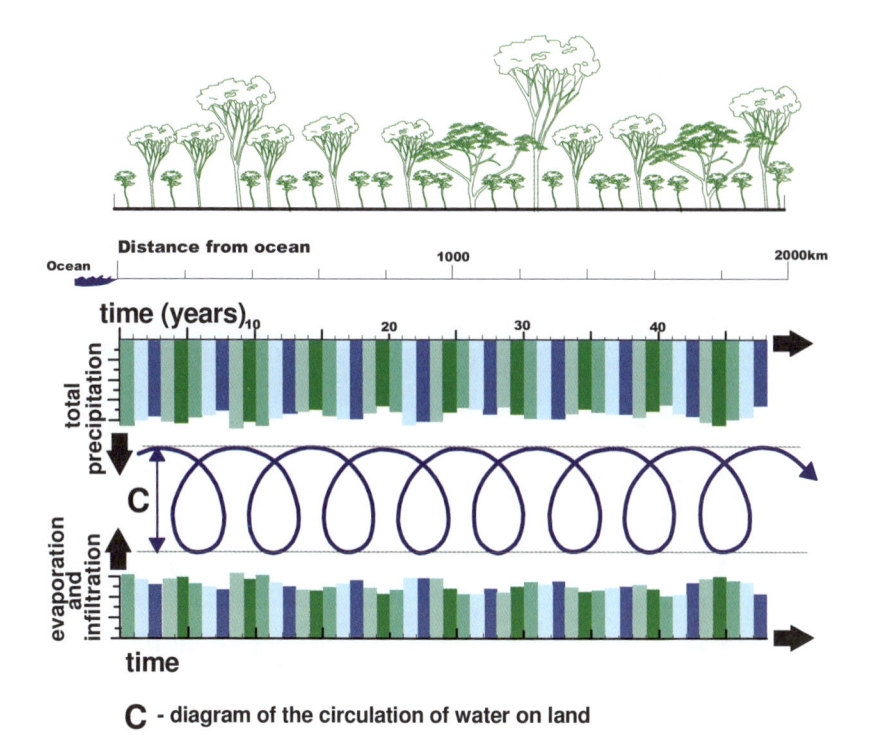

Figure 2-4. Diagram of the long term stable small water cycle on land with constant biotic pumping (maximum evapotranspiration with distance) within a tropical rainforest (Amazon or Congo). Adapted from: Michal Kravcík M *et al* 2007 Water for the Recovery of the Climate - A New Water Paradigm, Municipalia.s. and TORY Consulting a.s. 2007.

The vegetation, rainfall and evapotranspiration become an interdependent cycle, as shown in Figure 2-4, showing the smaller water cycle rolling water inland, renewed via evapotranspiration from the vegetative layer (tropical forest).

If the land contains insufficient water to promote maximum evapotranspiration, huge flows of solar energy cannot be transformed into latent heat by water evaporation but are instead changed into sensible heat, which further reduces precipitation from the small water cycle. In part this is caused by seasonality in the large water cycle (wet season and dry season) that does not keep the biotic pump operating at a maximum such that the amount of water cycling via the small water cycle diminishes with distance inland and vegetation adapts to

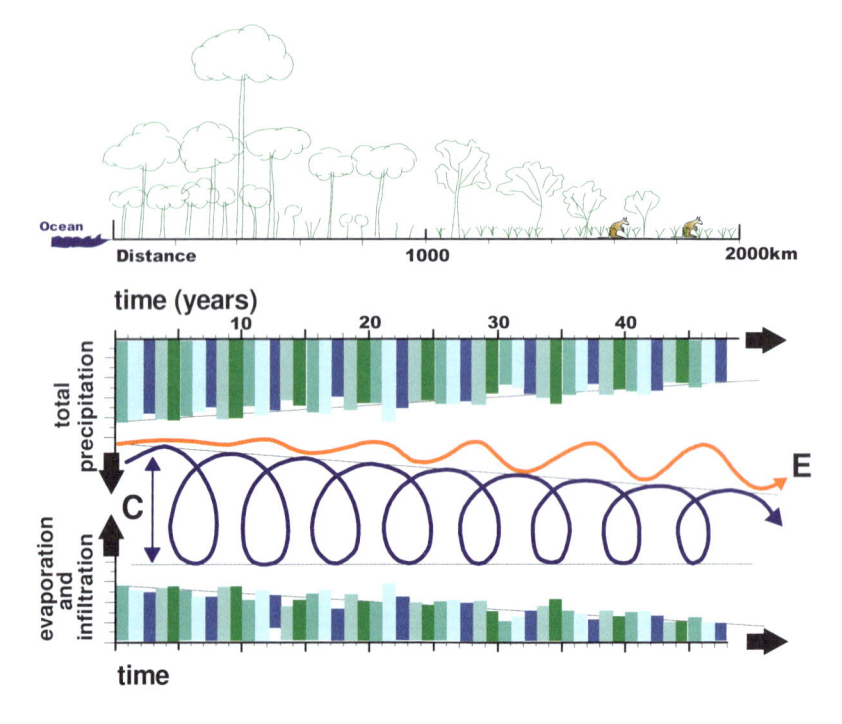

C - diagram of the circulation of small water cycle on land
E - diagram of extreme weather events

Note: Extreme events occur with intensity and frequency increasing inversely as biotic pumping (represented by vegetation types) diminishes

Figure 2-5. Stable small water cycle with diminishing biotic pumping on a subtropic/monsoonal continent with diminishing biotic pumping in-land with distance from the ocean (African Savanna, Australia pre-1788). Adapted from: Michal Kravcík M *et al* 2007 Water for the Recovery of the Climate - A New Water Paradigm, Municipalia.s. and TORY Consulting a.s. 2007.

periods without rainfall resulting in stomates, pores on the underside of plant leaves, not being fully open and therefore evapotranspiration is reduced even when water in the soil is maximised. As evapotranspiration is reduced so too must the small water cycle be reduced. This is depicted schematically in Figure 2-5.

Also, there is less free water on the land during the dry season, similarly resulting in less evaporation. This means there is less water in the atmosphere to maximise local precipitation. Thus, the small water cycle diminishes with distance from the ocean and extreme events start to occur and increase in intensity and frequency with distance from the ocean as the small water cycle diminishes. The biotic pump still works, but is less effective. The system is stable as the biotic pump is controlled by natural cycles in the regional weather system.

In mismanaged landscapes with little vegetative ground cover, or seasonally no-vegetative cover, soil absorbency of water is destroyed, the small water cycles are weakened or destroyed, more heat is radiated, and there is little transpiration to form local mists, fogs and rain, as shown in Figure 2-6.

C - diagram of the small water cycle events on land
E - diagram of extreme weather events

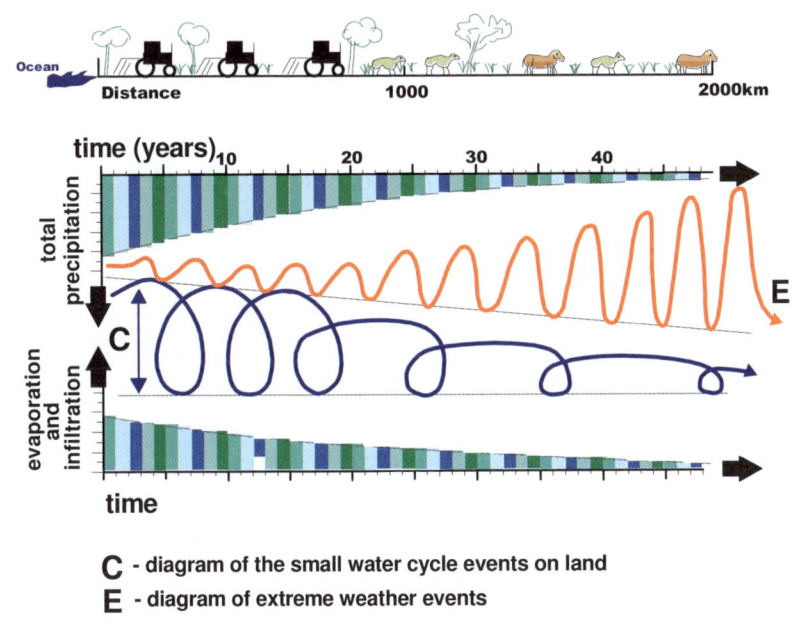

Figure 2-6. Diminishing small water cycle due to land use change. Adapted from: Michal Kravcík M *et al* 2007 Water for the Recovery of the Climate—A New Water Paradigm, Municipalia.s. and TORY Consulting a.s. 2007.

In Australia, typically the year before a La Nina event, a continental high traps cyclones to within 200 km of the coast. As well as coastal flooding—Townsville, February 2019 is an example—the resulting massive rain dump also causes flood waters to move into the interior of Australia via a series of braided rivers known as the Channel

Country. The vegetative response to this rain restores the biotic pump destroyed by the drought (and human activities) and pulls in greater rain the following year, dislodging the stable continental high that propagated the drought. The second season of rain falls onto a land already containing elevated moisture levels (latent heat) and results in river flow deep into the interior of Australia, all the way to Lake Eyre. Research has not yet interrogated whether the biotic pump that pulls water inland is what creates La Nina or whether the La Nina derives from temperature changes in the Pacific Ocean as the push inland restores the biotic pump, or if it is a bit of both.

It is evident, however, that the small water cycle is extraordinarily important and critically influences regional climate and potentially global climate. Without it, not only is rainfall less, but extreme events, including floods, droughts, cold snaps, heatwaves and fires increase, as depicted in Figure 2-6. But the role of the small water cycle within our landscape and its influence on atmospheric processes is not commonly known or well understood.

The small water cycle is dependent on evaporation of water from a vegetative landscape and the latent heat exchange, which in turn is dependent on soil security.

Human activities, such as deforestation, agriculture and urbanisation, have gradually reduced soil moisture, ground water and vegetation, which in turn have reduced on-land evaporation, completely destroying the small water cycle. During my lifetime I have seen the loss of light rain, mists, fogs and a reduction in summer thunderstorms. Restoring small water cycles will benefit local climates: summers will be cooler, winters warmer, droughts less severe, and rainfall more predictable and less extreme. Not only will you see and feel the results in your lifetime, the global climate will improve.

'It's good to be aware of the objective fact that water itself represents a financial value and adds to a country's wealth. The more water there is in the landscape and living organisms, the more life, biodiversity and food there will be and abundance affords protection to other water environments. Water is a treasure.' In 2007 Michal Kravcik elegantly set out the importance of retention of water in land use. 'Water in soil is a deposit in a high interest account. If there is money in the bank, the profit from it will pleasantly grow thanks to the interest rate. If, however we fall into debt in soil moisture and we don't want to lose our treasure of water stored in living organisms, the downward spiral of taking new loans from other surrounding water to pay the interest may suddenly threaten to destroy us. The draining of the land (for agriculture) is like living on debts. Water falling from the large water cycle is like a state subsidy. It comes for free but not regularly, often to the wrong recipients, and in the wrong amounts. It sometimes brings more harm than good. To rely on it is risky, because today it is here, but tomorrow it may not be. It is only the rainfall in the small water cycle which deserves credit for much of the profit we have today. Water in rivers is, if you like, a gift which the community higher in the water sheds hands down to the communities lower on the river. The society which acts as bearer of such a gift should not try to plunder it, but pass it down in a fit and cared-for state.'[37]

How does the conversion from net solar radiation to latent heat occur?

Incoming solar radiation plays a critical role in supporting life by providing energy to increase Earth's temperature. As shown in Figure I-1 on page 6, incoming solar radiation has several different fates. A portion of incoming solar radiation is reflected by surfaces back out to space. The amount of reflection is called albedo. The remainder is called net solar radiation.

The net solar radiation is mostly split between latent heat and sensible heat with about 10 per cent of the net solar radiation lost to the heat flux of soil and vegetation. Finally, a very small amount, about 0.5 per cent, is converted by plants to biomass by organelles in plant cells called chloroplasts, which use chlorophyll (the green colour of plants is a result of reflected light from chloroplasts). This small amount of net solar radiation powers life. Chlorophyll allows plants to grow sufficient biomass to create a functional vegetative layer. A functional vegetative layer depends on precipitation, in which the greater portion is the small water cycle. Earth, when covered by a functional vegetative layer, provides soil security which in turn promotes latent heat over sensible heat. Here's how.

A functional vegetative layer comprises vegetation and litter (mulch) covering the soil. Litter consists of dead plant matter. The decaying of the litter layer is what comprises the organic matter portion of soil.

Though there are other types of fungi, in soil fungi come in two modes of living; living interdependently with plant roots, and living free of plant roots but interdependently, with bacteria to break down dead plant matter, the so-called wood rot fungi (many of which are edible). Bacteria and fungi break down (decay) litter to produce soil organic matter, CO_2 and water.

Fungi are an essential component of soil security. When soil security is maximised, there is an abundance of soil moisture to convert the radiant energy from the Sun (felt as sensible heat) into latent heat. This in turn creates a vegetative layer which provides the soil with a healthy microbial biome. The fungi and sometimes plant roots produce the glue that binds organic matter and particles of soil together. In essence the roots either directly or indirectly (via rhizosphere biome) produce simple sugars that attract fungi to live in or close to its roots. They in turn produce glomalin, a glycoprotein exudated from fungal hyphae, that becomes the glue binding soil into aggregates. Hyphae are the micro hairs that fungi push out into the soil, which also assist in stabilising the soil into aggregates and create the right soil-water characteristic for the plant. Some fungal hyphae also produce oxidants and acids to break down rocks and mineral grains into soluble nutrients which, together with bacteria, bring it to the root in a digestible form.

The soil-water characteristic is the balance between water infiltration, storage and release from the soil. This is effectively the amount of water that infiltrates from rain and the water that drains by either gravity, suction from the plant or evaporation. That is, the plant needs fast infiltration from rain and increased water storage in the suction range that it can access. Fungi, via glomalin, does this for the plant. Gardeners know that the state achieved by glomalin is a fluffy friable soil, ideal for optimum plant growth. This is soil security manifested: tangible soil security.

Under infiltration, a friable soil has an appropriate spread of pore sizes, from macropores to mesopores to micropores, that allow maximum infiltration into the soil. These conditions also provide storage capacity that keeps the soil highly humid. This not only keeps the hyphae moist and functional but maintains humidity immediately above the soil. This in turn reduces the diurnal temperature variation, resulting in cooler moist days in summer and warmer nights in winter (less frosts).

In addition, vegetation prevents an increase in sensible heat by also converting solar radiation to vegetation by photosynthesis. Organic matter in the soil also disperses some of the radiation, being a portion of inbound radiation that is not converted to heat. This is immensely positive in reducing temperature variations and combating climate change.

Therefore, a vegetative layer is essential to protecting the soil from sunlight, keeping the soil moist and friable, and to prevent it from drying out. Dry soils lose their fluffiness—the capacity of the soil to rebound after it is compacted—and dry soil allows too much airflow, which results in the organic matter being mineralised (which means broken down to just minerals and CO_2 and water, bypassing organic matter). This is because aerobic bacteria dominate in a highly aerobic dry soil and, without the need of fungi, breakdown a large portion of the dead plant matter, thereby mineralising organic matter without the intermediary compounds that comprise organic matter in the soil. For example, the actinobacteria tend to directly mineralise plant polymeric sugars. Via the process resulting from excess bacteria, plant matter is quickly converted to CO_2 and oxides of elements without accruing organic matter in the soil.

Evaporation and transpiration are the processes by which water is changed from the liquid state to the gaseous state: moist, wet or saturated surfaces into water vapour. Transpiration is the movement of liquid water from the soil through the plant and into the air as water vapour via stomates. Unless there is excess water, stomates typically open at night and close during the day. Under vegetation cover some infrared emissions from the earth during the evening are converted to latent heat with the evaporation of water from the stomates. In this manner the vegetative layer further reduces the impact of sensible heat.

As a result of the vegetative layer, a baked soil has different characteristics to a soil in the moist state. A soil baked so dry that its organic matter mineralises, has a different soil moisture profile: it has a few macro pores, and then mostly micropores with nothing in between. It is described as massive and hard, 'crowbar soil'. Mineralogically it may be the same soil as the friable moist soil, but it has lost all organic matter. No organic matter means there is nothing to direct solar radiation away from the soil, meaning the land absorbs the heat leading to hotter days and nights. The cooling effect of latent heat from the vegetative layer is so great that cooling caused by just one medium-size tree is equivalent to 10 air conditioners, assuming sufficient water is present.[38]

To experience the impact of a vegetative layer and bare ground yourself, go outside about 20 minutes after sunset during a summer evening. Try lying on bare ground or tarmac for a few minutes, then go to a bushy area and lie down—ideally on multi-storied vegetative cover with leaf litter—then compare the two. Conceptually expand your sensory reaction, the warming effect, out to a global scale and it becomes clear how the land surface is affecting our air temperature and in turn our climate.

In summary, the volume of moisture in the land and within plants on the land, is key to influencing the impacts of solar radiation and the consequent energy exchange, resulting in either latent or sensible heat. Conversion from latent heat to sensible heat is therefore subject to changes in vegetation; type, cover and height, and consequent soil organic matter influencing surface heat and soil moisture. And that heat conversion is critical to regulating the surface temperature of the Earth. What we do to the land is crucial in regulating how much latent heat is created and inversely the amount of infrared heat released from it.

What happens when latent heat decreases?

Reduction in latent heat causes a reduction in the small water cycle. Understanding how to transform sensible heat to latent heat is critical to identifying and evaluating available soil security solutions. Latent heat is the energy required to change the state of water from liquid to vapour, which in the context of this book, is the process of evapotranspiration. Evapotranspiration is the transfer of heat energy from radiation or from a hot atmosphere by the evaporation of water directly from the ground and bodies of water or through transpiration of water from plants sucking up water from the soil. As the small water cycle accounts for between 30 to 90 per cent of precipitation—40 per cent is common, and above 70 per cent is exceptional[39]—evapotranspiration is the source of water in the atmosphere and therefore integral to the small water cycle. Evapotranspiration varies significantly throughout the day due to atmospheric and land surface heat exchange processes.[40] Simply, when vegetation and soil organic matter is reduced, water from the landscape is lost, latent heat is lost and the small water cycle is reduced. Loss of all vegetation ultimately results in loss of all organic matter, the cessation of the small water cycle and a drastic loss of annual rainfall.

The characteristics of the air near the surface will be impacted by the soil surface. A hotter surface means rising air has to reach a greater altitude before the atmosphere cools it to the dew point. The dew point is the temperature at which water vapour may condense into droplets and possibly fall as rain. So, a hotter surface may mean less contribution to annual rainfall by the small water cycle.

Vegetation, particularly trees, cause air turbulence and atmospheric turbulence promotes thunderstorms.

Rainfall in the small water cycle is characterised by rain events with mainly small water drops. Examples include mist, fog, and light winter rain. While late summer thunderstorms are also created by the small water cycle, they do not tend to be characterised by small water drops. Small raindrop sizes are a result of a thinner local surface layer caused by a smaller difference in humidity between the ground and the clouds, a smaller latent heat flux, as well as less heat in the ground.

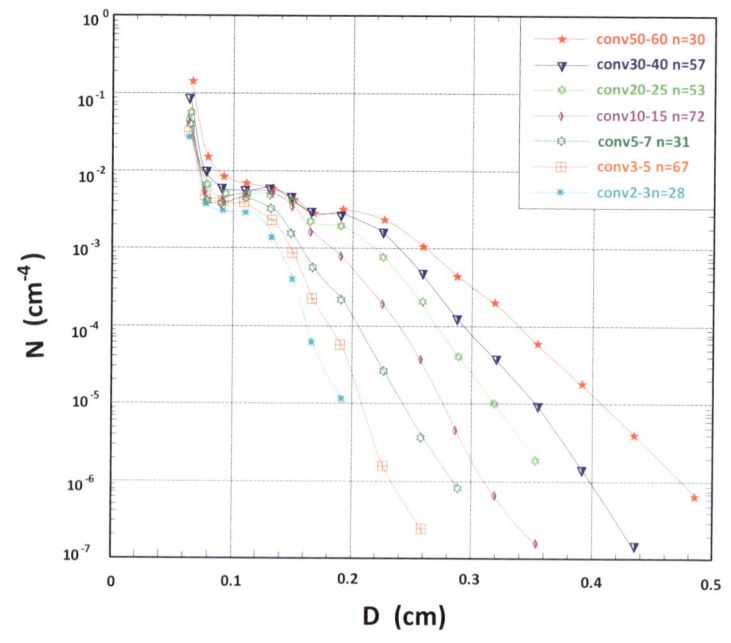

Figure 2-7. Example of distributions in convective rain in Florida with different rates of precipitation: i.e. frequency of rain drops (logarithmic scale of number N) versus raindrop size (linear scale of diameters D). Willis *et al*, 2006 'Rain Drop Size Distributions and Radar Rain Measurements in South Florida'[232]

Nevertheless, if rain does not fall, clouds may themselves be beneficial because white clouds have a high albedo to divert solar radiation back into space, reducing net solar radiation, thereby keeping the ground cooler during the day.

The small water cycle results in a relationship between raindrop frequency, raindrop size and seasonal rainfall. Figure 2-7 illustrates the frequency of raindrops versus raindrop size density during storm events. It charts storm events in Florida, and is useful for illustrating the contribution of the small water cycle to securing moisture in our land. Though it is difficult to say exactly what is locally sourced, the light blue, orange, dark green and purple lines shown, together with all raindrop size less than 0.2 cm, could be seen as representative of the rain caused by the small water cycle. That is, water sourced from local evapotranspiration.

Part of what happens when latent heat decreases as a result of less vegetative cover, is the reduction in plant available water (PAW): less evaporation and transpiration, less moisture in the soil, the air becoming drier, and in turn, the soil consolidates—resulting in less and less new plant regrowth, greater soil compaction and less infiltration — leading to less PAW. The consequences are less and less rain, and when it does rain, an increase of large, less beneficial raindrops and greater run-off occurs. What now falls is less effective rain.

Right across southern Australia we have already experienced less rain, and what falls is less effective as a consequence of this poor land management cycle. Measurably reduced rainfall has also been reported as having occurred in the recently cleared range lands of the Amazon.[41] This is not an impact of CO_2 but a regional impact of the loss of the small water cycle.

Though understood as early as 1996 in Australian academic circles,[42] the conclusion was categorically stated by Nair *et al* in 2011: increased heat from agricultural areas results in regional change in precipitation for all of southwest, central and southern Australia.[43] Furthermore modelling undertaken by several research teams have found that historical land clearing had a stronger regional effect than expected and is likely to be a first order forcing of climate change (equivalent to GHG) over the past 200 years.[44]

Speaking plainly, regional reduction of precipitation and a reduction in the proportion of incoming solar radiation that is converted to latent heat, is a key aspect of climate change and is due to clearing of agricultural land, not an increase in GHGs.

What happens when sensible heat increases

The ratios of latent and sensible heat are interdependent. If latent heat decreases, sensible heat increases. We have established that less latent heat means reduced precipitation, loss of the small water cycle and a reduced percentage of what falls infiltrating the earth. But what happens when sensible heat increases?

Simply, increased heating of the land, which consequently leads to less humidity and moisture in the soil, compacts the soil. This in turn leads to desertification, resulting in ever less moisture in the air and soil, causing larger raindrops, which in turn causes further compaction and increased run-off. All of these factors contribute to a cycle of droughts, wild fires and flooding which are all consequences of what happens when sensible heat increases, because sensible heat is a key driver of climate change.

Australia has no significant high mountain range and depends on seasonal and global effects for most precipitation, meaning that annual precipitation is more variable. Variability is reduced when the small water cycle is maximised. As sensible heat results in the land getting hotter, an increase in sensible heat can affect that system and the water cycle. If the humidity at the surface is low because of high sensible heat (low latent heat) and the difference between humidity at low and higher altitude is large, raindrops evaporate as they fall. If the ground is wet and has a relative humidity close to 100 per cent, almost no water is lost from the drop as it falls. So, when the land is very hot and dry, only larger raindrops overcome the loss to evaporation, and heat reflected from the ground causes further loss of water from the water drop as it falls. The ground may be so hot that the initially large raindrops evaporate before infiltration or runoff can occur. In very hot environments, most raindrops never hit the ground, let alone infiltrate or run-off. In Kuwait, rain that passes your eyes often evaporates before it reaches

Figure 2-8. Phil Mulvey's large sized foot photographed in Kuwait City in February 2019. Note the size of rain drops and the speed of evaporation from the hot surface

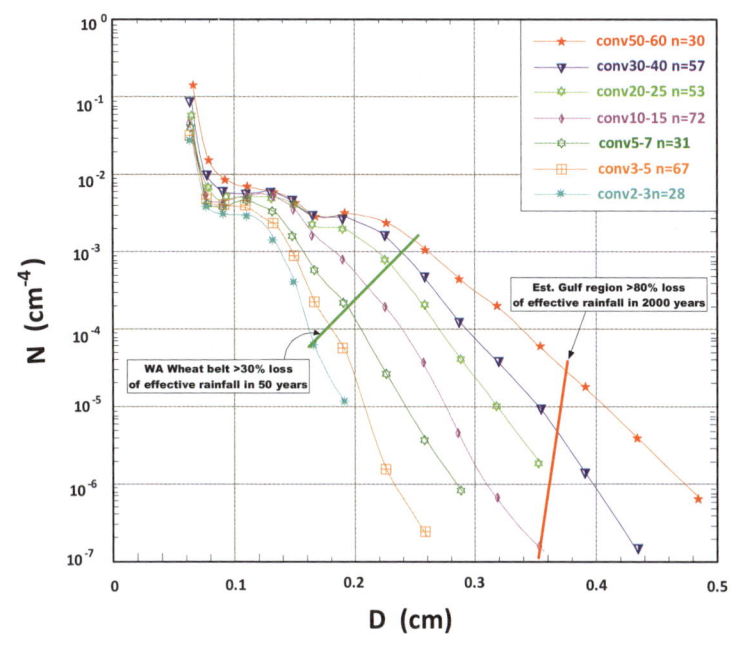

Figure 2-9. Likely loss of rainfall events due to loss of small water cycle as a result of alteration to almost complete conversion of latent heat to sensible heat (author's estimate). Base figure Willis et al, 2006 'Rain Drop Size Distributions and Radar Rain Measurements in South Florida'[233]

your feet. In Australia, this would be expected to occur more frequently when rain follows very hot days.

Consequently, as the process of desertification progresses, the raindrops must be larger and larger in order to actually reach the dry ground, as shown in Figure 2-8. They become so big that they hit the ground with such force they smash soil aggregates, causing fine particles which infill the larger pores, armouring the soil. This is made worse by the loss of organic matter, as a coating on the remaining mineral matter results in the soil being hydrophobic—repelling water. Hydrophobic soil armours the surface to such an extent that nearly all rain runs off. The ground is so hot and dry, the clouds so high, only the biggest storms which cause the biggest drops will hit the ground.

Receiving three months rainfall in one storm on an armoured surface means nearly all the water runs off. And a cycle of droughts and floods develops (precursor to desertification). The land is dry and the water falls in a way the land cannot use. Little water infiltrates, almost no rain replenishes groundwater and basal stream flow ceases. This causes the water table to drop beneath the level of the roots and beneath the bed of the streams and rivers. This hastens the loss of the small water cycle and all streams become ephemeral. Streams do not flow normally, they only flood. Not only has total rainfall diminished, as can be seen in Figure 2-8, rain frequency declines and rain drop size increases, and what falls does not infiltrate. What rainfall there is, from the landscape view, is no longer effective. The rain is destructive rather than restorative.

This effect was observed in Victoria, Australia, after the decade-long Millennial Drought ended in 2002. In some of the central Victorian water catchments, particularly the former goldmining areas within Silurian sediments, the underlying soil is more prone to adverse physical conditions after loss of the vegetative layer. These types of catchments were subject to the processes described above and consequently the precipitation pattern and groundwater level altered. This in turn has significantly reduced stream flow. Even a decade after the drought broke, and even though other catchments in Victoria have returned to their former patterns of flow, those Silurian sediment type catchments have not.[45]

The association of human activity on soil security and climate is strong. Loss of soil security not only increases the sensible heat at the expense of latent heat, reducing the small water cycle, but also reduces and ultimately eliminates base stream flow, creating a permanent hydrological drought following the precipitation drought.

Droughts and floods have always occurred in Australia, but as a result of loss of soil security, with increased desertification, anthropogenic climate change has increased the frequency, duration, and intensity of droughts and floods and their after-effects.

This notion is supported by the SRCCL IPCC Report through its discussion on desertification: 'Desertification exacerbates climate change through several mechanisms such as changes in vegetation cover, sand and dust aerosols and greenhouse gas fluxes. The extent of areas in which dryness (rather than temperature) controls CO_2 exchange has increased by six per cent between 1948 and 2012, and is projected to increase by at least another eight per cent by 2050 if the expansion continues at the same rate. In these areas, net carbon uptake is about 27 per cent lower than in other areas.'[46]

Interestingly the IPCC do not ask or model what happens if you reverse this landscape dryness, by returning or thickening the vegetative layer. Nor do they consider the impact of desertification on global heat.

How does our agricultural system impact the small water cycle?

Less organic matter leads to less evapotranspiration which in turn means a reduction in the small water cycle. Reduction in organic matter in general has been caused by, not simply agriculture but, the wrong agricultural practice for Australian conditions. This is a result of a lack of understanding of the system that achieves balance between Natural Capital and production performance in the Australian landscape. An understanding of the production systems imported into Australia and the reason for their failures compared to the production system that existed prior to the importation of agriculture and some reasons for its success are essential for deriving the principles of a production system that safeguards not only Natural Capital but maximises rainfall.

Australian soil and landscape are different to Europe's and European agricultural practices are not suitable for Australian conditions. When applied to the Australian landscape, European agricultural practices rapidly degrade soil organic matter. The First Fleet brought with them UK practices which had not significantly changed in the previous century, and were not only unsuitable for the Australian landscape but harmful. From the early eighteenth century, as a result of the renaissance period, agriculture in the UK underwent significant development. The landed gentry's (at the time only nobility and only the very wealthy were farm owners) openness to new ideas led to experimentation which improved drainage and impacted land titles and the tenure system. A freeing of tithed labour—as a result of the plague-induced labour shortages—led to adaption of European practices of management including crop and pasture rotation systems and use of legumes to restore the land. This became part of the concept of a managed landscape, known as the 'gentleman's estate'. A good land owner was expected to practise soil husbandry.

By 1780 a four-field rotation system had evolved in the UK: wheat, turnips, barley and clover. This system generally depended on:

- frequent regular rainfall (predictable)
- high organic matter
- high permanent charge (weathered primary minerals)
- stocking for an average year (to get you through a bad year)

In theory this system formed the backdrop for farming in Australia. Those from the First Fleet tasked with farming or who elected to do so, adopted the English system of agriculture. However, few had experience or the systems knowledge for sustained agriculture provided by experienced farmers, and there was the perception of an abundance of land. This meant that early Australian farmers unwittingly mined the organic matter from our soils.

The English system of agriculture was not transferrable to Australia. Australian soils being comparatively old and infertile did not have high charge, so they could not retain the organic matter when stressed by European agriculture practice, even though Australian soils initially had significantly higher organic matter than they do today. Furthermore, rainfall was not predictable.

'Charge' refers to a soil's cation-exchange capacity; a measure of soil's ability to hold positively charged ions. Charge is a very important soil property, influencing soil structure stability, nutrient availability, soil pH and the soil's reaction to fertilisers and other ameliorants.

Settler and author James Atkinson observed in 1826 that farmers in New South Wales were: 'so extremely slothful and negligent many even neglect this important point [rotations] in good farming, but sow wheat on the same land, year after year, for a succession of seasons … The consequence of this miserable system is that in a few years the land gets exhausted and is entirely covered with weeds.'[47]

From the outset the approach was exploitation of land. That is Financial Capital over Natural Capital, with innovations being driven by yield and profit regardless of damage to the landscape. That was the case even though the severe impact on the landscape by 1850 had become obvious. Ploughing down the hills, buried fences at the bottom of the hills with soil from up the hills. The impact of over 12 million sheep on the central slopes of NSW prior to the gold rush devegetated slopes and sent soil downhill too.[48] After World War I and World War II, degradation was compounded by encouraging the opening of marginal land in relatively small allotments as soldier settlements. Droughts ensued due to the poor land management and left many family farms broke.

Over the next century farming practices 'developed'. However, the driving motivation remained Financial Capital at the cost of Natural Capital. A weed control system developed using heavy tillage with crops followed by a fallow or a pasture ley using legumes. Constant tillage destroyed soil organic matter further, and fallows altered the soil biota to become bacteria dominated, which mineralised plant litter and organic matter.

Minimum tillage with the associated use of chemicals, the so-called modern farming system, or as author and farmer Charles Massy in his book *Call of the Reed Warbler* described it, 'Mechanical Farming', was introduced to Australia in the mid-1960s, but uptake was slow until about the 1980s. This is a typical lag for Australia, where it takes about 30 years between innovators demonstrating an improved technology and industry uptake.

The promotion of the use of knockdown herbicides allowed farmers to chase the perception of the greatest profit in the grain belts. Farmers were able to adopt a wheat-canola-wheat rotation, that is avoiding pasture leys or a pulse or legume rotation. But the extensive use of chemicals, particularly fertilisers in cropping, grazing and mixed farming systems, had severe unexpected consequences for our soils. The ultimate effect being degraded soil security: structural breakdown; fertility decline; salinity; acidity; and accelerated erosion. All making the soil vulnerable to variation in climate and consequently causing increased sensible heat. Though modern farming systems protected the soil from excessive mechanical destruction and sensible heat, it had a number of unintended consequences. Specifically chemical residues, loss of native flora and fauna, chemically resistant weeds and, reportedly, potential health effects. Unlike the 1960s, in which tillage and bare ground were common, more land was now subject to these changes due to replacement of sheep grazing with cropping and in the more arid areas, with increased density of grazed stock as polypipe allowed increased watering points.

Mechanisms and consequences of degrading soil organic matter

Most modern farming systems depend on use of manufactured chemicals for pest management and use of manufactured fertilisers to replace nutrients in the soil. Manufactured fertilisers are commonly introduced as acids or salts of acids. Over time, these ultimately destroy the soil, particularly in Australia because of the nature of Australian soils. A brief introduction to soil chemistry is necessary to explain why this is so.

Young landscapes are often fertile, as they are derived from geologically young rocks which have not been significantly weathered, or alluvium in glacial tills. Comparatively, Europe and the US are geologically young, and/or have had extensive relatively recent glaciation. Glaciation forming alluvium and glacial till (glacial sediments) spread widely, both depositional and windblown, from these young rocks. Most young volcanic, plutonic and metamorphic rocks are rich in the primary rock minerals such as olivine, pyroxene and K feldspars. These minerals weather to moderate and highly charged clay minerals. It is a permanent negative charge that attracts positive ions, cations, from the soil solution to balance that charge. This negative charge is offset by cations in soil solution, such as calcium and potassium, which are plant nutrients. This charge is called cation exchange capacity. As clays weather, getting older, the mineral alters to less charged clays.

Organic matter is also charged and can be linked to the clay by the cations in solution that have a double charge. These highly charged clay minerals bind more carbon to the soil than soil of a lower charge in a similar climatic zone.[49] Although organic matter can cover part of the clay mineral and reduce cation exchange capacity, this is compensated for by increasing charge and nutrient storage capacity of the organic matter in neutral soil. Ultimately, increased charge is a good thing for soil security.

Australia is old and glaciation has not influenced the formation of our landscape, except in Tasmania. Rock minerals in old landscapes have been subject to so much weathering that they have been altered to clays with almost no charge and many metal oxyhydroxides and oxides, collectively known as sesquioxide. Sesquioxide and organic matter have a charge but it varies with soil acidity, pH, and is not permanent or inherent to the compound. This means that for Australian soils, to ensure charge is maintained, it is important not to lower the pH.

The capacity of soil to resist chemical change, is called 'buffering'. High charge, together with increased organic matter, increases buffering, allowing the soil to be very resilient to change. Charge is also important for the preservation of organic matter and mineral charge, by binding dissolved organic matter (DOM) released during the initial breakdown phase of organic matter. This process prevents DOM loss downward or it being mineralised. The DOM then binds to the semi-labile non-soluble soil organic matter and charged minerals in the soil. Without bound DOM, soil organic matter more rapidly mineralises or washes out of the soil profile.

Though it is well known that soil organic matter is important for many soil functions and as the primary indicator for soil health, it's function in regional climate, as we have discussed, is not well known. But it is known that Australian soils have less charge and are less able to buffer against change, so introducing chemical fertilisers, the effect of which is to increase the acidity of the soil, is destructive to soil health. And it gets worse, as explained below, degrading soil organic matter can also occur as a result of chemical fertilisers impacting bacteria and fungi, which negatively influences both DOM and soil organic matter.

Carbon dioxide exists in the soil chemically as a component of organic matter, carbonates and chars. Soil carbonates, for example calcrete, are usually an outcome of evaporation exceeding precipitation for most months of the year, hence associating them with semi-arid to arid conditions. Chars, which are the end product of pyrolysis—that is, combustion with inadequate supply of oxygen—can occur in all soil. However, the greatest rate of production of char is associated with temperate woodlands which have the fastest degradation rate. Arid and semi-arid grasslands and woodlands produce much less char but breakdown is slower. Although these carbon pools, carbonates and chars can be increased by bio-geoengineering, the fraction overall in the soil is low.

The most significant CO_2 pool in soil is soil organic matter. Soil organic matter is approximately 50 per cent carbon, and occurs in all soil as a result of decaying roots, and in both living matter and dead vegetative litter. The degradation of vegetative litter, extraction of minerals and growth of roots almost exclusively depends on the relationship between bacteria, fungi and the root. Animals—nematodes, beetles, worms and so on—have a more minor but still important role.

Organic matter occurs in a number of phases: labile or DOM is usually produced as exudates from roots and fungi which only lasts in the soil from hours to days; particulate organic matter that lasts in the soil from months up to several years; and recalcitrant organic matter that lasts from a year up to decades. The recalcitrant fraction includes organic matter bound to clay and other charged minerals, sesquioxide, and within this fraction, chars and soots. Semi-labile carbon is not in the dissolved phase but is particulate organic matter made up of very biodegradable compounds that are rapidly consumed by microbes in the soil within hours and up to weeks.

As previously stated, the conversion of organic matter to microbial biomass and CO_2 is called mineralisation. Unexpectedly increased retained DOM, even though it only lasts a short time, is indicative of increased fungi in the soil and a slower rate of mineralisation. This is because leaf litter is converted to longer-term soil organic matter and entrapped in aggregates by DOM and glomalin acting as glues. Increased bacteria in relation to fungi results in less DOM and less glomalin, leading to less aggregation and increased mineralisation of litter bypassing sequestration to soil organic matter. Fungi in soil, with pH between 5.2 to 7, increases with organic matter and provides glomalin to bind the mineral matter with organic matter to form aggregates.

In most instances, when manufactured fertilisers are introduced into Australian soil, acid is also released. That acid reduces and ultimately negates the charge of organic matter and sesquioxides, as the permanent charge is too small to remove the acidity. Once the acidity drops below a pH of about 5.5, disaggregation starts: the soil becomes prone to erosion, shrink and swell, and hard setting. The DOM generated is washed down the profile and soil organic matter is mineralised. The soil biome is changed favouring bacteria which mineralises the organic matter. Glomalin is not produced. Once the soil is acidified and the buffering capacity is lost, neutralising the acidity by lime does not restore the system. There is one exception, when concerted effort is made to rebalance the soil biome to a system where fungi is greater than bacteria.

Liming after fertiliser addition only corrects pH. Most other soil functions are lost, including: home for diverse micro-organisms and macro fauna; the storage of nutrients and water improved infiltration; maintenance of the small water cycle and resilience against droughts and heavy rain. Liming of the soil may allow it to continue to act as a growing medium but there is no soil security, as resilience has not been restored by the balancing of the soil biome (particularly ensuring that fungi numbers are greater than bacteria numbers).

Some farmers have tried adding humic and fulvic acids with the lime to aid in balancing the soil biome. Though this assists in providing DOM, until the fungi numbers recover, gradual decline is thought to continue. Consequently, with the arrival of the first drought, even with the farm practices of not-tilling, with or without liming, the topsoil will be eroded—initially by wind erosion, and later by storms (erosion from water drops and sheet erosion).

For non-scientists this gobbledygook means certain kinds of chemical fertilisers are extremely bad for soil health, which in turn is bad for climate regulation.

Organic matter in Australian soil has fallen from a continental average of over 3 per cent to below 1.4 per cent.[50] This includes all forests and national parks and therefore the continental average for agricultural land is likely to be less than 1 per cent. We mine organic matter, that is, we are carbon miners rather than carbon farmers, and we are converting soil from a key function of our terrestrial ecosystems to simply a growing medium. What remains after removing organic matter is microbial poor sands or massive clays which are unable to provide the landscape functions required and expected of soil.

Pushing the soil beyond its buffering capacity without a drastic intervention and change of practice, irreversibly changes the soil for the worse, so it cannot perform the functions required of it, including the function of promoting and maintaining the small water cycle. This in turn changes the local climate—reducing latent heat and increasing sensible heat—leading to loss of precipitation due to the loss of the small water cycle and more extreme climatic events.

Historical and current land management practices impacts heat and climate

The real culprit of anthropogenic climate change is the change in ratio of latent and sensible heat. Increased sensible heat has a number of effects. As moisture is lost into the upper atmosphere, it drives down the humidity in lower levels. This dehydrates the land and the vegetation, creating a 'tinderbox' landscape, often exacerbated by strong hot dry winds and dry lightning, with the disastrous effect of widespread bushfires.

Droughts and extended dry seasons will continue throughout the Australian interior until organic matter and vegetative cover returns to shift the balance of sensible heat to latent heat. To achieve this, the land must be soaked with heavy rain and follow-up rains, which can only be achieved through a strong small water cycle and low-pressure systems. However, a long period of continuous rain is usually not capable of overcoming the constrictions placed on the land by sensible heat and this is why droughts are usually only 'broken' with a flood and follow-up rain to produce vegetative cover.

Figure 2-10 is a representation of the change of heat expressed through an increase in extreme temperatures across Australia from

1920. Extreme heat events typically result in bushfires. Though not part of Figure 2-10, two major 19th century bushfires, one in the 1850s and one in the late 1890s, are likely to be the only extreme events prior to 1910. Considering these earlier events as part of the record shown in Figure 2-10, the pattern reflects the change in agricultural practice explained above and also the concomitant reduction of remaining

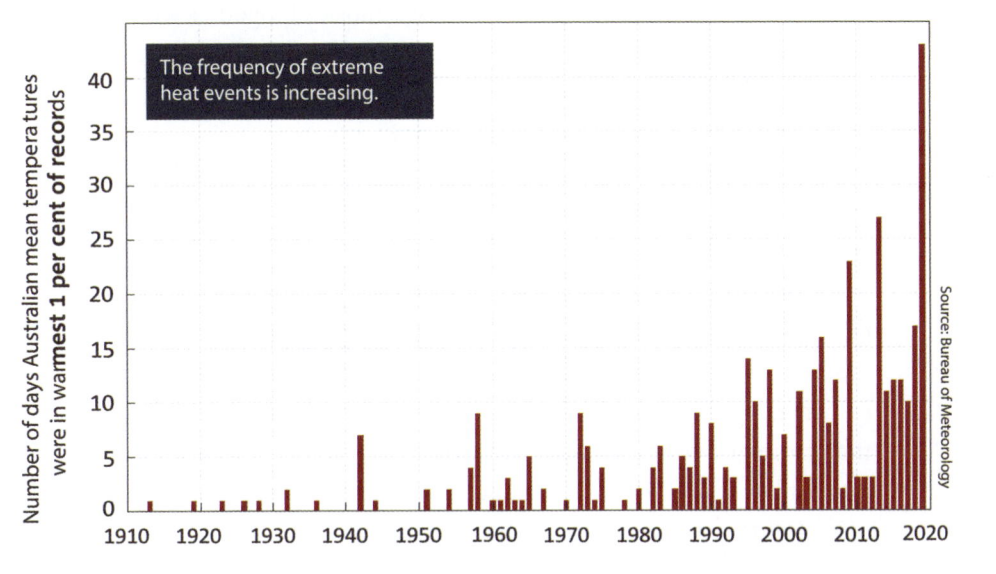

Figure 2-10. Number of days each year where the Australian area-averaged daily mean temperature is extreme. Extreme days are those above the 99th percentile of each month from the years 1910–2017. These extreme daily events typically occur over a large area, with generally more than 40 per cent of Australia experiencing temperatures in the warmest 10 per cent for that month. Bureau of Meteorology *State of Climate 2020*.[234]

wilderness as similarly reported by David Attenborough in his 2020 documentary *A Life on Our Planet*.

In Australia, droughts are no longer episodical but have become common occurrences, with regional droughts present somewhere in Australia every year and continental droughts every three to five years. It is concerning that this trend is escalating. Before 1920 it appears, there was a drought cycle of one drought every five to 10 years, resulting in one extreme day for 40 per cent of Australia. Land clearing increased in the 1920s as a result of the impact of the returned soldiers land stimulus scheme and for horticulture in the Murrumbidgee Irrigation Area (MIA). The introduction of mechanised tillage or weed control in the 1930s and the government policy of encouraging returned soldiers to clear the land, increased the severity of droughts but not their frequency. The introduction and widespread use of manufactured chemical fertilisers from the mid-1950s (supported by a subsidy) together with the use of polypipe to extend watering points into the arid zone, increased the area of bare ground, resulting in a reduced period between droughts and increased severity and duration of droughts.

Without a significant continental mountain range, which would cause the air to rise and increase local rain, Australia has always had cycles of drought or drying events of varying duration caused by Earth, solar and interplanetary cycles.[51] This is why the Indigenous people developed sophisticated landscape management systems that optimised production of food, while minimising tinderbox conditions. Now there is increasing evidence that not only is total precipitation declining in the centre and southern part of Australia as a result of the change in ratio of latent and sensible heat, but both the frequency and intensity of droughts in the last 50 years has increased.

Altering landscape for maximum soil security

As a result of the break-up of the big pastoral stations in the 1880s, the authors' family had a farm enterprise for over 100 years on the Western Plains of NSW. Over the last 100 years or so, most families on farms west of Dubbo sent their children to boarding school because of the isolation. Thus, the number of children that a farm business can afford to send to boarding school compared to 100 years ago, is a good way of comparing profit over time when the value of money is variable. During the time of our family's management of the land there has been a loss in organic matter and a significant reduction in profits, as shown in Figure 2-11—represented by the line marked "costs of inputs". This represents a typical farm on the Western Plains of NSW where Financial Capital was prioritised over Natural Capital, consequently

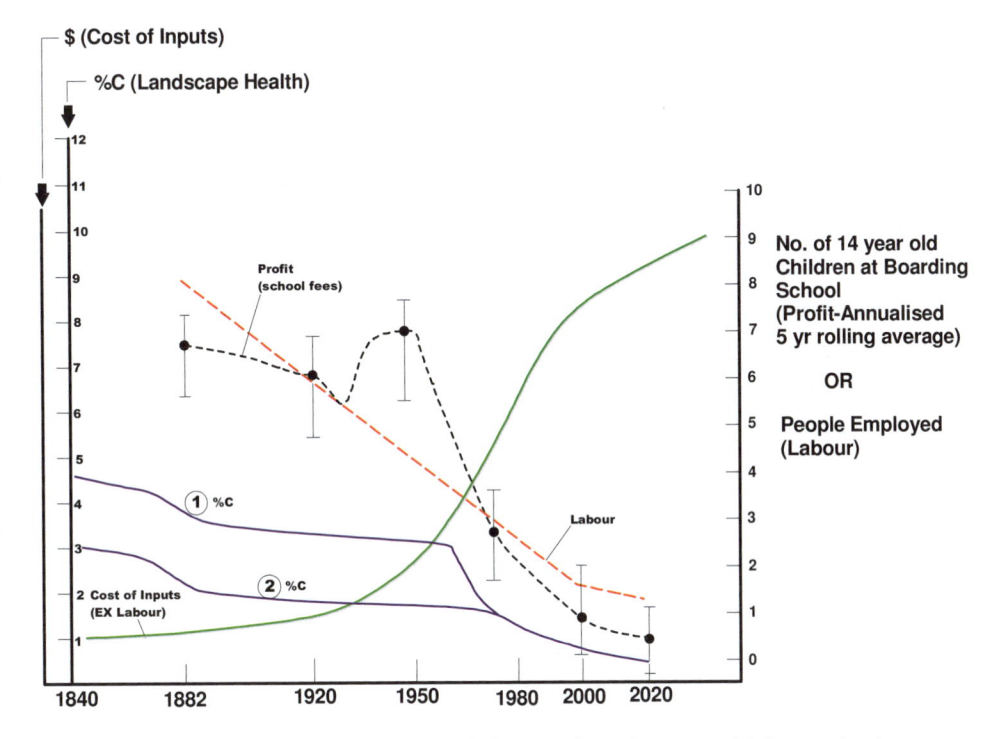

Figure 2-11. Estimated Profits, Inputs, Labour and Landscape Health for grazing/mixed farming enterprises (approx. 2200ha) Western Plains NSW, since 1880

degrading the Natural Capital. Profits shifted from the family to agrichemical and farm machinery providers.

In 1839 polish explorer, surveyor and scientist Pawel Strzelecki undertook exploration and survey of NSW, which at that time included Victoria and Tasmania. In 1845 he produced an extraordinary book, *Physical Description of New South Wales and Van Dieman's Land*, the first detailed scientific investigation of Australia. In many ways Strzelecki's work was more important than Sir Joseph Banks'. Strzelecki provided the first geology map, the first classification of soils with over 40 soil profiles and the first warning by a scientist backed by measurement and observation that reduction in vegetation by agricultural in turn reduces soil organic matter, relative humidity and local rain (the small water cycle). He even warned the government, recorded in Parliamentary Papers for 26 August 1841, of the consequence of overstocking, poor intensive cropping results in hotter drier conditions. Additionally in his work Strzelecki noted that the 'removal of thick interwoven forests must have necessarily rendered the climate drier... however though both drier and hotter is far from improved'.[52] Strzelecki is discussed further in Chapter 4.

Strzelecki's observations were over 50 years before Svante Arrhenius developed Fourier's argument that infra-red radiation was being trapped by some gases and then re-emitted in all directions. Unfortunately this unheralded extraordinary scientist lost many specimens and soils during his southern exploration when horses were forced to be released due to dense thicket in the Gippsland. Consequently only 4 of the 40 soil profiles Strzelecki collected are on uncleared land:

- one from basalt soil at Mount Tomah NSW (15 per cent organic matter)
- one from Lake country in Tasmania (20 per cent organic matter)
- one from the slopes of the Huon River in Tasmania (18 per cent organic matter), and
- one most likely from flats of Silurian meta-sediments of the western slopes of NSW, and subject to pastoral activity (4 per cent organic matter)

It appears likely that prior to pastoral activity the flats of the Western Plains of NSW may have been a little higher in organic matter. Thus organic matter on the flats of the western slopes potentially started at between 5 and 6 per cent organic matter (2.5 to 3% Carbon) and by 2010 were below 1.5 per cent organic matter (0.75 per cent Carbon). That is a decline in soil carbon approaching 75 per cent.

Over this time, as soil carbon has drastically fallen, so has profit and labour. However, the cost of sales, fuel, fertilisers and chemicals have increased. Farms have generally become less profitable as the farm chemical and fertiliser sector increasingly became more profitable. Operating a farm is now commonly a minimum 60-hour week operation.

Based on records made by explorers and early settlers, and known

Aboriginal practice for maintenance of healthy country and rectifying sick country,[53] there were probably less trees pre-1788 than there are now across the continent but the land had complete vegetation cover. Bruce Pascoe in a recent seminar estimated that mature tree cover of Australia was maintained by Aboriginal cultural burning practice at 10 trees/acre, 22 trees/ha (presumably not in tropical forests and other former Gondwana wetland forests) unlike current sclerophyll forest and plantation forest densities of up to 400 trees/acre.[54] A recent publication using pollen studies to estimate historic fire patterns calculated low regional tree cover as being 45 trees/acre.[55] Clearly, most agricultural areas do not achieve 10 trees/acre while national parks way exceed this density.

Simply put, we have failed to collect or listen to prior knowledge on successful landscape management, causing the vegetation system Australia-wide to be out of balance.[56]

After the arrival of the Aborigines many species of mega-fauna became extinct and it is likely that the Aboriginal system of land management developed as a consequence; principally for two reasons:[57]

- to ensure that the land was optimised for efficiency of harvesting food and water during even the worst season and
- to ensure species were not pushed to the brink of local extinction as happened in the first 10 000 years after the arrival of humans in Australia

Before the end of the last ice age a landscape management system appears to have been developed, and after the end of the last ice age, this was modified to suit the changed conditions. Ongoing widespread propagation (not necessarily cultivation) had occurred in regard to yam daisies (*Microseris lanceolate*), black bean tree (*Castanospermum austral*) and in particular the Australian grains, kangaroo grass (*Themeda australis*) and Australian millet (*Panicum decompositum*). Kangaroo grass and Australian millet were propagated over widespread longitude and climate zones. In 1974 Norman Tindale defined an Aboriginal grain belt that includes the northern portion of the wheat belts in existence today, but extended it right through the inland deserts of Australia.[58] Furthermore, Peter Ampt of Sydney University said that seeds were collected, traded, sown and irrigated,[59] and in 1833 Sturt recorded millet being harvested and dried in bunches prior to willowing.[60] Additionally, as noted by Bill Gammage, fire, the daily work of land management by Australian Aborigines, was observed during almost all early European encounters; the most well-known example being recordings of extensive smoke.

Most explorers who had visited the east coast prior to 1788 or explored inland prior to 1825 noted the land was verdant and soft underfoot, and the river surfaces were level with the land, contained a lot of fallen and submerged timber, and were full of fish.[61] The Aborigines harvested plants and had a system of controlled grazing.

This same land, the tablelands and western slopes and plains of eastern Australia, is where mixed farming by family farms dominates today. In these areas, rivers and creeks are now carved into the land and are ephemeral, while organic matter is typically less than 1.4 per cent. That's less than 25 per cent of what it was pre-1788. The land is now rarely verdant and tree dieback is extensive. Though the intensity of use is now greater, cropping and grazing was the dominant activity both then and now. It is estimated that Aborigines spent less than three or four hours a day on harvesting, hunting and fire management work, the remaining time being spent on cultural activities and leisure.[62] Some of this time was spent making tools, baskets, nets, and string, which would also be considered as work. The modern owner of a mixed family farm now spends most of their daylight hours working on the land and the evenings on accounts.

Maximisation of profit and production, of food and energy output, over Natural Capital and sociocultural values, has crippled our land and many of those who work our land.

How did Aboriginals manage land to maintain soil security?

An absence of known aspects of agricultural plant husbandry (nurturing and protecting the crop) in Australia prior to 1788 does not mean that Aboriginals did not optimise the landscape to increase ease of harvest of meat and plant foods. Fire was how aboriginals managed soil fertility, weed management and ease of animal harvest, a proto agriculture process which was successfully utilised for around 30 000 years prior to 1800. From recent and emerging research, it is now apparent that Aboriginals developed a sophisticated system of culturally based landscape management that preserved Natural Capital while making sourcing food as easy as possible.

Many people have a romantic view of the Australian Indigenous people living in harmony with an unaltered environment. In 1992 Keith Helyar was among the first to challenge that view. In a lecture to the NSW branch of Soil Science Australia, Helyar proposed that Australian Aborigines did not live in an unaltered landscape but actively managed the landscape for their own needs. As evidence he noted that the soil in the Pilliga in NSW was not consistent with the parent material and natural regolith processes. This soil had an alkaline top soil, which is advantageous for vegetation in the very poor soils of the area. This environment could only be achieved by intentional and sustained low temperature burning.

Tim Flannery in his 1994 book *The Future Eaters* implied that after the arrival of Aborigines in Australia it took them some time to develop a landscape management system, and during that time some megafauna became extinct.[63] Others are strongly of the opinion that the megafauna extinctions were caused by the Aborigines.[64] The explanation may not be binary. After the end of the last ice age, it is likely Aboriginal Australians developed a landscape management system. As emerging science shows the extinction of megafauna coincides with major climatic and environmental deterioration both locally and regionally, including increased fire, reduction in woodlands and loss of freshwater.[65] Arguably these sustained climatic changes were the result of new anthropogenic landscape management systems.

In *The Biggest Estate on Earth* Bill Gammage proved the thesis that the Australian landscape was intentionally managed for the long-term benefit of the Indigenous people. Effectively, the landscape was changed to suit the people. The practice of management was coded in a system of obligation to land, as well as all flora and fauna on and within it, a management system stemming from what Europeans call the 'Dreamtime'. While the system allowed slow change, it was vulnerable to sudden changes, such as the invasion and occupancy of Australia by Europeans, and all that resulted from it during the 18th and 19th century, which had a significantly detrimental effect on Dreamtime knowledge.

The elders, the keepers of knowledge of landscape management and living systems, were the most susceptible to the diseases introduced by Europeans. Many, if not most, likely died before passing on all knowledge of country.[66] This resulted in the loss of the finer points for management of districts, particularly on the east coast. Nevertheless, the principles have been preserved in fragmented groups who still possess and teach traditional knowledge. See for instance *Fire Country* by Victor Steffenson and *Treading Lightly* by K Sveiby and T Skuthorpe.[67]

It is estimated that when Europeans arrived, Australian Aboriginal land management systems had already been in place for over 30 000 years.[68] These land management practices were followed consistently across Australia: continual management of all landscapes by aggressive weeding and removal of trees (all with fire); reducing animal abundance during times of plenty to maintain resources for droughts; rotating culling so as not to spook animals through developed patterns of human behaviour; and managing human population. The management was optimised to maximise biodiversity and not to drive any more species to extinction.

By the time most explorers trekked further into the inland, they found it was largely depopulated and already 'sick'. In 1826 James Atkinson, in An Account of the State of Agriculture & Grazing in New South Wales, recorded that in the great chain of plains from the Liverpool plains, around Moree, to the Monaro, south of Canberra, the grassed plains were 'destitute of timber' and 'abandoned by Aborigines, and shunned by Kangaroos'[69] which graze on short rather than long grass. Only five to six years earlier, John Oxley had reported an abundance of kangaroos and observed a grave site of a youngish man who

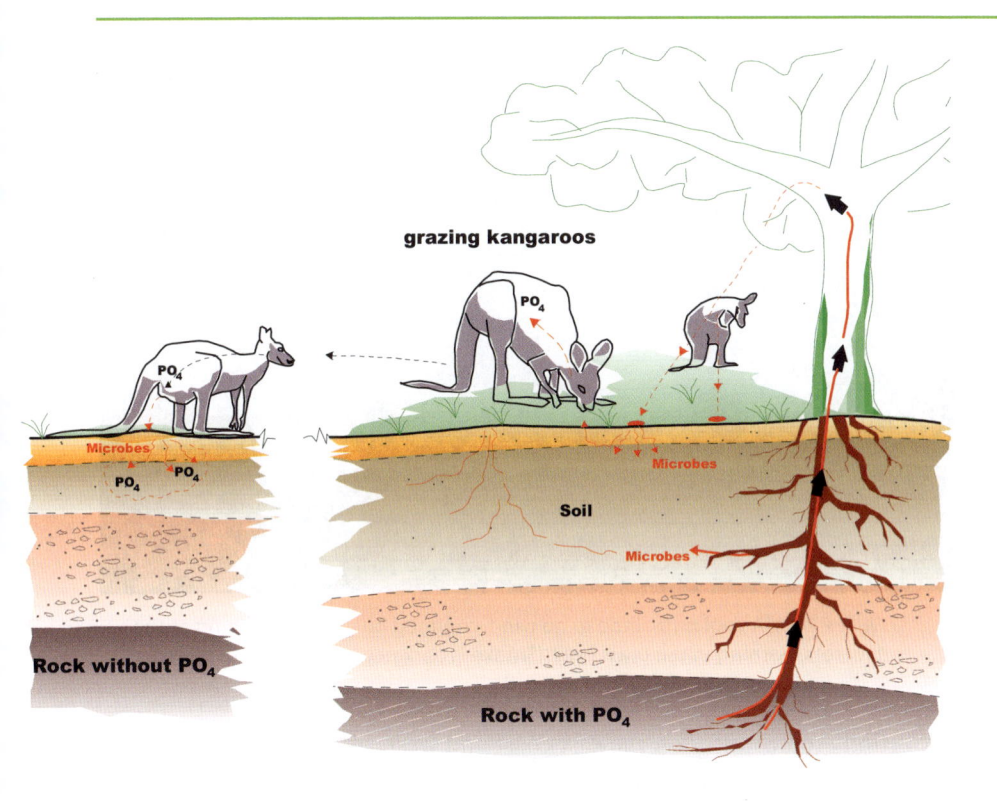

Figure 2-12. Movement of phosphate in the landscape by native animals

had been buried within the previous nine months, potentially representing evidence of European disease impacts on Aboriginals.[70] The death of so many indigenous people from disease meant the landscape was no longer being actively managed. As grasses were not kept short through Aboriginal burning practices, kangaroos left the area for lack of food. This likely meant that, though not currently recognised, the impact of the lack of landscape management in inland NSW was already apparent as early as 1826.

The key practices for landscape management by the first Australians were fire and may have included what is now called pasture sowing—edible crops are sown into pasture without tillage but probably following fire. It is simplistic to define Aboriginal burning practices as pattern burning or hazard-reduction burning, because a fire hazard or tinderbox was never allowed to occur.[71] In more heavily

Figure 2-13. A cool burn: little to no wind, confined burn in the evening as the dew sets, burning in the grass only. (Smoke is dark because of sunset, not soot)

timbered country on the east coast and western slopes and tablelands, corridor burning was practised for management of game (in this case macropods).

Burning by Aborigines was substantially undertaken according to a landscape management plan, which was maintained orally via the Dreamtime, on a cycle to achieve the primary objective of the plan: the ease of sustained living for humans and their support system. This included maintenance of all flora and fauna, access to native animals to be caught easily for food, runs of grass separated by bush fences, tree covered ridges and upper slopes for maximum water infiltration for maintenance of groundwater and base stream flow, as well as, management of kangaroos' numbers during times of plenty. The location of a burn and the reason for it informed the type of burn performed.

A cool, damp burn generates more char and a hot burn more soot and ash (more alkalinity). These different outcomes were manipulated for advantage. Depending on the region, a cool burn in the evening is preferable after a hot, still, cloudless day in spring or autumn. A clear night means dew will form as the sun sets and this ensures more

Figure 2-14. Burnt grass: green pick seeks sustenance from ash in the short term, and char in the medium term

char with less ash. A cool burn produces white to light grey smoke, as the burn temperature is too low to condense soot. Grass burnt in a low-temperature burn produces char that has small round balls of aromatic compounds (tight rings of carbon) linked by chains of aliphatic compounds (chains of carbon), and this will bind the plant phosphorous, nitrogen and sulfur in heterocyclics (loose ring structures with other compounds as well as carbon in the ring) in its matrix, which are like lollies to fungi. These are essential for the general health and vigour of all plants, and to extract these lollies, fungi detach the aliphatic chains and charges the aromatic residues. These charged residues form in the first 12 months after the fire, becoming the loci for DOM, allowing soil organic matter to accrue, improving soil fertility.

Along with this cool burn process comes the fresh grass, the new regrowth bringing in kangaroos from land that is likely to have more phosphate as a result of the type of bedrock or phosphate-rich soil. Naturally, the kangaroos defecate, which in the first few months contributes phosphate to the soil of the burnt patch, another contributor to the restoration of soil fertility (see Figure 2-12).

The intensity of the rainfall and the nature of the chars from the first fire dictate how long it takes for grasses to become lank and sour, nutrient deficient, and the need for another fire. The timing is typically between three and 10 years, but in the monsoonal tropics can be seasonal.

Knowing how to rotate burns to optimise phosphate distribution would have taken thousands of years to learn. From observing that kangaroos prefer to eat short green grass, Aboriginal Australians were able to determine the optimum pasture rotation system and move kangaroos by low-temperature burns, not by fences. Figure 2-13 shows an example of a cool burn and Figure 2-14 the post-fire regrowth.

There are also advantages to hot burns, which are typically used to control trees. For instance, mountain ash takes longer than a decade of growth from germination to set the first seed. Therefore to remove mountain ash trees from the landscape, a hot burn every decade for three decades is required. Mountain Ash take longer than a decade to set the first seed. To promote acacias for seed before a big tribal gathering, a hot burn would be carried out early enough for seeds to be ready for the future corroboree, typically three years. A hot burn creates a lot of ash but mineralises nitrogen which volatilises into the atmosphere, leaving the soil post-burn nitrogen deficient. This means that the first species to emerge and flourish after the burn are nitrogen-fixing species, such as acacias, which have an advantage because they have nodulated roots with nitrogen-fixing bacteria, which most trees do not. A hot burn produces dark grey to black smoke as the hotter fire results in soot condensing in the flame. Soot aerosols are known to nucleate rain and therefore locally in the presence of elevated humidity increase rainfall—rain may follow late season burns. There is some evidence in explorers diaries that Aboriginals used hot burns to cause local rains during drought.[72]

These plausible scientific explanations are an indication as to why Indigenous land management was effective, but so little is known of the burning system undertaken in specific areas that the science behind it is unknown. The science behind burning as a land management tool is complex and not yet well understood. While burning projects in the

Kimberley, Arnhem Land and Kakadu are lauded, more recently the efficacy of those regimes are being questioned, particularly the carbon abatement programs which may be, through too frequent or mistimed burning, having a perverse effect on the ecology of those areas.[73]

Because Europeans did not take the time to study Aboriginal landscape management in any given area, it does not mean Aboriginal landscape management was not a sophisticated, productive, sustainable landscape system designed to be fit for purpose. We believe that the thought processes would have been on improvements to systems, not on why the system works.

Based on their values, the Aboriginal system managed land to their 'economic' advantage; less than 30 per cent of their time being required to collect food and manage the landscape and any unpredicted events. If individual effort was not valued over fulfilling community needs, group comfort and group values, then there was no incentive to work harder. This may be why evidence of experimentation and rejection of plant husbandry, a pre-requisite for a more sedentary, village, agricultural life style, in northern Australia and southern Western Australia occurred. A more likely explanation is that for the landscape, climate and dominant soil type, propagation, weed management and stock management was achieved more easily, with less effort and in less time, using fire. Some have argued the absence of wool in kangaroos or any human need for textiles removed one of the drivers for the development of agriculture.[74]

Unfortunately, the recognition and communication of landscape management systems was mired by cultural differences, as well as indifference. While Australia is still learning to understand and appreciate its First Nations culture, it is now recognised that the Aboriginal template for land management had an enforceable system of title ownership and transfer. The Dreamtime had rigorous standards for enforcing land stewardship, and a strong feedback loop, with oral communication for record keeping.[75] Through this system, though climate change was not prevented, weather and climate variability were less common than what we have experienced in recent decades.

Chapter 3

Climate Change
Expanding the debate

The focus of discourse on climate change has two aspects:

- whether climate change that may be happening—as measured by mean annual global temperature—has been caused by increased carbon dioxide in the atmosphere
- whether this increase in carbon dioxide, and to a lesser extent, other GHGs, is caused primarily by our industrial emissions.

The intensity of this debate has been so politically dominated it has overwhelmed a proper discussion on the subject. In the past, people who were against the hypothesis that climate change is principally caused by increased GHG emission from industry, were condemned as climate deniers, leaving little room for nuanced and robust debate. Now we are in the absurd situation that, if you take the position that the assumptions underpinning the hypothesis that carbon emissions, as a proxy for GHGs, are the only cause of climate change, you are regarded as progressive and pro-environment, and if you argue against any part of this hypothesis, you are regarded as conservative.

Here we explore the link between the increase in annual global temperature and atmospheric CO_2, carbon emissions. Then we explore the correlation of atmospheric CO_2 and land. Land clearing required for agriculture is also a major contributor to GHG activity, and land clearing is modelled on global population, so it must be considered whether population also correlates with atmospheric CO_2.

Because the climate debate is confused by the almost exclusive focus on the increase in average global annual temperature rise, we test the assumptions underpinning the premise that carbon emissions are causing global warming. To demonstrate the nuances of the debate, we also explore other measures of climate change at a continental scale, such as precipitation, extreme heat events and the frequency of significant bushfires. Importantly, while all these measures are accelerating due to anthropogenic factors, none are principally caused by GHGs.

What is climate change?

Climate has always changed and will continue to do so. It is a long-term alteration in the average weather patterns that have come to define Earth's local, regional and our global climate.

Serbian scientist Milutin Milankovitch theorised about Earth's long-term climate cycles a hundred years ago, hypothesising that changes in the position of the Earth in relation to the Sun are a strong driver of Earth's long-term climate, including triggering ice-ages. Plate tectonics also have a long-term effect on climate through altered ocean and wind currents.

There are also exceptionally short-term impacts on climate, the most severe in recorded history being the impact of a volcanic eruption over 536 and 537 BCE, which wiped out two summer seasons in the Northern Hemisphere and cooled summers for up to 50 years. This climate event caused about half of the population of Europe to starve to death and the consequent social upheaval led to the Viking raids and ultimate colonisation of Europe, and then England via Normandy, effectively creating Europe as we know it today.

Climate is subject to many influences including human impact on landscape. In the 1970s there was concern in the media over the world's climate cooling, and more recently, beginning in the late 1980s

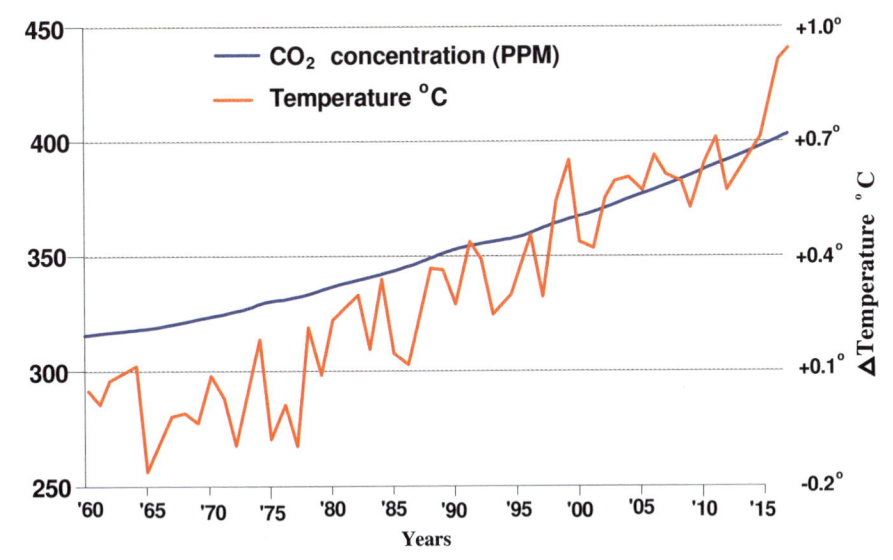

Figure 3-1. Global temperature change (relative to average temperature from 1951-1980) and CO₂ measurements made at the Mauna Loa Observatory in Hawaii. Adapted from NOAA.https://www.weforum.org/agenda/2018/05/earth-just-hit-a-terrifying-milestone-for-the-first-time-in-more-than-800–000-years

and accelerating, the world's climate heating, as shown in Figure 3-1. Figure 3-1 clearly shows that since 1980 there has been a global average temperature rise and a correlated rise of CO_2 in the air. Therefore, as measured by global mean temperature, climate since 1980 has been changing and this change can be correlated with a rise in atmospheric CO_2.

Are we causing the climate to change?

Climate is the summation of daily weather events over a year or more, and can be measured by changes in mean temperature, frequency, duration and intensity of extreme events, and the change in periodicity and level of precipitation. Climate change, as reported by the media, has primarily focused on global temperature increase, particularly the frequency and intensity of extreme weather events. A secondary impact of climate change is rising sea levels around islands, which is also frequently presented as a measure of the threat of climate change.

This reporting has led to the majority view that the rise in Earth's temperature is solely caused by GHGs of which CO_2 is the main culprit. Noting, although significantly less abundant in the atmosphere, other GHGs such as methane and nitrous oxide have a greater impact on climate than CO_2. Water vapour, though more abundant than CO_2 is also a GHG.

Reporting has also shaped the majority view that climate models can and do accurately predict the future. This is not so. And we are causing climate change by at least one factor other than GHG emissions.

A key and often ignored question is: what do GHGs do? GHGs prevent heat accumulated on the Earth's surface during the day from leaving the earth's atmosphere at night as thermal radiation into space. This prevents the night-time temperature from dropping to natural lows and results in an accumulated temperature increase the following day. GHGs trap heat like a blanket on a bed.

Separately, CO_2 causes modification of the acid/alkali balance of the ocean, reducing alkalinity. Although this is important, it won't be discussed in this book, which focuses on continental climate change.

Many landscape scientists and meteorologists disagree with the consensus view that GHG is the only or the major first order impact on continental climate change. Though GHGs, from carbon emissions and fossil fuels, are clearly an important component of global climate change, land management, principally agricultural practices, are the key factor causing continental climate change. Our reasons for drawing this conclusion follow.

Over time, there is a correlation between CO_2 levels and average global temperatures. Carbon dioxide entrapped in air bubbles in polar ice and Greenland icesheets have been extracted and compared with average global temperature. From sea-level rise expert John Englander's website,[76] Figure 3-2 shows a correlation between CO_2, mean global temperature and sea level rise. It shows that CO_2 in the Holocene rises above the sea-level induced plant growth maxima of 300 ppm. This is the maximum recorded natural increase of atmospheric CO_2 up to the Holocene—the end of the last ice age—in the last 500 000 years.

Climate Change

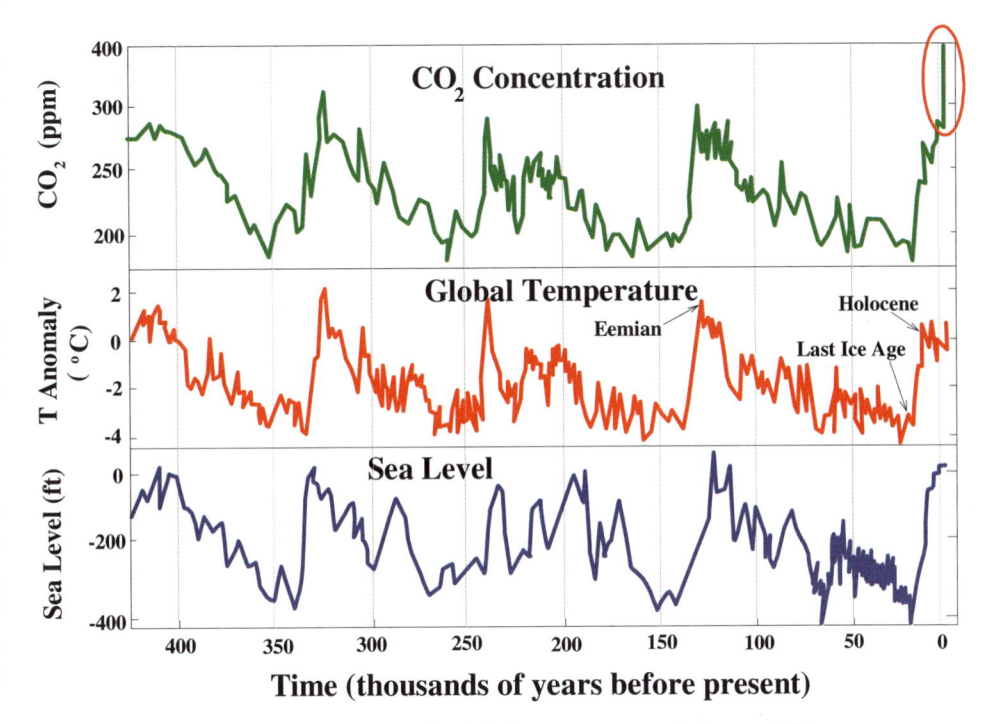

Figure 3-2. Correlation of sea levels, global temperature variation and CO_2 concentration Adapted from and redrawn from data on sea-level rise climate-change expert, John Englander's website: johnenglander.net

This level was exceeded after 1945 and, as seen in Figure 3-3 has risen ever since.

Figure 3-2 shows that prior to the Holocene, lower temperatures likely resulted in increased sheet ice and glaciers, and reduced sea levels. Conversely, reduced sea levels also led to an increase in land area at the temperate and tropical latitudes, in turn resulting in increased vegetation growth and less CO_2 in the atmosphere.

John Englander's figure is not from an official source. Figure 3-3 from the US NOAA shows a similar graph.[77] Figure 3-3 shows that in 2019, CO_2 concentrations had exceeded the Holocene interglacial maxima by over 30 per cent, therefore, it is clear from Figures 3-1, 3-2 and 3-3 that CO_2 concentrations in the atmosphere have definitely increased due to human activity.

However, it is a given in science that correlation does not mean

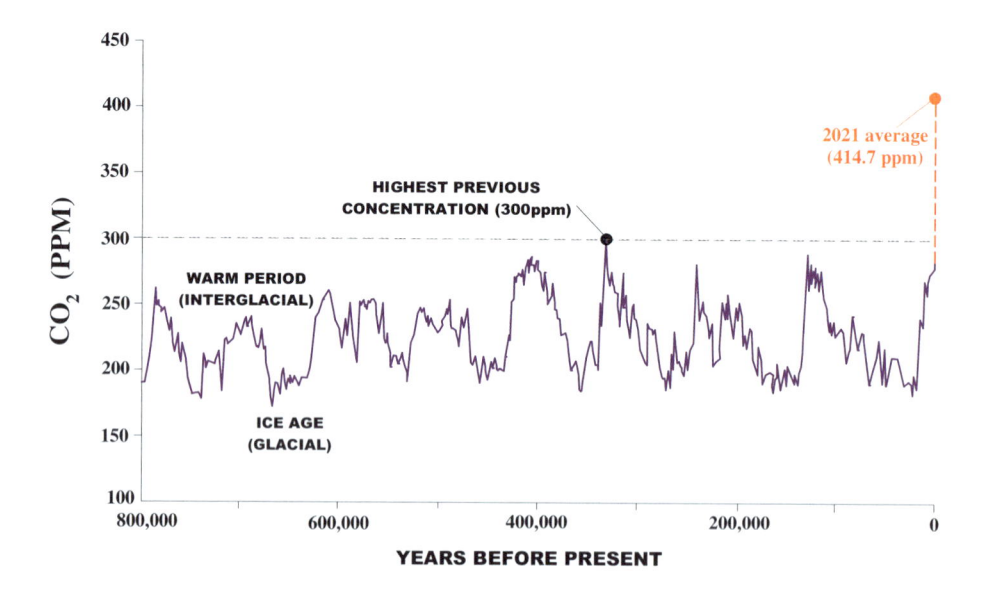

Figure 3-3. Atmospheric CO₂ levels 800 000 BP to now. Adapted from data of NCEI, NOAA Climate.gov

causation, so although CO_2 is correlated with global temperature rise, CO_2 alone may not have caused the global temperature rise.

Does CO_2 in the atmosphere equate with fossil fuel emissions?

It appears that at least one other significant cause, apart from GHG emissions, underlies not only CO_2 increase but in particular anthropogenic climate change. The rise in CO_2 emissions does not correlate with a rise in emissions between 1750 and 1870. Although elevated CO_2 in the atmosphere is undoubtedly influenced by fossil fuel emissions, Figure 3-4 which shows global CO_2 emissions plotted against atmospheric CO_2 between 1750 to 2019, indicates that there may be another process impacting atmospheric CO_2 emissions.

The public is left with the impression that imperfection of fit with time between gas emissions of atmospheric gas concentrations is probably due to sorption into water, as there are many articles on acidifications of oceans as a result of elevated atmospheric CO_2. All gases can be sorbed into solids or water, and the rate at which this occurs is called 'the partitioning coefficient'. The partitioning coefficient

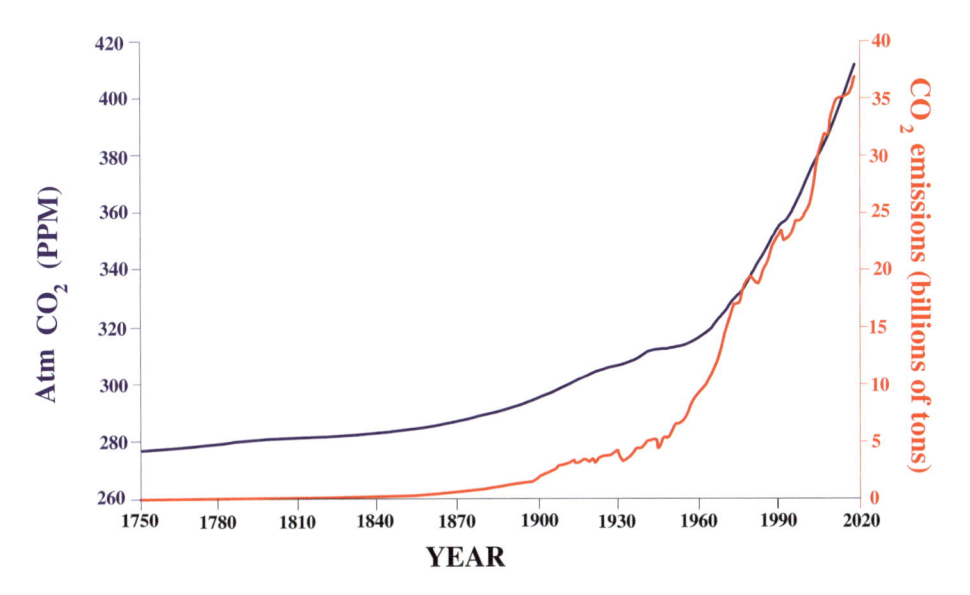

Figure 3-4. Plot of CO_2 in atmosphere and CO_2 emissions. Adapted from data and figures from NOAA, ETHZ, Our World in Data, NOAA Climate.gov

between air and water is significant and is impacted by temperature as well as the CO_2 concentration in both water and air. As CO_2 in air reduces, CO_2 is released from water, so water is a sink for rising CO_2 in the atmosphere. This means changes in partitioning of CO_2 into water and solids will affect atmospheric concentrations of CO_2. Partitioning of CO_2 into water is comparatively rapid, so the amount of partitioning in 250 ppm and 300 ppm in air compared with 300 ppm and 400 ppm would not be sufficiently different to account for the difference between emissions and CO_2 in the air as shown in Figure 3-4. Consequently, given the speed of the expected dampening, CO_2 concentrations in air do not directly reflect variability of emissions. Put simply, something other than fossil fuel emissions, appears to be affecting carbon dioxide in the air.

As noted, the trend in Figure 3-4 seems to correlate to the history of global use of fossil fuels. Burning of coal to generate electricity commenced in 1882 and by the 1960s coal had become the major fuel used to generate electricity in the US. At the same time as we began to see the rise of oil, closely followed by gas. Figure 3-4 clearly shows that the emissions rate (red line) accelerated in the late 1950s but plateaued in 1980 before accelerating again.[78]

Again, there is a strong correlation between atmospheric CO_2 (blue line) and CO_2 emissions (red line). However, on closer inspection it is evident that atmospheric CO_2 was rising *before* CO_2 emissions, and CO_2 emissions do not mirror changes in the rate of atmospheric CO_2, thereby indicating other factors are at play.

The principal factor is that fossil fuels as a new power source transformed economies and enabled the industrial revolution. Prosperity and progress also drove population growth which in turn spurred greater development and global food demand, causing more land to be cleared of natural vegetation. This notion is supported by a dip in CO_2 emissions in the 1930s during The Great Depression, before the widespread use of tractors, but CO_2 continued to rise.

Land clearing releases CO_2 from vegetation and the soil. Increased CO_2 emissions after The Great Depression reflect population growth and a shift to large-scale industry, and sitting behind industry is primary production. Increased primary production required more land, and drove the industrial revolution. Consequent advances and innovations in agriculture technology changed how we used land. There is also a compelling correlation between developments in agricultural technology and increased agricultural land with CO_2 emissions.

Therefore, it must be concluded that factors other than greenhouse gas emissions have caused CO_2 to rise, so lowering CO_2 emissions from fossil fuel use and sequestering carbon may not be sufficient to stop global temperature rise, particularly if land clearing continues.

Heat waves as a measure of climate change

Various atmospheric processes influence climate change and examining only CO_2 emissions fails to capture the broader atmospheric influences and systems at play. In this and the following sections we evaluate extreme events and rainfall as other measures of climate change, asking questions such as, is the number of extreme hot days also rising? Is rainfall rising or falling? Do floods and cyclones occur more frequently or with greater severity?

Heat waves are increasing. Every two years, the Australian Bureau of Meteorology produces a report on the state of climate in Australia. In 2020 the report revealed that the number of extreme hot days since 1980 are increasing exponentially as shown in Figure 2-10 on page 59. The bureau reports the area average daily mean temperature as being extreme when the 99th percentile of each month is exceeded. This generally means that more than 40 per cent of Australia is experiencing temperatures in the warmest 1 per cent for that month.

Figure 2-10 also shows that the frequency and duration of extreme heat events have increased steadily from 1910. The number of events increased in the 1920s and again in the 1950s. Apart from an extreme event of seven days duration in the early 1940s, increases in duration did not occur until the late 1950s. From the 1980s, growth in extreme heat events was exponential, both in number and duration. Emissions from fossil fuels, as indicated in Figure 3-4, accelerated in the late 1950s but plateaued in 1980 before accelerating again. This is not consistent with the record of extreme temperature events shown in Figure 2-10. At best, correlation with CO_2 only broadly matches.

The fact that heat waves are increasing exponentially in Australia is arguably the most shocking statistic of climate change. The impact of extreme heat events is horrendous, with heat waves reportedly killing more Australians than any other natural cause, both directly and indirectly, as many road deaths and suicides can be attributed to heat waves.[79] Additionally, and as witnessed during the 2019–20 Black Summer bushfires, heat waves can devastate the landscape and wildlife. This alone makes it imperative that we find a mitigatory solution to anthropogenic climate change. However, addressing only fossil fuel emissions and GHGs is not the answer as they are *not* the primary cause of extreme heat events.

An increase in heat waves with time does not align well with CO_2 emissions or atmospheric CO_2 concentrations. Figure 3-1 shows that average global temperature did not begin to rise above the mean level until the late 1970s but CO_2 has been rising constantly since about 1700, increasing more rapidly from 1870, plateauing between 1930 to 1960, before increasing exponentially. Though the frequency and number of hot days has also grown exponentially since the mid-1980s, the slower but still significant increase from the 1920s to the 1960s correlates poorly with CO_2 emissions and atmospheric CO_2. Also, despite CO_2 emissions decreasing as a result of Covid-19, 2020 remained the second hottest year on record. CO_2 emissions do not correlate with heat waves.

Using heat waves as a measure, anthropogenic climate change in Australia is happening. As demonstrated by mean global temperature and extremely hot temperature events, our climate is definitely changing and it is clearly not a natural phenomenon. The question is not so much is climate change happening and have humans caused it, because clearly the answer is yes, but what combination of factors have caused it and what is the most effective way to stop and reverse it.

Precipitation changes as a measure of climate change

Precipitation is an alternative measure of climate change. Changes at a regional level often appear earlier or are at least more defined than global climate change, which is inherently based on world-wide averages and suffers from a blurring effect of variability of the rate of change across the globe. As set out below, precipitation provides a more accurate regional model compared to global average temperature rise as a measure of climate change.

Precipitation patterns have also changed considerably in the last 50 years, with rainfall in continental temperate zones experiencing significant decline in contributions from polar lows (that is, winter precipitation) and therefore less rainfall, whereas rainfall in tropical areas has become more intense.[80] Though precipitation data is variable across the globe, and even more so with accelerating climate change, regional long-term precipitation trends become apparent earlier than temperature change and provide a more reliable indication of changing climate. For the reasons discussed earlier, diminished rainfall and desertification precede increased temperature rise.

One area well studied that was previously considered by many meteorologists as having the most reliable rainfall of all Australian agriculture areas, is South Western Western Australia (SWWA)[81], which has suffered at least one significant drop in rainfall since the 1970s and potentially another more recently, 2000–2020.[82] This is shown in Figure 1-2 and Figure 1-3 on page 26.

Figure 1-3 shows a regional mean, and as you can see, in some areas mean rainfall has diminished by up to 15 per cent, with another 15 per cent in the last 20 years.[83] This reduction is associated with a change in the frequency and intensity of cold fronts, particularly during the period May to July. Rain from storms associated with prefrontal troughs has diminished both through the absence of requisite weather formation and from less rain when troughs do form.

Due to our warming climate, the autumn and early winter lows are being displaced by mid-latitude highs moving to higher latitudes during winter. This condition does not result in frontal troughs and rain occurring because when the frontal troughs do occur, they generally produce less rain.

To examine this phenomenon further we looked at the combined inflows into all Perth's water supply dams, their catchment area being the Swan Basin lying within the eastern portion of SWWA, as shown in Figure 3-5, Figure 3-6a and Figure 3-6b. Inflows into dams are a combination of rainfall and landscape factors. As can be seen by comparing Figure 3-5 with Figure 3-6a, though rainfall had fallen by roughly 15 per cent, dam inflow had fallen between 70 and 80 per cent. An interplay of rainfall frequency and intensity, and landscape changes has caused this radical change. Are these landscape changes impacting climate?

Some authors have suggested that these changes in SWWA are part of natural regional climate change. Citing as evidence rainfall data at Rottnest Island, located just off the coast of Perth, which had a long

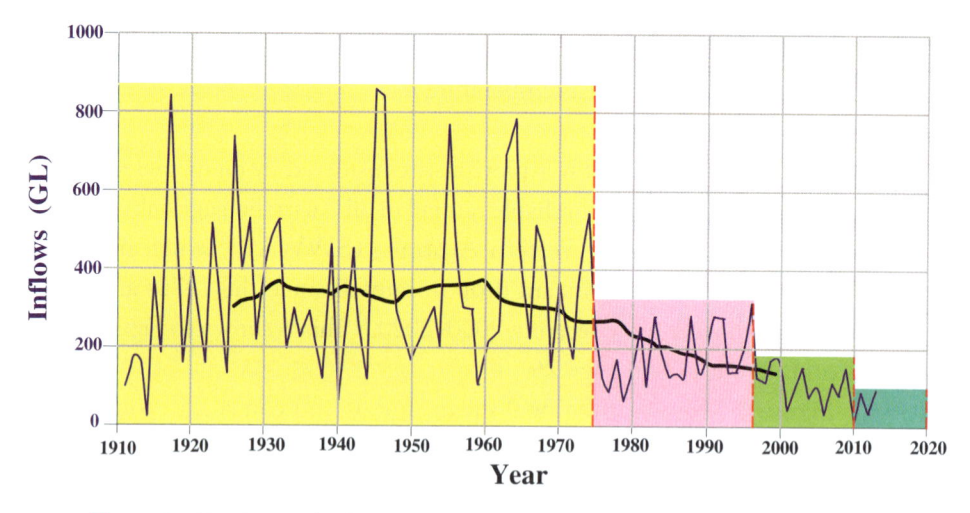

Figure 3-5. Total annual inflows to Perth dams 1910–2020. The black line is a time-weighted average– 31 year running averages. Adapted from Smith, I and Power S, 'Past and future inflows into Perth WA dams', *Journal of Hydrogeology: Regional studies* 2 (2014) 84–96

dry period prior to 1920 (a mean rainfall of about 410 mm), as shown in Figure 3-7[84]. Perth data in Figure 3-5 and Figure 3-6a shows that rainfall during the decade between 1910 and 1920 does not support a step change in rainfall between that decade and the later decades. Though 1911 and 1913 was a drought for Perth, 1912, 1914, 1915, 1917 and 1919 are in the average range of the later decades, and 1916 was a very wet year. Dam inflow data (Figure 3-5) does indicate that the latter half of the previous decade (1900–10) was dry, as inflows for the first year of record at 1910 and 1911 are low. Consequently, as the Rottnest data does not show the same trends as Perth data for the period 1910–1920, we reject the idea that the loss of rainfall is part of a normal step change in regional rainfall.

Temperature correlation with reduced dam inflow does not demonstrate causation. In the Perth dam inflow study some 12 years after this period, Smith and Power conclude that,[iii] though there is a correlation

---

iii   Smith is also part of the Indian Ocean Climate Initiative team.

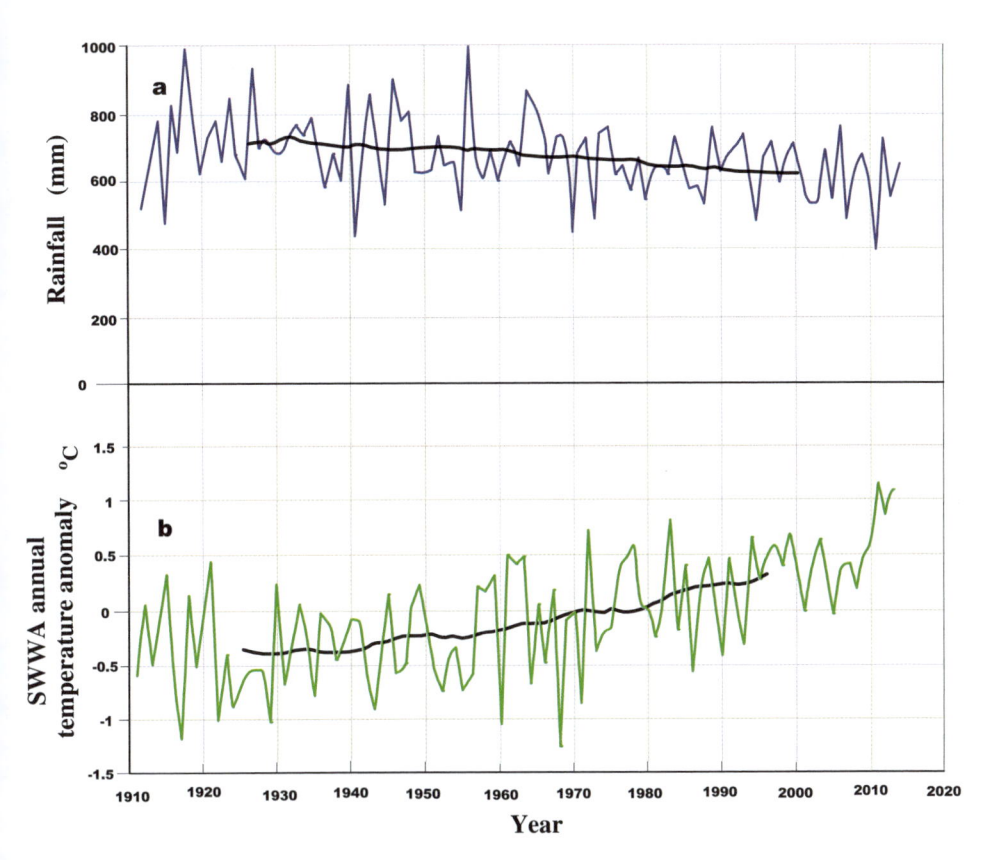

Figure 3-6. As for Figure 3-5, except for SWWA, (a) annual rainfall and (b) annual average temperature, both expressed as deviations from the long term (1960–1990) average values. Adapted from Smith, I and Power S, 'Past and future inflows into Perth WA, dams' *Journal of Hydrogeology: Regional studies* 2 (2014) 84–96

between temperature and dam water inflow, when the data is considered on an annual basis there is no causation between temperature and lower inflow.[85] The effect is simply that temperature reflects the lack of rain resulting from a hotter land surface. Temperature is simply the wrong measure for understanding lower rainfall and the inflow to dams. Elevated air temperature is not the cause of the lack of inflow; a hotter land surface is.

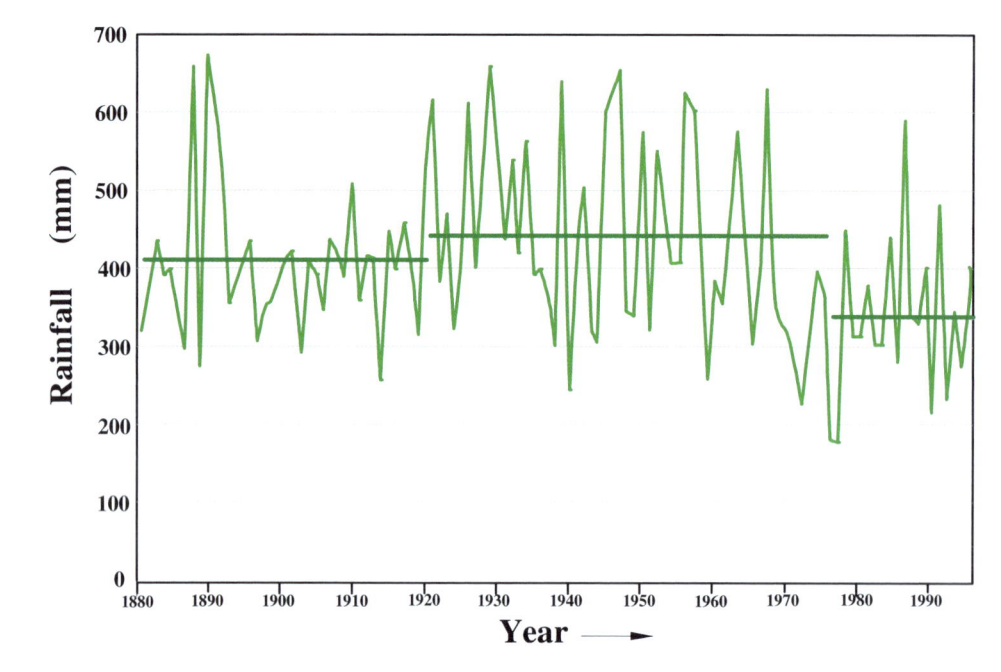

Figure 3-7. Rottnest Island Lighthouse May-July rainfall from 1880 to 1996. Horizontal lines are means for 1880–1920 (408 mm), 1921–75 (439 mm) and 1976–95 (337 mm).[235] Adapted from IOCI 2002 *Climate variability and change in south west Western Australia.*

Rainfall and dam inflow as predicted by climate models

Climate models can be wrong or insufficiently accurate so as not to be a useful prediction of what actually occurs. Nevertheless, regional climate models are important for predicting rainfall and resultant inflows for water dams, and such models would be expected to have the potential to be more closely correlated with regional data than with global models. All models including regional models are based on theoretical concepts considered relevant to the site known as 'site conceptual models'. In regard to rainfall models, the Indian Ocean Climate Initiative (IOCI) undertook a study reported in 2002 to predict the impact of climate change caused by doubling CO_2 emissions from 1980 atmospheric concentrations, using a variety of different climate models.[86] Interestingly, while trying to calibrate the models, they concluded that the climate models significantly under-predicted the amount of rainfall loss currently occurring. They believe, although no evidence was presented, that though GHG is a first order cause of this rainfall loss, landscape impacts are likely to be a second order impact, a quiet acknowledgement that landscape changes may be a significant driver of climate change but that climate models do not yet adequately consider these impacts.

Climate models are not only a poor correlation with measured data but underpredict climate change. Figure 3-8 and Figure 3-9, from the study by Smith and Power in 2014, show measured rainfall data and dam inflows from the Swan Valley. Also shown is the output for seven individual climate models used for the Coupled Model Intercomparison Project—Phase 5 of the IPCC Assessment Report of 2013 known as CMIP5, as well as the minimum, maximum and median values of 31-year averages of all the 38 climate models used in this study. All models were coded to simulate GHG emissions' impacts on regional climate to predict either rainfall and, coupled with a hydraulic model, to predict inflow. The extraordinary thing is that not only were all models poor predictors of actual data, but they badly under-predicted the reduction of rainfall and totally underpredicted what the loss of inflow actually was. This is probably because an unknown factor was not considered, or a known factor underestimated as a result of input assumptions not being questioned and therefore not included in sensitivity analysis. That models underpredict climate change has been seen time and time again; when run in 2002,[87] and even as models improved in 2014,[88] and most recently in June 2021.[89] Simply put, it is likely that the conceptual model is wrong and other factors are having a greater impact than CO_2 emissions.

Recent research has established that landscape factors are having a significant impact on catchment hydrology, with long-term step changes in river flow occurring, after return of precipitation following drought, with apparently minor reduction in long-term mean annual precipitation.[90] This effect for Swan Valley (and potentially the greater SWWA) is shown in Figure 3-5.

Rainfall and dam inflow data as climate change measures are being

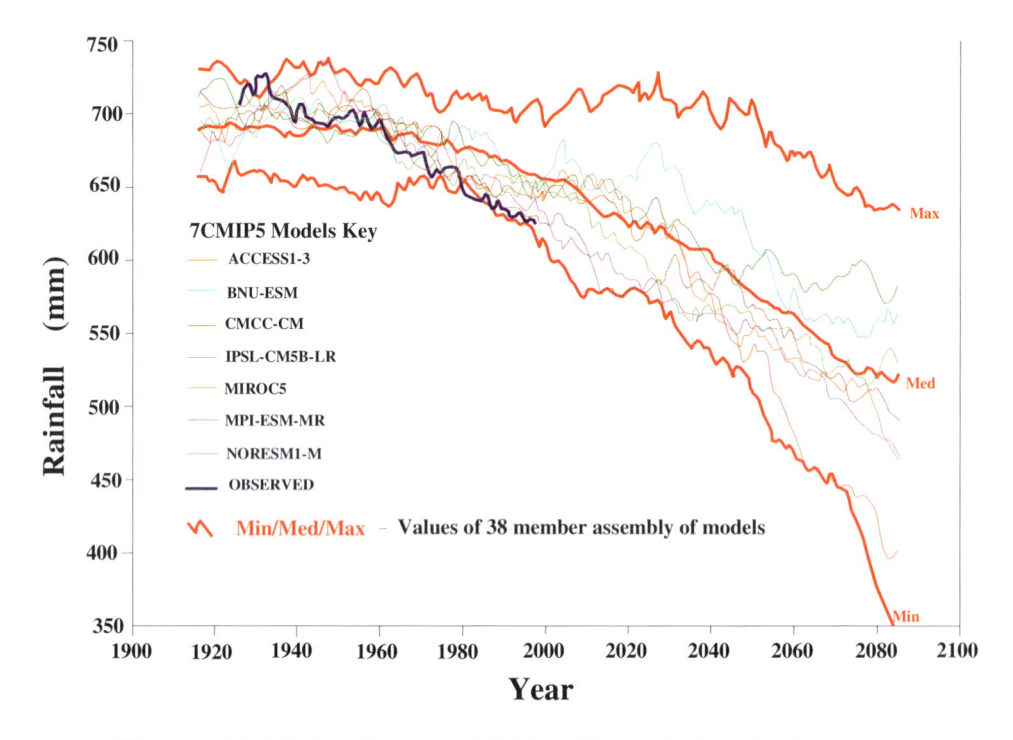

Figure 3-8. Modelled prediction of rainfall from 38 models plotted against observed values for the SWWA on a 31-year running average. Adapted from Smith, I and Power S, 'Past and future inflows into Perth WA, dams' *Journal of Hydrogeology: Regional studies* 2 (2014) 84–96

impacted by factors other than temperature. Temperature is a significant outcome of increasing CO_2 emissions, therefore it is understandable that these climate models would be poor predictors of actual climate change as measured by precipitation and dam inflow data. So, it can be concluded in SWWA and potentially all continents that, in regard to rainfall and temperature, GHG is not the only nor potentially the main driver of climate change. Some other anthropogenic factors are at play because the change, particularly in the last two decades in regard to river flow, is outside the known natural variation and enhanced greenhouse climate change predictions. Similar problems for prediction have occurred at global scale.[91] Models of climate change for the last 20 years have consistently under-estimated the rate of climate change,

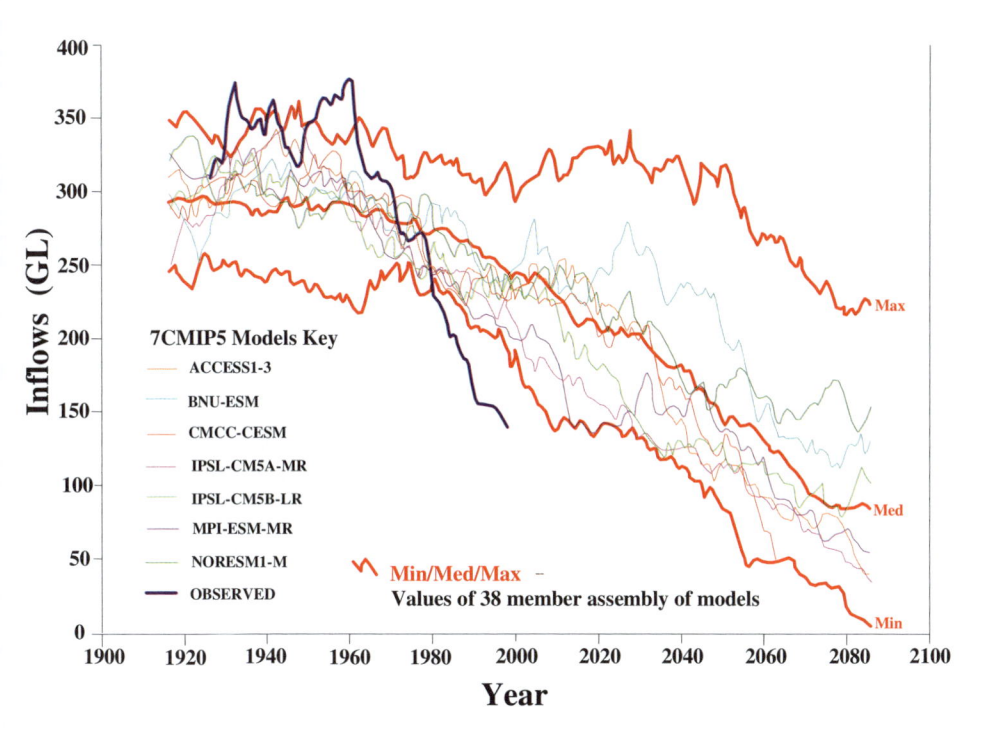

Figure 3-9. As for Figure 3–8, except for observed and modelled flows Adapted from Smith, I and Power S, 'Past and future inflows into Perth WA, dams' *Journal of Hydrogeology: Regional studies* 2 (2014) 84–96.

not only for global climate indicators like mean global temperature, but also local measures of climate change such as rainfall and heat waves. Clearly another major factor apart from GHGs is at play.

What other anthropogenic impacts could alter the climate

Land use changes the fate of solar radiation. Human population and land cleared for agriculture use have increased significantly between 1750 and 2020, as have urban areas and paved surfaces like roads etc. The effect has been a greatly increased cleared land area which has substantively altered the relationship between latent and sensible heat, lowering the former and increasing the latter.

It is well known that clearing land for agriculture often leads to deserts in low latitudes,[92] and Neolithic agricultural land degradation likely caused some of the peats and moors to form at higher latitudes. Loss of rainfall has recently been observed in land cleared in forests in Brazil.[93] As discussed earlier it is also known and evident that clearing land releases CO_2.[94] Could agriculture be both a source of CO_2 and, via other factors, climate change?

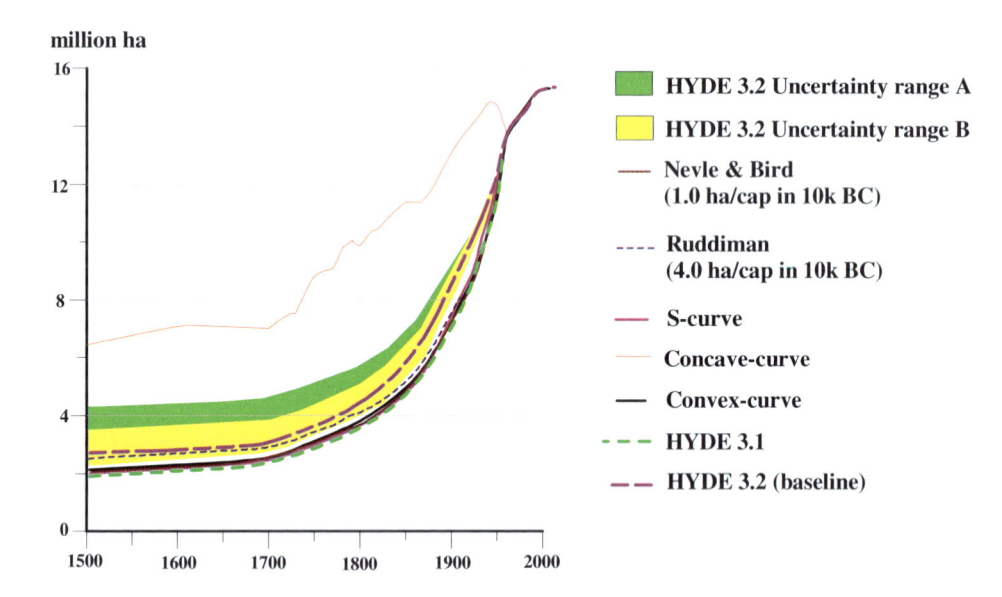

Figure 3-10. Modelled amount of land used for agriculture with time. Hyde 3.2 (baseline) is used in Figures 3–11 and 3–12 Adapted from: Goldewidj K, Dekker S and van Zanden J, 'Per-captita estimation of long-term historical land use and the consequence for global change research' *Journal of Land Use Science*, Vol 12, No 5, pp 313–337, 2017.

Establishing how much cleared land is currently *used for* agriculture is difficult, let alone establishing land cleared *for* agriculture, both cropping and grazing. One way is to equate human population with land needed for food production based on rainfall and latitude; a per-capita estimation. Figure 3-10 has been prepared by Goldewijk *et al* 2017 using this methodology as a means of evaluating a number of models to predict a time series increase in agricultural land.[95]

The old adage, initially stated by statistician George Box, requoted recently in relation to Covid-19 by virologists,[96] that 'all models are wrong but some are useful', applies in this instance. One limitation of the modelling is that per-capita estimation does not consider recent changes in the developing world's preferences for beef and the use of agricultural land for aspects other than food and fibre production, that is bio-oils,

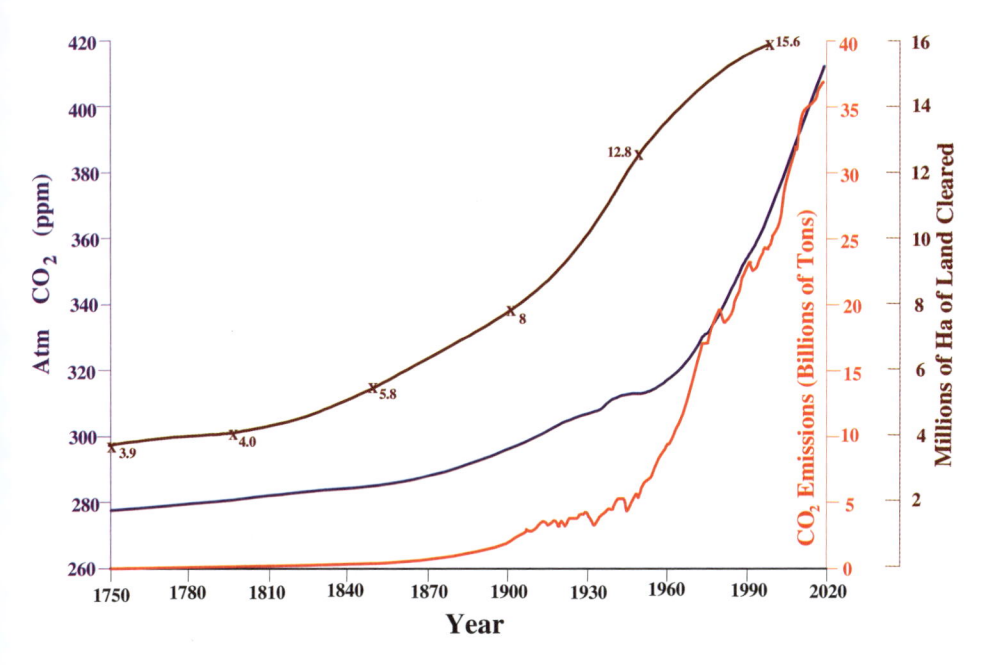

Figure 3-11. Is an overlay of Figure 3-10 on Figure 3-4—CO_2 in the atmosphere compared to annual emissions and millions of hectares (Ha) used by agriculture. Adapted from CO_2 and emission data and figures from NOAA, ETHZ, 'Our World in Data' Climate.gov

biofuels and tobacco. Consequently, it is likely the HYDE 3.2 Baseline adopted by Goldewijk *et al* (as shown in Figure 3-10) underestimates the pace of land clearing for the last 50 years. The dotted red line (shown in Figure 3-10) is considered to be the best prediction and the pink line the maxima. Overlaying the dotted crimson line from Figure 3-10 with CO_2 concentrations in air in Figure 3-4 is shown in Figure 3-11.

Modelled land cleared for agriculture also correlates with CO_2 rise and has a rapid acceleration after about 1930. Figure 3-11 shows a correlation between land clearing and atmospheric CO_2. Prior to 1870, land clearing more closely mirrors atmospheric CO_2, because land clearing predates CO_2 emissions—indicating causation of both CO_2 and temperature. Shifting the two curves until they overlay for most of the curve, illustrates that the correlation is good up to about 1990 for CO_2 in the atmosphere, as shown in Figure 3-12. There is a shift of about 45 years between land cleared for agriculture, based on population, and increased CO_2 in the atmosphere. After 1960 the Green Revolution occurred and the amount of land clearing for agriculture compared to population no longer correlates. After about 1980, as fuel prices increased, agricultural land was also used for biofuels and increased

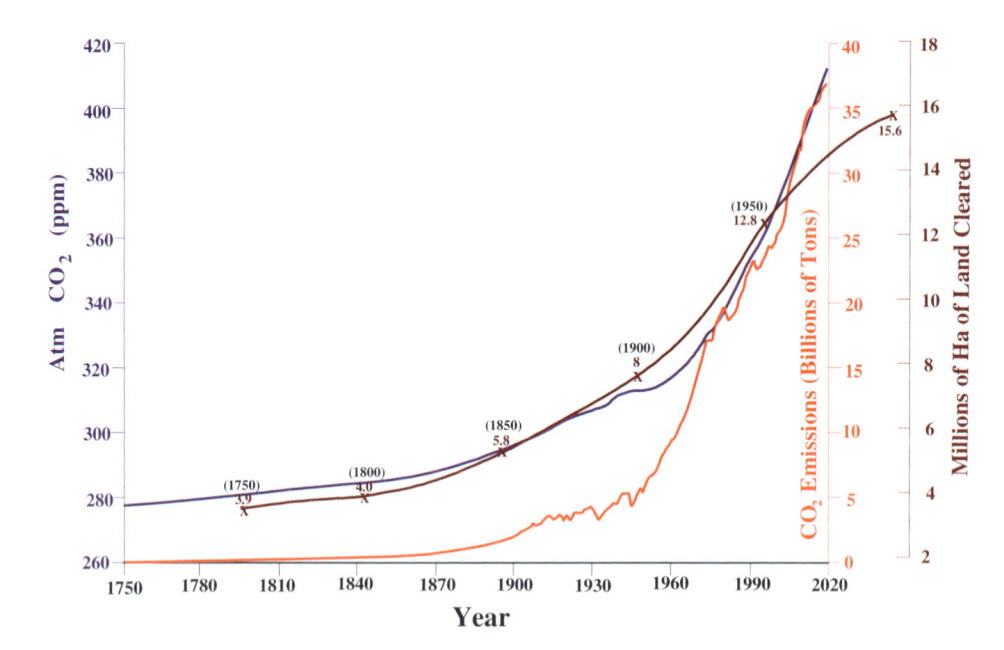

Figure 3-12. CO_2 in atmosphere and CO_2 emissions plotted against land under agriculture offset forward by 45 years. Adapted from CO_2 and emission data and figures adapted from NOAA, ETHZ, 'Our World in Data' Climate.gov

tobacco use worldwide, as well as, widespread clearing for beef consumption and bio-oil by the developing world. Nevertheless, once shifted by 45 years, the fit, as shown in Figure 3-12 appears good before 1990. The greatest acceleration of the rate of emissions occurs post-1980 as industrial development occurs in Asia and South America, particularly India, China and Brazil—this development corresponds with the greatest clearing of land for beef, bio-oils (palm oil) and biofuels. The land cleared for this purpose has not been captured in land clearing based on population-growth models but is evident in land satellite imagery.[97]

Land cleared for agricultural use contributes more to climate change than just what is released as greenhouse gas emissions. In the last 40 years agricultural practices have severely mined organic carbon from the soil. Causing latent heat to diminish, and loss of, or a severely diminished small water cycle. Loss of organic matter in soil impacts the CO_2 in the atmosphere. Though latitude rainfall and charge strongly impact organic matter, both on the starting amount of organic matter and the final degraded value, we estimate that overall worldwide soil organic matter loss due to agriculture is between 4 and 6 per cent in any given area.[iv] Though this is small compared to fossil fuel emissions and vegetative loss, the nature of the curve would suggest that if elevation of GHGs in the atmosphere is a cause of climate change, so too could be the increase in land clearing for agriculture. Both are correlated with CO_2 in air. But only land clearing is directly responsible for increased infrared radiation. This is the source of heat that is raising global temperature.

The IPCC acknowledge that clearing vegetation and agricultural practice releases CO_2 and other GHGs into the atmosphere. But it fails to understand that the contribution of GHGs by land clearing is not the only landscape factor that is affecting rainfall and heat waves.

---

iv Between the 200 years from 1750 and 1950 approximately, an additional 10 million ha was added for agricultural use. At a depth of 30 cm and a bulk density of 1.3, this is equivalent to 286 t/ha, which is equivalent to 2860 million tonnes of CO_2 emissions from soil being released to the atmosphere in that time. Note this does not account for the reduced capture of CO_2 due to vegetation loss, or methane loss in the tundra, or CO_2 loss from draining of acid sulfate soil.

Cleared land has a greater impact than just increased temperature. In SWWA significant expansion of the grain belt occurred with the advent of modern fertilisers and soil testing, and resulted in a significant expansion of cropping in the 1950s. Again, in the 1980s, the introduction of dwarf varieties of grain and knockdown herbicides facilitated expansion into previously marginal land. Based on Figure 3-6b, temperature in these regions went above the long-term average in 1976 and has climbed ever since. Dam inflow, Figure 3-5, reduced enormously in this year and has never recovered. Though rainfall, Figure 3-6a, only recorded a slow gradual decline from the mid-1960s.

Clearing land reduces precipitation over a region. Figure 3-13 overlays cropping land with the loss of rainfall for SWWA. Given the limited number of recording stations, as discussed in Chapter 1,

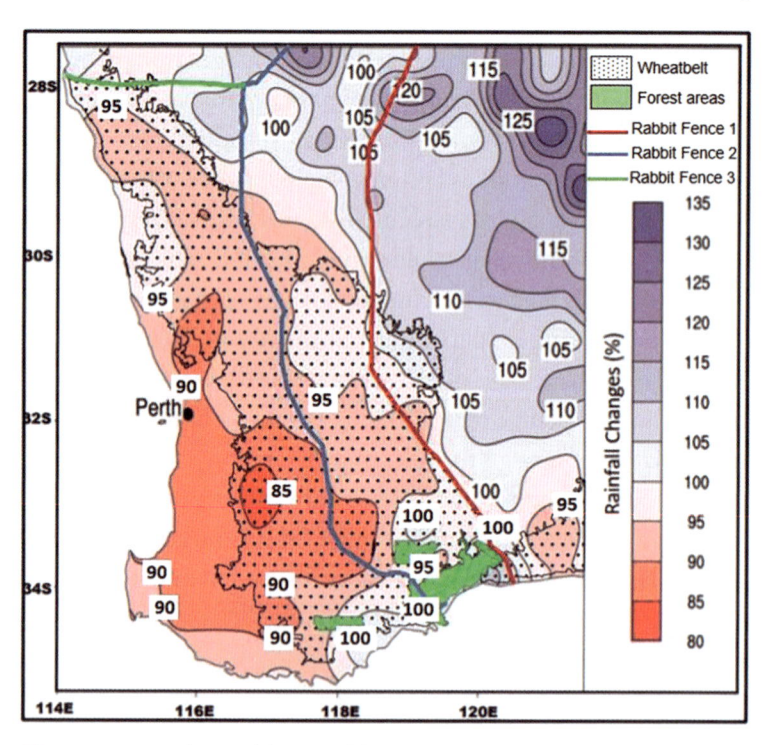

Figure 3-13. Landuse, rabbit proof fence and percent rainfall change for SWWA. Rainfall Change as Percentage for the Average May-October Rainfall of 1976-2001 compared to that of the same period of 1925-1975. Base Map Source: IOCI 2002, Climate variability and change in SWWA

Figure 1-2 and Figure 1-3 on page 26, this overlay shows a very good comparison of agricultural land and loss of rainfall. For the sake of comparison, the Rabbit Proof Fences are also shown in this figure. Evidently cropping land is correlated with the reduced rainfall zone, but it also impacts the partly cleared timbered country to the west of the cropping land on the Darling Ranges east of the Swan Plain.

Cleared land increases heat waves. Across the continent, land clearing accelerated during post war periods, in 1920–30 and 1947–60 due to Soldier Settler Schemes, and again in 1970–80 with mechanisation, chemical fertilisers, crop health products and improved crop varieties. These known increases in land clearing in Australia have a close association with the heat waves shown in Figure 2-10 on page 59 and could explain the increase of heat events from 1920, before global temperature rise was apparent.

Changes in the frequency and duration of heat waves and measurement of the loss of precipitation predates agreed measurable global temperature increase by at least 20 to 30 years.

Reduced rainfall and dam inflows in SWWA and heat waves across Australia can be correlated with land clearing for agriculture, but we contend it is more than just correlation, it is causation, and that agriculture as predominately practised, is a first order factor in climate change.

Anthropogenic climate change

There is no doubt that climate change is happening at a rate above the natural rate of change, but the causes and the solutions needed are still subject to debate.

The essayist Henry Louis Mencken stated 'there is always a well-known solution to every human problem—neat, plausible, and wrong'. CO_2 as a first order cause of climate change is a plausible but not a neat solution. It is plausible but wrong to assume that climate change is caused solely by GHG effects, because it is clear that other factors are also at play. It is in fact an unhelpful and misleading simplification. Terrestrial systems and atmospheric processes are interdependent, and individually and collectively complicated. Continuing to focus only on

CO_2 because the problem is complicated, as Charles Keeling suggested, would be annihilistic.

Climate change represented by an increase in extreme heat events on the Australian continent occurred before mean global temperature showed a rise, with local continental effects seeming to be at play. It appears that precipitation changes, or at the very least dam inflow, predated temperature changes. Dam inflow loss is not due to temperature but landscape factors in association with precipitation. We acknowledge there is a correlation with fossil fuel emissions, there is too a correlation between modelled per-capita estimates of land clearing over time and CO_2 in the air.

Agriculture is the prime cause of climate change in SWWA. Climate studies in SWWA have concluded that autumn rainfall associated with fronts has decreased due, not only to less of this type of weather pattern (fewer fronts), but also fewer frontal troughs.[98] The reduction of precipitation from frontal rain, also noticeable on the east coast of Australia,[99] is due to a reduction of relative humidity as a consequence of less evapotranspiration. Agriculture has resulted in this loss of evapotranspiration.

Many landscape scientists and meteorologists disagree with the consensus view that GHG is the only or the major first-order impact on continental climate change.

Put simply, the impact of GHGs is significant, but land management is crucial as it leads to increased sensible heat at the expense of latent heat. Land management causes the increase in infrared radiation for the GHGs to reflect. Poor land management, though done with the best intentions, generates excess sensible heat which is a major cause of global warming and climate change. GHGs in trapping and holding heat in the atmosphere are part of the effect, exacerbating the problem, but not the primary cause of the heat.

Chapter 4

Should We Have Known?

Professor Lyn Abbott from the University of Western Australia's (UWA) School of Agriculture and Environment was Australia's first professor of soil biology and a previous National President of the Australian Soil Science Society. Phil and Lyn were discussing the unique nature of studying poor soils when she remembered an international colleague who, upon hearing of her appointment to UWA for a new position, offered commiserations for her studying soil biology in such highly weathered soils as those in south-western Australia.

Years later she realised it was an ideal location to study soil biological fertility. With hindsight Lyn came to appreciate the best way to understand a stressed system was to start with a system of low resilience, because the impacts of stress in the system become apparent earlier.

Australia's landscape and climate systems have been stressed for a long time—so much so, it is now self-evident. However, could we have known earlier? Or were stressed environment systems a substantive outcome of the industrial age? And who first drew the correlation between degraded landscape and climate change? Was it a scientist or a farmer? Was it here in Australia or overseas?

Learning from the past

In pre-literate societies, stories with great lessons attached to them were passed down as myths, legends, or songlines.

According to Greek myth, the goddess Athena and the god

Poseidon competed for the Kingdom of Attica. It was said that whoever gave the city the best gift was the one fit to hold the position of guardian of the kingdom. Poseidon gifted the city a well of salt water. Athena bestowed an olive tree on the city.

And so, Attica came to be rooted in the merits of the olive tree and in the name of the goddess whose gift it was. Olive trees provide shade, flourish on degraded mountain slopes, survive long periods of aridity, and provide useful fruit, oil and wood. They were essential to preventing further loss of soil from the arid and degraded hills of Attica. Olive trees were one of the few trees that grew on the denuded slopes and had an agricultural value. They represented a life closely bound to the preservation of Attica's steep, degraded land from further degradation—the roots of settlement.

The myth of how Athens got its name served to illustrate and preserve through generations the importance of the olive tree to fostering the previously degraded land of Attica and, with it, a life of relative domesticity. It was antiquity's version of putting up a sign saying *Do Not Cut Down Olive Trees*.

From the beginning of the 6th century BC (2550 bp) olive trees were protected by special laws, first instituted by the legislator and statesman, Solon. There are numerous ancient Greek myths affirming the protection afforded to olive trees, for which its reverence was as much practical as it was spiritual. In addition to Athena, the olive tree's virtue was championed by other famous Greek characters such as Aristaeus, Hercules, and the Myrtle Nymphs.

The olive tree was also central to Ancient Rome. The Roman Empire's economy was centred on agriculture and trade. For a time, territorial expansion meant that as land within the empire became exhausted, the Romans could supplant grain fields with olive estates and rely on imported grain from elsewhere. However, when the granary of the eastern Mediterranean desertified, they could no longer sustain their population.

The sanctity of the olive tree is almost universal. Numerous myths and parables, from disparate civilisations and religions (including

Judaism and Christianity in which the olive oil is sacred) explain the need to protect olive trees.

Cautionary tales from nomadic people on the margins of originally more fertile agricultural land have throughout history in sharing their lessons preserved humanity. Neolithic farming in Ireland and resultant land destruction took place some 2600 years before the first written version of the Old Testament of the Bible.[100] Similarly, and closer to the source of Bible stories, desertification in the hotter area of the Levant and Anatolian plateau is the result of degradation, caused or precipitated by agriculture with such a cycle having been completed more than 6000 years before the written record of the Bible.[101] Some of these people became the tribes of Israel. Their shared lived experience could well have become the biblical allegory of Adam and Eve in the Garden of Eden.

Australian Aboriginal Dreaming myths and songlines also describe how to thrive in their world: Australia. They tell of water holes, rivers, food sources, and maintenance of the ecological landscape, for the holistic wellbeing of the living system, inclusive of humankind. Aboriginal tribes in northern Australia reportedly experimented with agriculture.[102] It is logical that they would, when a level of agronomy appears to have afforded benefits to both people and the land. Benefits they observed from their neighbours in New Guinea who practiced primitive agriculture (there was a land bridge between Australia and New Guinea >8000 bp).

It would seem from the end of the ice age, as humans experimented with cropping, adverse ecological and climate impacts became apparent, and cautionary tales were woven into oral history to inform and warn of the perils of pillaging the land.

Plato and Ancient Greece

The connection between healthy soil and a moderated climate was clear in Plato's time. In fact, Plato used the phrase 'attempered climate' in his work *Critias* to imply moderation or control of the climate by the land.

Plato writes of Attica, a peninsula projecting into the Aegean Sea which includes the city of Athens. When describing the Attica peninsula, Plato notes that there used to be an abundance of wood in the mountains. In his work he reflects that between the peninsula's natural prime, of about 9000 years earlier,[v] and his time, excessive rains removed the topsoil. He laments more primitive but fertile times when the land was well covered with soil: 'not as now losing the water which flows off the bare earth'. In his writing he labours the suffering of the Attica Peninsula from soil erosion and degradation. Speaking not only of the lost landscape, but also of lost knowledge: 'husbandmen's awareness of the balance between agriculture and nature'.

Plato records that appropriate husbandry of the soil was necessary to prevent being left with the mere skeleton of the land. In an environment in which evaporation dominates, as Plato witnessed, aridity is the outcome. Conversely, as an outcome of prolonged farming in the Neolithic period in Ireland, where rainfall exceeded evaporation, the outcome was anaerobic putrefaction. The land was near drowned, manifested by the formation of peatlands and moors. The importance of those who work the land then cannot be overstated. Indeed, Plato speaks fondly of 'true husbandmen, who made husbandry their business, and were lovers of honour, and of a noble nature'.

Plato's description of a prosperous near past, in which high infiltration of rain into the groundwater nourished streams during the drier season to provide a base stream-flow year-round, demonstrates a rudimentary understanding that rich soils supported an abundance of water in the landscape and together influenced an 'attempered climate'.

People may have been aware of connected environmental systems, including landscape, soil, and climate, as early as sometime between 9000 bp and Plato's time 2500 bp. Plato's work demonstrates a nuanced understanding of the land, potentially even that landscape and climate are interlinked.

Given Plato's writings, should we have known earlier that loss of soil security leads to climate change?

---

v   Noting, the dawn of agriculture is estimated in that region to be approximately 9000 bp.

Bogged down—Neolithic farming in the British Isles

It was apparent from archaeological digs in the 1940s to current day that early Neolithic farmers also impacted the soil and landscape.[103] For instance, in the British Isles, while archaeological investigations revealed those areas to have been fertile tree-covered landscapes at about 4600 bp, those areas are now infertile moors, peatlands and bogs.

In subtemperate land, where rainfall exceeds evaporation, degraded land does not produce deserts, but the wet equivalent: moors, peatland, and bogs which make the climate wetter. Soils known as podzols often form on sedimentary and granite parent material. Podzols from these parent materials in subtemperate environments produce soils that are highly susceptible to degradation.[104] Neolithic farming started on these soils in the British Isles (Bodmin Moor and Dartmoor, England; and Ceide Field, Ireland), as woodlands predated widespread fire events which were followed immediately by grazing with some cropping.[105] It was thought that fire was used to clear the land and it is apparent from archaeological records that the climate in those regions prior to farming was drier and warmer than post farming.[106]

In Neolithic Ireland, over a period of about 400 years,

Figure 4-1. Ciede Fields near Ballycastle Island. Photo showing the top of Neolithic Stone fence showing overlying peat. The peat at this location was about 3m deep to the former pasture surface and less than 1 metre deep to the top of the paddock fences. The North Atlantic Ocean is in the background.

farming reduced the resilience of the land which caused the loss of topsoil. The removal of topsoil exposed a clay subsoil on the sedimentary parent material and granitic bedrock elsewhere. The exposed clay or bedrock interfered with normal drainage allowing water to puddle and pond. The ponded water resulted in anerobic putrefaction, causing organic matter degradation to dominate over both humification and mineralisation, creating moors, peatland, and bogs. Excess water collected at the surface and, in turn as the small water cycle dominated with mists and light rain, the climate became wetter.

Maximised evaporation for the latitude also meant the climate was not just wetter but became much cooler too. Any changes that occur within the bigger climate cycles cause a greater incidence of extreme events because the landscape now has less resilience to modify those normal variations. This amplified impact on degraded landscapes made the land unusable for farming.

This pattern, of landscape degradation acting as a climate forcing agent, evident throughout many of the Neolithic landscapes (both semi-arid and subtemperate) was not identified even in the detailed papers of the last twenty years.[107] Till now the opportunity to learn from this has been lost.

European Knowledge of Agricultural Impacts from 1650

Jethro Tull forewent a legal career to become a gentleman scientist. He took a Grand Tour of Europe in the late 1600s and again in the early 1700s. Having been raised as a gentleman farmer he was not so much interested in antiquities but in agriculture, and his tours of Europe allowed him to observe different agricultural systems.

While abroad, Tull became interested in the agricultural problems of the day, three in particular (1) soil structure, (2) soil nutrition, and (3) inefficiencies in yield due to seed placement. Prior to 1700, seed was broadcast by hand and, if practiced, rotation was haphazard. Tull studied different soil types and farm systems in Europe. Though he did not solve the three problems he set out to address, he made a significant contribution to the resolution of all three and a huge contribution to the theory of good husbandry and the development of modern agriculture.

Upon returning from his first European tour, in 1700, he invented the horse-drawn seed drill that placed seed in neat rows. Adoption was slow and his ongoing trial work was expensive. He made no money from his invention. Later, in the 1720s, he invented a horse-drawn hoe that pulled grasses and roots to the surface to dry as a mulch overlying the tilth.

Tull erroneously assumed that small particles of soil could enter the pores of the roots and that constant ploughing and crop rotation would overcome the need for manuring, which was limiting cropped land. Though this quickly proved to be incorrect, his discussion of rotation with artificial pastures (sown lucerne which is a legume) had a huge impact on the gentleman farmers in Europe. Tull's work led to research into crop rotation systems in the early to mid-1800s and ultimately the understanding of nitrogen fixation.[108]

As a pioneer for his day, Tull was encouraged to collect his thoughts into a book and, in 1731, he published *The New Horse Hoeing Husbandry*.[vi] His inventions and book are considered by many the most important herald of the industrial age, proof he was not *as thick as a brick*—the barb thrown at his namesake 1960s rock band and the title given to their fifth album.

While Tull recognised that the growing of crops degraded the soil, he did not go the next step to evaluate its impact on climate. Admittedly this is likely because farming in the UK did not significantly impact regional climate as precipitation exceeded evaporation, rendering impacts less obvious. Additionally, degraded land was not regionally widespread, as hunting estates kept by the nobility remained forested rather than cleared and, in particular because of the rewilding of landscape that occurred from the mid-1300s through to the mid-1700s as the Black Death plague depopulated the land.

Although there was no knowledge of the adverse impact of farming

---

vi Husbandry after the 14th Century had the meaning of proper management of crops and animals.

on landscape, by 1700, Tull had shown that agricultural improvements were best made through studying a wide range of soils and landscape systems. By the turn of the next century, however, the connection between degraded land and changes to the climate may have been made.

In 1813, Sir Humphrey Davy, a British chemist, noted in a series of lectures on the *Elements of Agricultural Chemistry* that exporting grain (straw and hay) from a country which does not receive in exchange substances capable of giving a manure (bone dust or guano), must ultimately exhaust its soils.[109] He does not state what exhaustion is but the implication is loss of soil fertility leading to crop failure. He reflects that: 'some of the spots now desert sands in northern Africa, and Asia Minor, were anciently fertile. Sicily was the granary of Italy: and the quantity of corn carried off from it by the Romans, is probably a chief cause of its present sterility.'

It is evident from Davy's commentary that he too was interrogating land management practices. He conducted experiments to understand the nature of grasses best adapted to permanent pasture. Examining their comparative merits he concluded that 'a grass that supplies green nutrient throughout the whole of the year, may be more valuable than a grass which yields its produce only in summer, though the whole quantity of food supplied by it should be much less'.[110] His writings demonstrate a slightly more nuanced understanding of a broader systems approach.

Across the continent, German agronomist Albrecht Thaer and German scientist Justus von Liebig were similarly making major contributions to agriculture, respectively through applying scientific methods and knowledge to the practical business of husbandry and to agricultural and biological chemistry. In the years since Tull, from the 1700s to early 1800s, farming had evolved to commonly include rotational systems alternating sown pastures with lucerne, and the discourse had come to be dominated by how to avoid crop failure by applying manures and humus.

In 1802, Thaer established an agriculture school (practical training) and founded the first German Agricultural Academy (farming theory).

His work focused on experimentation with rotation to improve yield, and on how different kinds and combinations of manure impacted the nature of the soil. In this way, his work contributed greatly to the profession of agronomy and the practice of farming. Between 1809–1812, Thaer published his four-volume work *The Principles of Agriculture* (translated into English in 1844). Although he demonstrates an awareness of what we would describe as the connection between soil and the small water cycle, Thaer does not appear to draw larger or more longsighted conclusions on environmental systems.

In 1840, Justus von Liebig, the pre-eminent chemist of his day, published *Chemistry in its application to agriculture and physiology*. His work was largely based on the analysis of ashes independent of farm studies.[111] Data is fundamentally two things: measurement (which Liebig did) and observation (which he did not). Liebig was under the impression that a scientific hypothesis could be tested in the laboratory with chemical analysis alone. He did not foresee that, for example, although nitrogen was present in manure, not all of it was available to the plant at the time it was needed. Thus, he erroneously concluded that manure (which at this time also included composts) provided all the nutrients the plant needed.

In neighbouring France, from 1836, at the first agricultural research station at Pechelbronn, agricultural scientist and chemist Jean-Baptiste Boussingault studied the impact of a greater suite of legumes (clover) with and without manure. Although he began his studies without formal training, he later became professor of chemistry at the University of Lyon, France, and professor of agricultural chemistry at the Conservatory of Arts and Crafts, Paris. Boussingault was the first to introduce modern field trials supported by chemistry methods. Based on observing the rotation of crops and evaluating laboratory studies, Boussingault proved that nitrogen from air was fixed by the root of legumes for uptake by plants. He also suggested (but not proven by him) that the method of fixation may occur via some sort of microbial mechanism.[112]

Boussingault's work with rotational crops and sown pasture swung the focus back to mineral systems and biology, further contributing to developments in the study of soil fertility. In 1857, Boussingault argued that soil fertility was controlled by mineral fertility. He was the first to understand the potential application of chemical fertilisers (rather than natural manures, both plant and animal, examined by the likes of Thaer and Liebig) and to encourage its use.[113] Boussingault published an agriculture textbook in France in 1843, *Economie rurale*. The English translation was published in 1845 as *Rural Economy*, released immediately before Paweł Strzelecki's seminal work *Physical Description of New South Wales and Van Diemen's Land*—a text discussed at length below.

With the exception of Strzelecki, the above distinguished individuals studied comparatively fertile and robust systems with limited exposure to soils formed under different environments.[vii] During this period, as the twin sciences of agriculture and meteorology were developing, the study of differences in soil fertility within soils of significantly different types or impacts of non-nutrient minerals on fertility (i.e. CEC) remained largely neglected. Rather, scientific attention focused on the emerging science of chemistry at the start of the 1800s and then on biology at the end of the century, i.e. on the disciplines of science to define the components of a system. Only Strzelecki wrote about the impacts of agriculture on climate.

With the exception of Tull and Strzelecki, the written record from 1700 to the 1880s would suggest no scientist or gentleman agronomist studied a variety of soil systems from different geographies, latitudes, and climate zones, and none studied landscape interaction with climate. It would seem there was little to no knowledge that agriculture could impact climate.

Across the globe in Australia

Agriculture was adopted and common in Papua New Guinea from approximately 10,000 years ago and, possibly as early as 28,000 bp (the age of tools covered in taro starch). There is evidence to suggest that

---

vii Though Boussingault had been to countries with different climates his interest in soil developed after his youthful travels.

agriculture had developed in Papua New Guinea earlier than anywhere else in the world—earlier than the Fertile Crescent in the Middle East (10,000 bp to 12,000 bp), or the Yangtze and Yellow River Basins in China (11,000 to 9000 bp).

However in Australia, New Guinea's less fertile and more arid neighbour, agriculture was not practised, although there is evidence that Aboriginals of northern Australia experimented with agriculture.[114] In the less resilient soils of Australia, had the Aboriginals already understood that sedentary life was destructive to the land? On less resilient land, had they witnessed and quickly understood the stress that agriculture puts on systems, and drawn the connection that land and climate were to some extent interrelated?

Australia and New Guinea were connected by a land bridge for thousands of years. There is, however, an important difference between the two islands that must be highlighted and understood. Both are part of the Australia Continental Plate, New Guinea being the leading northern edge and Australia the centre. The leading edge of continental plates is subject to collision with oceanic plates, the oceanic plates are forced under the edge of the continental plates, creating both volcanic activity and (through uplift of the leading edge of the continental plate) mountain ranges—which in turn enable more regular rainfall. These tectonic movements gave New Guinea young, enriched soils for its foundation.

New Guinea's advantageous latitude, mild temperature, and near constant rain (i.e. rainfall exceeds evaporation), coupled with its fertile soils mean that land degraded by agriculture in New Guinea can restore rapidly. Some land is so fertile that fertility decline does not readily occur. However, the same cannot be said for Australia, which was formed from the centre of the continental plate.

Non-edge zones of continental plates have old and weathered (and thus poor) soils. Australia missed the benefit of continental uplift from collision with oceanic plates, so is also comparatively flat, and has low rainfall and low cloud cover. It is also a large land mass and, in holding thermal heat, causes evaporation to exceed rainfall. The land in terms of rainfall and soil is simply not resilient. Furthermore, northern

Australia is monsoonal (less predictable) whereas New Guinea is equatorial (more constant).

It stands to reason that a common feature of agriculture practice in northern Australia was failure, due to degraded soils and unpredictable weather (particularly late or poor monsoons and cyclones) creating a trying and labour intensive practice.

Aboriginal Australians arrived in the northern part of Australia at least 65,000 years ago. The death of most megafauna (approximately 46,000 years ago) would have been understood as a significant warning that a stable population with stable practices is certainly desirable; if not necessary. Over thousands of years, it would have also been apparent that the practice of agriculture in northern Australia would not deliver stable or repeatable outcomes.

If you study landscape, or are a long-time observer of landscape systems like the Aboriginal peoples were, why would you persist with something that is neither advantageous for you nor your people? Perhaps Aboriginals understood acutely that population growth should mirror the carrying capacity of the land.

During the invasion by Europeans, Aboriginal knowledge of landscape was not considered. Should we have at least asked? Undoubtedly.

Invasion and colonisation of Australia

In January 1788, the Australian colony, without even having unloaded its ships, moved from Botany Bay to Camp Cove due to unfavourable land. It should have been a forewarning of the lack of resilience of the land, particularly its infertility, but at that time its inhabitants only perceived a land of plenty.

David Collins arrived on the First Fleet and wrote one of the most complete accounts of the colony's first years. He was the colony's deputy judge advocate and lieutenant-governor. In May 1798, the first volume of his diaries was published: *An Account of the English Colony in New South Wales*. In it he recorded:

- day temperature in Sydney in February 1788 as 105°F (41°C);[115]

- intermit heavy rain for six months in 1789 from February to June, in what we now call prolonged east coast lows;
- prolonged drought from 1791 to 1792 and again 105°F (41°C) in February over several days, during which a strong north-westerly wind blew.

Flying foxes were recorded as falling from their perches and dying, and dead birds fell from the sky. During this time water storage tanks were dug into the sandstone bed of the stream at Camp Cove, which is now known as Tank Stream. Fires readily started in the cleared land of the colony—but not in the Aboriginal maintained land (for the reasons discussed in Chapter 2).[116]

Collins' diaries set the scene, establishing that Australia's natural cycle at the end of the 18th century was characterised by extremes of flood and drought, with associated extreme heat.

Several decades later in 1815–1819, under the administration of Governor Macquarie, surveyor-general and explorer John Oxley discovered the Lachlan-Murrumbidgee river system.[viii] On 21 April 1818, Oxley describes the landscape in the immediate neighbourhood of Bathurst in his work, *Journals of Two Expeditions Into the Interior of New South Wales*, as 'much wooded with ill-grown gum and stringy bark trees (all of the eucalyptus genus); the grass good, and tolerable plenty, and much more so than the appearance of the soil would seem to promise.'

Later, on 23 April, Oxley wrote, 'I never saw a country better adapted for the grazing of all kinds of stock than that we passed over this day'.[117] Several months later on 3 July 1818, having followed the Lachlan River for some months, marshes prevented Oxley in his primary object of tracing the Macquarie and Lachlan Rivers. Oxley infamously speculated mistakenly about an inland sea, writing 'if an opinion may be permitted to be hazarded from actual appearances,

---

viii Botanist and explorer Allan Cunningham accompanied Oxley on his first exploration expedition in 1817, and over his career distinguished himself for pairing discovery with botanical research, providing thousands of botanical specimens.

mine is decidedly in favour of our being in the immediate vicinity of an inland sea'. A circumstance visually apparent in the same area in late 2022, two centruies later.

In 1824, a prolonged drought occurred, commencing with below-average rain and deepening into a major drought right through to 1826–9. This created the ideal conditions to explore beyond the impenetrable marshes encountered by Oxley in 1817—which is exactly what Charles Sturt did in 1829.

Sturt was from a military background and travelled to Australia in 1827 with a detachment of his regiment, charged with accompanying convicts to the colony. Soon after his arrival Sturt was appointed Military Secretary to the Governor and Major of Brigade to the Garrison. In 1829, Governor General Darling dispatched Sturt to look for the inland sea spoken of by Oxley.

By the mid-1820s Sturt had noted that in NSW a major drought occurred every ten to twelve years. During his exploration for the inland sea in late 1829, beyond the Macquarie River Marshes, he recorded extreme drought-affected vegetation. Sturt observed: 'Those seasons in which no rains fall … occur every 10 to 12 years … rains of excessive duration decrease gradually year after year until they wholly cease for a time. It seems not improbably therefore that the state of the interior, does in some measure regulate the fall of rain upon the eastern ranges which appears to decrease in quantity yearly until the marshes become exhausted, and cease altogether when they no longer contain any water. A drought will naturally follow until such time as the air becomes surcharged with clouds of vapour from the ocean.'[118]

Similarly, Sturt, in the prologue to his book *Two expeditions into the Interior of Southern Australia*, suggests that for inland NSW there is a strong connection between the moisture in the landscape and rainfall. Sturt's writings suggest he observed and was able to draw connections between different components of our climatic and landscape systems.

Concurrently, James Atkinson, a civil servant to the colonial secretary and gentleman farmer in the Southern Highlands of NSW was writing his *Account of the State of Agriculture and Grazing in New South*

Wales.[119] He documented the problems of adapting European plants, animals and farming methods to a strange environment. In 1822, Atkinson obtained two grants of land totalling 1500 acres (607 ha), though he had occupied part of the property from 1821. In 1825 he returned to England, then travelled to Saxony in eastern Germany with Charles Macarthur to buy sheep in 1826. He returned to Australia in 1826 where he pursued his interest in farming and its improvement, and was actively involved in the Agricultural and Horticultural Society and its Stock Club. Having been born in Kent, Atkinson had experience with Kentish farming and had an active interest in the innovations of the 'agrarian revolution'. Atkinson is described as a progressive farmer, though he did not observe any regional effects of land degradation, he is clear in his book that degraded land due to poor practice occurred rapidly after settlement.

Despite Atkinson being labelled a progressive and his active attempts to raise the efficiency of farming in New South Wales, only a small number of farms, less than one hundred, practised a rotational crop system. In 1826, Atkinson described his crop rotations as including 'wheat, turnips, barley or oats, grass ley with clover and peas'. The peas were recorded as having an 'excellent yield following a wheat crop without manuring'.[120] But this system was not widely adopted and much of the area surrounding Sydney, Newcastle and Bathurst had been cleared of trees and subjected to substantively monoculture farming, which was commonly abandoned within a decade or two due to loss of soil fertility.[121]

Even by the 1820s, degradation of the land had already occurred. As documented, a number of observers of the early colony are very clear that widespread land degradation soon followed clearing. The system of land grants and a government floor on wheat prices, coupled with inexperienced farmers, encouraged a merciless rotation of wheat-corn-wheat or wheat-wheat rotations until the land was exhausted and overridden with weeds. However, while land degradation became apparent to many, it would seem there was little to no knowledge that agriculture could impact climate.

Strzelecki's exploration of NSW and Van Diemen's Land (Tasmania)

Pawel Strzelecki was unusual. He does not appear to have studied at a well-known university, and like Boussingault, was an autodidact and polymath. He was competent in survey, meteorology, geology, and soil as a subset of geology and agriculture; and—like many of the distinguished individuals mentioned above—he was an explorer.

Prior to visiting Australia, he had visited Germany, Scotland, Mexico, California, and Chile, observing landscapes and visiting high-performing farms of the country. Though he did inherit a fortune most was forfeited during a dispute and was insufficient to live a life of luxury. He did not marry. Furthermore, he did not stay in a country long enough to have a sponsor for membership of the prestigious scientific societies of the time. He also, regrettably, did not publish an explorer's diary but instead chose to publish a scientific study of the landscape, geology, and agriculture of NSW and Tasmania: *Physical Description of New South Wales and Van Diemen's Land*.[122] Although that work gained Strzelecki some acclaim from his professional colleagues, including Charles Darwin, it appears through the long glass of history that his work was not popular. We speculate that it was not received more grandly by history for the reasons discussed below.

Strzelecki's work, published 1845, was at a time of relatively prolific publication. Released a short eight years before the Gold Rushes Memoirs were published and after printed recounts of the colonies and exploration of foreign lands had been popularised. Further, as Strzelecki was not a member of any prestigious scientific society, his work did not carry the weight of such societies behind it.

Additionally, Strzelecki was somewhat politically unpalatable. It would seem being a scientist he was a stickler for the tenets of its institution—the paramountcy of 'fact' through applying the scientific method. In this way, he did not share the Government's view on Aboriginals. He describes terra nullius or as he calls it 'illegitimate possessors of land' as a 'sophistry of law' and writes that Aboriginal Australians are 'as strongly attached to … property, and the rights which it involves, as any European political body'.[123] But more damning was that he was involved in a small (but historically very important) controversy.

In September 1839, Strzelecki discovered traces of gold near Hartley and Wellington (in the area of Bathurst)—possibly the first to do so—for which samples were sent to eminent geologist Sir Roderick Murchison of London. But the Governor of New South Wales at the time, Sir George Gipps, asked Strzelecki to keep his discovery quiet, due to 'the apprehension of the disorganising consequences of such a disclosure' (i.e. in the interests of discipline in the colony).[124] And so it was kept quiet—this is apparently so even though Strzelecki's gold discoveries were noted in published House of Commons papers on 28 November 1841.[125]

In 1853 (some 14 years later) Edward Hargraves, a gold prospector, was officially recognised for discovering gold in Australia. This announcement was a little perplexing as in May of 1846 Strzelecki had been awarded the Royal Geographical Society's Gold Founder's Medal. Understandably, controversy ensued and in 1856—following Strzelecki publishing in London a brochure to supplement his work patently titled *The Discovery of Gold and Silver in Australia*[126]—Strzelecki's scientific priority was acknowledged.

It is a saucy read indeed! Strzelecki wrote in the preface: 'My object in publishing this Supplement is less to claim honour or credit as a discoverer of gold in Australia, than to protect myself against the imputation of negligence or incapacity as a geological and mineralogical surveyor…This is not the place to speculate on the wisdom of the course adopted by the Governor, but it will be admitted that if he had ordered or authorised the immediate prosecution of the requisite researches in the direction indicated by me, the prosperity in which the colony is now revelling, together with the reflected benefits which the mother country enjoys, would have been accelerated by several years …'

It was during this period that Strzelecki potentially fell out with the Administration and the opportunity to undertake further surveys in NSW evaporated. Some historians speculate that the outcome of this dispute may have led Strzelecki to stipulate in his will that all his writings be destroyed after his death. Such thinking was endemic to the time, where diaries were considered primary sources by historians but mischief by scientists. The destruction of Strzelecki's diaries is a further reason why his works may have faded with the years.

We must pause to reflect on Strzelecki's experience and how he has been remembered (or not) in the records of history. There is an important takeaway and that is that scientific discovery is not operating in a vacuum, it is subject to the policy and politics of the time.

No matter the reason, Strzelecki's backseat in history has been to the detriment of us all.

Strzelecki published the first geological map of Australia, albeit only surveying parts of the east coast. He also likely did the first comparative survey of soils from different soil types (potentially anywhere in the world but certainly in Australia). He explored large parts of SE Australia yet to be explored by Europeans; as far as 250 kilometres inland—greatly assisted by his Aboriginal guides Charlie Tarra, a young man from Gundungurra near Goulburn and local Djilimitang man Jackey.[127]

In August 1839 Strzelecki set off on a self-funded geological survey of the country. In undertaking fieldwork for his geological map of New South Wales he zig-zagged the state. On his journey Strzelecki named many localities, most famously Mount Kosciuszko (which my Polish friends tell me that Australians mispronounce). In April 1840, after passing the La Trobe River in Gippsland, he and his party, obstructed by tight thickets, impeded by almost constant rain, and on the brink of starvation, abandoned their horses, which were carrying all of their specimens collected from the Monaro, the Southern Highlands, and Gippsland. They survived for three weeks, thanks mainly to their Aboriginal guides Charlie and Jackey, and arrived in Melbourne completely exhausted on 12 May 1840. But for those samples being lost, Strzelecki's published survey would have been more comprehensive.

The first analysis of Australian soils in an Australian laboratory was undertaken by William Pugh MD of Launceston in the first six months of 1843. Strzelecki routinely collected and had samples analysed and we can surmise that some or all of the soil he collected in Tasmania was analysed by Dr Pugh. Upon returning to London in early 1844, Strzelecki had the rest of his soil and rock samples analysed by the leading chemist in London, Mr Richard Phillips, a fellow of the Royal Society, in the Laboratory of Economic Geology.

Strzelecki had more of a systematic approach than both earlier and contemporaneous publications which focused on the mineral content of ash of humus in comparative studies of soils from different geology, geography, and climate. Strzelecki's work incorporated respective aspects of interacting systems and may have been the first such approach in the world, certainly the first to apply such an approach from a European perspective. Strzelecki understood the concept of different mineral charges in the soil a full fifty years before the concept started to be explored.

In general terms, there are two defining features of the early agricultural areas of Australia compared with the agricultural soils of Europe and North America:

1. In Australia, evaporation dominates over unreliable rain, whereas Northern Hemisphere agricultural soils have reliable rain which dominates evaporation;
2. Typically, European and North American soils are young and have a high clay mineral-based (pH-independent) negative charge (i.e. cation exchange capacity), while Australian soils are old, having been subject to prolonged weathering in situ. This means the CEC is not only low but dominated by pH variable charge which is supplied by sesquioxides and organic matter.

Strzelecki associated increasing silica content in soil with reduced fertility, predating the concept of the Bowen Reaction Series by over one hundred years.[ix] Silica content is inversely related to mineral permanent

---

ix Bowen Reaction Series is the crystallisation of rocks from a melt on cooling which correlate with the reactivity of the rock to weathering and inversely correlate with silica content.

CEC, a concept not known in Strzelecki's time. However, he found that lower silica is associated with about three times more organic matter than the sterile soil with higher silica, thus predating the work of Jon Gray's thesis in 2015 by 150 years, in which it was found that CEC is correlated with organic matter.[128] Strzelecki further associated increased silica with reduced fertility, increased sensible heat, and thereby increased infra-red radiation released by the earth surface.

All of Strzelecki's achievements are extraordinary in their own right but by far the most significant were his measurements and observations that correlate the interconnectivity of land, solar radiation, and climate as being part of one system.

Physical Description of NSW and Van Diemen's Land by Strzelecki

Rather than summarising Strzelecki's findings it is best to provide a few extracts, presented below in italics (with explanatory comments inserted by us in roman text):

- *The experiments ... have rendered evident the influence of the physical character of the soil not only upon the vegetation, but upon the climate.'*[129]
- *The reflected heat and the high radiating power of the surface in NSW* (granitic and sandstone soil) *must cause an oppressive high temperature during the day time and an insufferable cold one during the night compared to the more fertile soil of Van Dieman's Land.'*[130]
- *Doing away with vegetation—a practise which far from improving the grass, as some have imagined, only subtracts from the soil the most essential conductor of moisture, or medium of condensing it in the form of dew of showers'* (i.e. loss of the small water cycle).[131]
- *Accumulation and decomposition of organic matter ....plays a prominent part in the effects of solar heat and moisture. And while this, in connection with vegetation tends to explain the difference in condition of the atmosphere as regards moisture ...'* (he means dew, light rain and maybe clouds).[132]
- *Removal of vegetation and talus* (plant litter) *to expose bare ground caused a sudden access of air, light and heat which accelerated the*

- *decomposition of vegetable deposits accumulated for ages.*[133]
- *Soils under tillage and pasturage have deteriorated in an agricultural point of view* (at 1839–1841). *Furthermore they have deteriorated in a climatic point of view, as the power of absorbing moisture from the atmosphere has been curtailed* (dews and light rain etc.), *and heat of adsorbing solar heat has increased* (here he means sensible heat, as latent heat was not yet measured or greatly understand at this point), *while that of retaining heat during terrestrial radiation has decreased* (outbound infra-red radiation).[134]

Above, Strzelecki directly correlates increase in sensible heat with increase in infra-red radiation of the earth. Increased organic matter does take up more water from a saturated atmosphere and, conversely, converts more incoming radiation to evaporation. Furthermore, increased organic matter also increases infiltration of precipitation into the soil, but based on the experiments conducted increased infiltration is not what he meant.

- *Fertile soil emits through radiation, an amount which is 2/3 less than that yielded by the sterile soil (<3.8% OM).*[135]
- *The amount of vegetable fibre in a soil regulates not only the proportion between its absorption and emission of heat, but also in greater measure its power of adsorbing atmospheric moisture* (dew, light rain etc.).[136]
- *During experiments, whenever the soil was found to be drier it was deficient in the base of humic acid* (a component of organic matter); *and whenever it was moist and retentive of moisture, it had of that base from 20–40%.*[137] We have assumed that this is equivalent to the modern day experiments for humic acid.
- *The restitution, then, to the soil of what is subtracted to it from cropping becomes an imperative and sacred duty of every farmer: to withhold it, with the knowledge of injury thus inflicted upon the soil and entailed upon its next possessors, borders upon a crime against society; at any rate it becomes the most flagrant abuse of the gifts of nature* (i.e. natural capital)*).*[138]

Strzelecki observed a system in distress and then measured the soil's response to solar radiation in an extraordinary set of experiments. And then warned us. It is an outstanding piece of work still not appropriately acknowledged to this day.[x]

Strzelecki was so concerned by the hypothesis he generated from his observations and measurement that he transmitted to his Excellency Sir George Gipps, which was published in the Parliamentary Papers of 26th August 1841: 'and in which I took the liberty of pointing out the bad consequences which would accrue to the colony from the doing away with vegetation, by overstocking the pasturage or by burning it'.[139]

That correspondence was written before he visited Tasmania, in which it became more evident to him that the kind of rocks that form the soil, vegetation and organic matter all influence the character and interaction of solar heat and moisture in the atmosphere.

Just sixty years after the great experiment of the Colony of NSW began, and fifty years before Svante Arrhenius stated that increasing carbon dioxide was heating the earth, Strzelecki proved (at least on a regional scale by experiment and observation) that agricultural practice affects local climate. He drew these conclusions over forty years before the first coal-powered electricity generation plant, at the bare beginning of the industrial age, ahead of any significant elevation in greenhouse gases.

We are of the opinion that his legacy as a scientist in Australia, and his pioneering work on the fate of solar energy and its impact on climate rates him as one of the most prominent scientists of his day.

So someone knew, but should we have?

You see, Lyn Abbott indirectly alerted us to why Strzelecki could likely see what his Northern Hemisphere colleagues had not. Though he may have been an extraordinary scientist, he was seeing a poorly resilient

---

[x] Though noting Strzelecki received the Founder's medal of the Royal Geographical Society and South Australia's Strzelecki Track and Victoria's Strzelecki Ranges also honour him.

system pushed past its buffering point. He was observing a system that was collapsing. Because the soil of many of the NSW sites he visited was so poor and the degradation widespread, its influence on climate was likely more obvious.

As Lyn told us, if you wish to study system dynamics, a system that has poor resilience which is then subject to prolonged stress, creates the best circumstance for such study. Additionally, if you wish to study components of the system, a resilient system is best, because a component can be varied while the other components can be held stable without having system variations affect the experiment.

From the 1840s to the 1930s, knowledge of the science of soil developed but knowledge of the system of soil did not progress beyond Strzelecki's findings. Mechanisation, fertilisers, new methods (e.g. ring barking), and chemical crop protection changed the practice of agriculture. In Australia, droughts continued to occur at frequent intervals, approximately every decade. After the drought of the early 1880s, the government of the Colony of NSW set up a Royal Commission into Water Conservation who collected scientific evidence from around the world. It concluded that wholesale clearing of forests reduced rainfall by up to 50 percent in some districts.[140] By the time of the Federation Drought of 1895–1903 (an ecosystem destroying megadrought as a result of an extreme El Nino) the idea that trees were essential for attracting moisture from clouds was frequently reported in newspapers. The concept that continual removal of forests will inevitably result in less rainfall was also reported.[141] But the Federation Drought, though massive, was overshadowed by Federation itself and an official investigation into the accepted observation that droughts were getting worse. The next drought, though not a megadrought, was overshadowed by the First World War.

Then big droughts appeared across many continents in the 1930s, and into the 1940s in Australia (you can almost hear Strzelecki saying *I told you so*) and topsoil blew away from agricultural land in most continents (recalling President Roosevelt's salient words in response to the Dust Bowl years, 'the nation that destroys its soil destroys itself').

Books proliferated on soil science, agriculture, and erosion control.[142] Though some had provocative titles, e.g. *The Rape of the Earth*, which focused on a worldwide review of soil erosion, none connected landscape degradation with climate change.[143]

Walter Lowdermilk was commissioned by the USA Government in the mid-1930s to undertake a world review of what causes soil erosion. The publication of his work was delayed by the war and so not released until 1953. Lowdermilk concluded that degraded land and subsequent droughts ultimately wiped-out civilisations but not that agriculture impacted climate.[144]

Although evidence was starting to accrue in the meteorology literature, it wasn't until 1991 that Professor Hillel in his book *Out of the Earth: Civilisation and the life of the soil* that another scientist since Strzelecki articulated clearly that degraded landscape alters climate. Professor Hillel wrote: 'forests moderate the local microclimate, and where they cover extensive areas the regional macroclimate as well. With their accumulated organic matter—living biomass and its dead residues (in soil)—they serve as dynamic sponges, adsorbing and then gradually recycling water and nutrients thus regulating their flows.'[145]

But again, unlike Strzelecki, Professor Hillel's focus was on the water cycle, not on what this means to incoming radiation and heat. The relationship between landscape change and climate change is lost in Professor Hillel's discussion on deforestation.

The scientists who worked on the Bunny Fence Experiment as discussed in the prologue, started at a local level in 1996 and became an international study from 2003 until 2007 when the project was cancelled. By this time a series of papers had been published setting out how landscape, particularly the impact of agriculture on landscape, may influence climate. Additionally, a series of papers were published at about the same time on the impact of hydraulic changes caused by agriculture with land clearing and drainage that changed the local climate and possibly regional climate.[146]

Modelling studies in Australia between 2007 and 2010, that considered vegetative cover reductions with stable GHG found that reduced vegetation cover increased droughts, floods, reduced rainfall and increased mean temperature by several degrees in SE Australia.[147] Similarly in the USA in 2010, a warning was issued by over 40 Meteorologists that land use changes induced by agricultural use are a first order human induced climate forcing factor and addressing factors that correct this are essential to mitigate climate change. That warning also noted that land use changes are poorly addressed in models. Worse, impacts of changes in soil moisture, as a result of decreasing organic matter and vegetative cover, are ignored, not even considered in the models. They argue that regional factors associated with landscape change (soil security) are a better measure of climate change and its mitigation then the current focus of most of the scientific world on modelling the global impact of greenhouse gases and its reduction.[148]

But the huge debate on the occurrence of anthropogenic climate change between 2007 and 2015 and its focus through a GHGs lens effectively silenced a broader discussion on other forcing agents of climate. For example, as noted earlier, Roger Pilke Senior, a meteorologist with NOAA, and his co-authors mentioned above, were accused of being a climate change deniers because of Pilke Senior's publications on agricultural practice being a climate forcing agent.

Should the world have known? As our brief review of literature up until about the mid-1990s suggests, probably not. But certainly by the mid-2000s we should have been aware. For Australia there is no denying that we should now know that mismanagement of land is a powerful forcing agent of climate change. Now we know, what do we do?

Landscape Management is the new currency

Every civilisation grew on the back of agricultural development. Not just Greco-Roman civilisations but also the civilisations of Sumeria, Egypt, the Indus Valley, Central America, Neolithic Britain, the Levant, and Colorado's Mesa Verde. Many of these civilisations exceeded populations of many millions but all experienced a collapse and a dark age in which the population substantially declined, resulting in a reversion to subsistence living.[xi] Prior to 1700, at a social or cultural level, in Britain, parts of Europe, South East Asia and India, and surprisingly Australia and North America, systems of landscape management were developed and encoded into law, lore and cultural practices. Though these systems varied according to local culture, landscape, and technology, the general purpose was to achieve a balance between population, human activity, and land – with ecosystem and landscape nurturing (effectively to reverse desertification from the preceding civilisation).

The need to achieve balance was made apparent up to centuries earlier when species extinction, landscape degradation, and local climate change occurred as a result of significant droughts. All these societies sought to limit population growth and/or human activities on the land to prevent further ecosystem decline. This occurred via trial and error over time and, to ensure societal compliance was encoded in lore.

When an activity promoted landscape restoration it was propagated. When an activity caused desertification (or moors, bogs, and peats in the subtemperate landscapes), the activity was censured or the people practising it ceased to exist and the landscape recovered but to a lower (biological) energy state. What worked can be readily defined as what allowed society to function. This does not necessarily mean grow but simply not to retract or collapse. Thus, what worked in these different landscapes varied as humans determined site-specific solutions to manage the landscape at a biologically optimum state.

European colonialism broke these managed landscape systems, principally through the introduction of new tools, resources, and methodologies from other continents without regard to the balance established by native people. For example, more recently Japan, Malaysia and China have harvested tropical hardwood timbers from South East Asia and the Pacific Islands to the detriment of these economies, particularly the fragile tropical islands. As consumers were external to the centre of production and absentee landlords and managers held

---

xi The soil and the precipitation have probably not returned to the former state in Central America, Neolithic Britain, the Levant, and Colorado's Mesa Verde.

no accountability for future loss of production, practices evolved that effectively adopted the most primitive type of slash-and-burn agriculture. Such practices favoured Financial Capital over Natural Capital, resulting in negative externalities at the cost of the local communities.

Externalities are generally environmental. An externality is a cost or benefit caused by a producer that is not financially incurred or received by that producer. The most common example is a business that causes pollution to another property, diminishing that property's value. That is an example of a negative externality but externalities can be positive too. 'Externalities' is an apt term for referring to the kinds of impacts discussed above: off-site, incremental, multiple or diffuse source impacts. The adverse externalities of agriculture are typically seen in terms of pollutants in ground water, such as dairy effluent from intensive agricultural industry, a common problem in New Zealand and recently Tasmania. Such negative externalities characteristically impact nearby land and water. But the more insidious externalities impact the region and beyond, and include dust storms, droughts, floods, extreme heat events leading to fire, increased sediment in water, and de-oxygenated waterways and estuaries.

While adverse externalities became evident as a result of land clearing, it was arguably too early to draw a connection between landscape degradation and climate change because the components of the system were yet to be understood. However, multiple off-site, incremental, and diffuse source impacts by their nature necessitate a systems approach. We can no longer turn a blind eye to the fact that various components of the system are connected such that agriculture is adversely contributing to our increasingly unpredictable climate.

Additionally, from examining the above evolution of agriculture (even if relatively superficially), another connection must be made and said plainly, there is a connection between Natural Capital and Financial Capital—that they too are very much interconnected, and a balance must be struck for the collective good, to sustainably secure our future prosperity (see Chapters 3 and 12). Effectively the identifiable pattern is that if too much weight is put on Financial Capital at the expense of Natural Capital, over time Financial Capital will diminish. In nourishing our Natural Capital we are sustaining our Financial Capital at a greater optimum. In this way, while it is easy to be paralysed by the cost to act, we must ask ourselves what is the cost of not doing anything—increasingly frequent and ever more intense extreme climatic events, diminishing fertile land—hunger and hardship—and at some point, our own demise.

The good news is as much as collective mismanagement destroys the landscape, collective and co-operative management can restore and sustain the landscape. A country as harsh as Australia requires citizens to act collectively and co-operatively. Australians have a long history of co-operative endeavours to manage co-existence in this harsh and barren land, from the Dreamtime, to more recent collective effort by bush fire brigades, surf lifesavers, Landcare, Pasture Protection Boards, growers' co-operatives, and the Country Women's Association—to name but a few. Working together we can minimise the externalities of agriculture. When externalities are minimised through collective practices which secure our soils and return the small water cycle, we will stabilise thermoregulation of regional climatic conditions and, further afield, regulation of stream flow consistency and quality, and create more biodiversity.

In recent times we have forgotten what it means to operate as a collective, instead favouring individual benefit and reward. But we are beginning to see a shift. Increasingly, under general duties to the environment and general duties to manage land written into recent changes in Queensland and Victorian environmental legislation and the Resource Management Act of New Zealand introduced twenty years ago, managers must not generate adverse impacts from their land upon other's land. This is a step in the right direction, but in Australia, such general duties are yet to be applied to agriculture. We propose to accelerate achieving a collective response by implementing National Landscape Regeneration Plans and Regional Planning—see Chapter 12.

Landscape management will be the currency of the coming

decades. There will be winners and losers, but we think a more collective approach, at least in the short term, is in the national interest. In the past, commonly applied practices (whether illegally or legally) privatised profits and socialised the cost of externalities. This cannot be allowed to continue. The *better off overall test* (BOOT) should be applied to determine if current activities result in unacceptably adverse environmental conditions for future generations (akin to, but an extension of, ecologically sustainable development). Doing nothing or failing to look beyond GHGs will result in all of us being worse off.

Managing land to moderate and even reverse anthropogenic climate change, as with mitigating carbon emissions, will result in winners and losers. Change is necessary to ensure that all emerging and future generations meet the test of being, at least, no worse off than our current generation. The solution proposed will only work if undertaken collectively and co-operatively, with the support of all levels of government and most of the population. The cost must be born collectively too, with subsidies for those substantively worse off.

Last century, the Czechoslovak plant biologist Vladimir Ulehla wrote: 'We cannot annul any of what distinguished our age from what went before. On the contrary we have to lift everything to a higher level. That is why we cannot keep the country side in a state of economic primitivism. Nothing remains but to alter the current state of the country, but to alter it more intelligently, more naturally, more professionally. And this is a task so noble that all missions of the nineteenth century pale before it.'[149]

With every new day, that noble task is renewed. And we now know. We can and we must do better.

Chapter 5

Agricultural Practices' Impact on Soil

Tilled to death and then poisoned to death

Stark dead trunks of lone trees stand like sentinels in paddocks or in rows at the end of paddocks, killed by spray drift. They no longer guard the fecundity of country, but write against the sky and into the landscape their warning of doom, a symptom of a sick country.

Other signs of a sick landscape are also writ large: muddy rivers, bushfires, massive growth of understory acacias, increased and persistent invading weeds, savage scars of deeply incised gullies, dust filling the air … Sick landscape affects communities with loss of youth, services and clubs from towns, as well as increased suicide rates; social symptoms of a sick country where agriculture is in decline.

A crop rotational system focused on financial gain at the expense of Natural Capital destroys soil security, our land and our communities. Cropping and mixed farming typically follow a system whereby paddocks are sown with different crops or pasture each year over a cycle of years in what is known as the rotational system. Although in most years grain crops produce a greater or at least easier financial return, to maintain Natural Capital, spelling of cropped land for pasture, or including legume and pulse crops in the system, is essential. Excessive tillage, annually repeating grain crops without spelling or legume or pulse crops in the rotational system, exacerbates the decline in Natural Capital. During average seasons or dry seasons before a drought, it is tempting to pursue profit to improve Financial Capital at the expense of Natural Capital. But before, during and immediately following drought, the land is most vulnerable to erosion.

Every 50 years or so, usually after a prolonged drought, it is evident land management practices which prioritise Financial Capital have led to substantial wind erosion, and spelling from grain-cropping has to be re-introduced. Usually, as we realise that land needs to be rested, recovered and rejuvenated, the degradation of the landscape is paused in response to the degradation of Natural Capital. But in certain systems, such as irrigated land, the effect of loss of Natural Capital can be masked. Perversely, off-farm impacts from irrigation such as dust, erosion and even fire, become worse than in non-irrigated agricultural areas. With irrigation, conserving water in the profile becomes less necessary, and practices such as excessive tilling, burning and heavy herbicide use can mask the loss of organic matter in the soil. The emphasis in these systems tends to be more focused on weed and fungal control. In a good season, apart from water-borne sediments and dust, off-farm impacts tend to be local but in a dry season when water is not available for irrigation this is not the case.

In March 2021 Phil toured the western and south-western NSW cropping belt, particularly the MIA, the Murrumbidgee Irrigation Area, principally to see if the increased symptoms of sickness from the previous parched three years had resulted in changes in landscape management. The MIA is similar to the Bunny Fence Experiment in being a paired-climate area of vegetation pattern. There is better vegetative cover and soil moisture when irrigation is available, but the reverse occurs during late summer, particularly during protracted droughts when sensible heat within the MIA is much greater than in the surrounding grazing land.

It was worthwhile visiting at the end of the great season of 2020 to evaluate whether a return of rain has seen a greater reliance on the malpractices of the past that mine organic matter, including excessive tillage and widespread burning of stubble. Simply, the answer was yes. In most instances the damage caused is done without malevolence, but as a result of ignorance or poor knowledge. Nevertheless, it has been long known that they are poor and destructive practices. Given the disastrous symptoms, can we continue to claim ignorance?

Why did we till?

Inspecting parts of south-western NSW in the MIA in 2020 after a great season, it was obvious that excessive tilling and harrowing was still occurring (see Figure 5-1 and Figure 5-2 on page 130). Given that we know it is destructive and promotes soil erosion, why do we continue to do it? An understanding of why we heavily tilled in the first place informs us why we continue to do so today.

Weeds compete for water and nutrients and interfere with the quality of crops. Traditionally, in an attempt to combat weeds, a seed bed was prepared by destroying the weeds with several passes of the plough and then, a number of weeks later, harrowing the tilth to destroy any weeds sprouting from the dormant seed stock in it. However, preparation of the tilth has the unintended consequence of destroying the soil's structure. Complete destruction of clods was often achieved by using a scarifier or a cultivator or both to break the soil down to very small aggregates. Through this level of cultivation, weed's growth was minimised or eliminated. A side benefit of a summer till was the absence of summer weeds and development of a loose soil mulch cover during late summer, minimising evaporation from the soil. Nevertheless, the disadvantages were many; principally the physical destruction of the soil and the loss of organic matter, which was laid bare to bake in the sun, resulting not only in wind and water erosion but the destruction of soil biota that benefits the crop, as well as a loss of nutrients.

To maintain fertility, this damage could be offset to some extent by crop and pasture rotation and mixed farming. But during prolonged droughts, when financial constraints become significant, rotational practices of mixed farming are often given up. Similarly, ignoring restorative rotational practices occurs on land that is leased or subject to share-farming. Both tenure arrangements focus on profit from the current season, as the temporary farmers are usually not incentivised to maintain long-term fertility.

Figure 5-1. Excessive Till. Four willy willies can be seen at the end of the paddock, an indication of loss of soil security

Figure 5-2. Harrowing to prepare a seed bed in the Griffith Region, March 2021

Agricultural Practices' Impact on Soil

Figure 5-3. Dust storm during the middle of the day when top soil fills the air

Figure 5-1 and Figure 5-2 show the damage caused to our land and landscape from excessive tilling. The top soil has both eroded and, laid bare, blown away, as in Figure 5-3. This is most clearly seen from the willy willy at the end of the paddock in Figure 5-1, and the billow behind the tractor in Figure 5-3 where top soil is blowing away, polluting the air and rivers, and reducing rainfall.

Sulfate-laden dust particles form part of the increasing number of aerosols in the atmosphere, together with soot from high-temperature low-oxygen fires. The Australian landscape is old and as it has not, to any great extent in the last 100 million years, been subject to the renewal processes of volcanism, glaciation or tectonic uplift, so it has accrued sulfate. These aerosols, particularly sulfate dust, result in smaller raindrop size, which over hot land further reduces rainfall.[150]

Repeated tillage destroys soil organic matter by breaking the physical structure of the soil and results in a more aerated soil. This, in turn, allows bacteria to dominate over natural soil fungi, to the detriment of soil structure. Aerobic bacteria mineralise plant litter to carbon dioxide and water, bypassing the creation of soil organic matter, in particular bypassing dissolved organic matter and glomalin, the glue that holds soil together. Tillage degrades our soils' security.

Tillage can also cause an increase of pathogenic fungi species such as crown root and rust. The solutions for the symptom of rust—rather than facing the disease of poor tillage practice—includes crop rotation and spelling the land with a pasture crop, fungicides or stubble burning. The cheapest short-term solution is burning followed by fungicide, but the unexpected consequence of burning stubble, historically a common practice, perpetuates the cycle of mineralising the litter, reducing populations of natural fungi and increasing pathogenic ones, eroding soil security. This not only results in a greater dependency on fire or fungicides but causes the need for more fertiliser to address declining yields, further perpetuating the cycle of declining soil and landscape health.

From the 1990s it was realised that excessive tillage and stubble burning was detrimental to the long-term viability of the land and new practices or a return to rotational mixed farming was required. Concerns in regard to profitability, productivity and sustainability were being raised by farmers and the public, so in 1992 Professor Ted Wolfe chaired the 21st Riverina Outlook Conference themed 'bridging the gap between the philosophies of organic farming and conservation farming'. Papers presented included alternate farming systems for the Riverina.[151] Almost 30 years later, as farm profitability and environmental well-being continue to decline, it is clear that regenerative agricultural practices have not been widely adopted and the gap between traditional farming practices and more sustainable practices remains, as shown by my March 2021 site inspection photos Figure 5-1, Figure 5-2 and Figure 5-4.

This intensively tilled region in the southern central part of NSW has greatly increased sensible heat during dry periods and caused measurable off-farm impacts, including well-reported significant pollution of our rivers, with dust contributing to making them anaerobic.[152] Could bushfires, floods and heat waves similarly be associated with agricultural practices?

Figure 5-4. Burnt stubble in the mid-ground and extensively in the background of farms in the southern central part of NSW in March 2021. Note the near complete absence of trees or ecological corridors.

Bushfires and agriculture

It is impossible to say whether regional bushfires occurred after drought before 1788. But it is apparent that long droughts of 1826–1829 (Sturt) and 1836–1838 (Strzelecki) did not have regional bushfires even though cultural burns were recorded. There is a strong correlation, however, between increased fire in the archaeological record and arrivals of humans around 50 000 years ago.[153] The fire-tolerant dry sclerophyll forests lost many of the she-oaks and at the same time expanded into the residual Gondwana wet forests of southern beech at this time, suggesting conscious landscape management by fire started then. The increased frequency of fire impacted on certain plants of the dry sclerophyll, like she-oaks and some types of banksia, which have difficulty in regenerating if burned repeatedly.

Colonisation in Australia again disrupted the landscape as Aboriginal people were dispossessed. Prior to the colonisation of

Portland in 1834 and Melbourne in 1835, the introduction of European diseases may have already occurred in Victoria. For example, introduced from the attempted settlement at Sullivans Bay at the mouth of Port Philip in 1803–4 and due to contact with seafarers, whalers and explorers, including from the Hume and Hovell Expedition of 1824. The spread of disease dramatically reduced populations, resulting in a substantial reduction in cultural activities for the maintenance of country using fire. Arguably, interference with traditional landscape management practices over time caused increasing wildfires, particularly if, as stated by Bruce Pascoe, the density of the trees gradually increased from 10/acre to 400/acre.[154] Though numbers differ the significance increase post colonisation is supported by a recent review on cultural burns and wildfires.[155]

The first major bushfire recorded in central and eastern Victoria, known as Black Thursday, occurred on 6 February 1851. It was proceeded by a prolonged drought in 1850, and several days of heat wave. A quarter of Victoria was burnt and 12 people died. The fire cleared the undergrowth, aiding the detection of gold later that year and the rapid expanse of alluvial mining sites.[156] It was not until Red Tuesday, on 1 February 1898, that another major bushfire occurred in Victoria. Again 12 people died, and this time 260 000 ha of south and east Gippsland were burnt. The fires of 1925–6 peaked with Black Sunday on 14 February 1926, which burnt 390 000 ha and resulted in 60 deaths. Less destructive and widespread fires burned in the early 1900s in central and eastern Victoria, including 1905–06, 1912, 1914 and 1919 but none met the definition of a major fire, over 150 000 ha burnt and loss of life. Following colonisation, there was a major fire very 2.5 decades. But after 1926 this increased to one to two each decade and has recently spiked,[xii] with two to three major bushfires occurring each decade.[xiii] The impact of the millennial drought is apparent in the bushfires from 1997 to 2009, terminating with the tragic disastrous

---

xii   1932, 1938–39, 1943–44, 1952, 1962, 1965, 1969, 1977, 1983, 1985, 1997.
xiii 2002–03, 2005–06, 2006–07, 2009, 2013, 2019–2020.

Black Saturday fires of 2009. This rapid escalation of wildfires is shown in Figure 5-5, which charts bushfires in Victoria from 1851 to 2010, noting the cumulative addition of fires from 1850 to the end of any given decade, shown at the start of the decade.

Figure 5-5 shows a correlation between an increase in bushfire frequency in Central and Eastern Victoria and the opening and expansion of the MIA. Operations in the MIA commenced in 1909 and it was substantially cultivated by the mid-1920s. The completion of the Snowy Mountains Scheme in 1974, delivering water via Blowering Dam, resulted in the MIA expanding in the late 1970s. In Figure 5-5 the opening of the MIA is labelled A and its expansion in the 1970s is labelled B, represented by the A and B blue arrows. The red arrow represents a period of about 15 years after the irrigation channel expansion in which the interval between bushfires in Central and Eastern Victoria accelerated. Correlation does not mean causation. The question then becomes: is this a natural phenomenon or exacerbated by agricultural activities post-1788?

It is well known that bushfires have increased, both in intensity and frequency, in all states since the 1980s. The difference for Victoria is the trend post-1926. As well as the fact that Central and Eastern

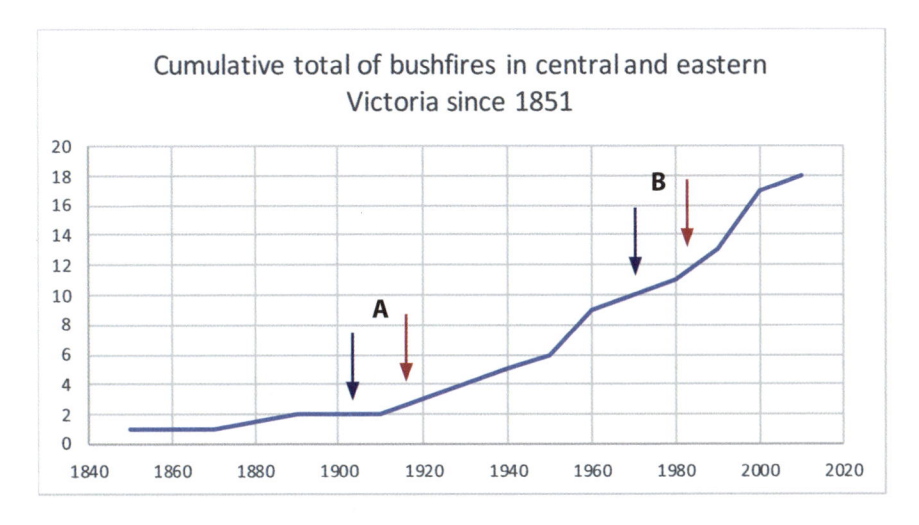

Figure 5-5. Cumulative total of bushfires in Central and Eastern Victoria since 1851

Victoria, representing just 2 per cent of the Australian land area, have suffered over 25 per cent of Australia's significant bushfires. And that this increase in frequency of bushfires corresponds with the opening of the MIA and the associated increase in sensible heat.

The 1908 map of the MIA (Figure 5-6) shows the proposed area that could and has been developed for irrigated agriculture. That area lies to the north and northwest of Central and Eastern Victoria respectively. Severe regional bushfires in these areas of Victoria strongly correlate with drought, heat waves and wind from the north and northeast. Evolving poor agricultural land management practices enabled by the MIA are likely causative of these developing and worsening climate changes.

Before clearing land for irrigated cultivation, the area comprising the MIA had a seasonal rainfall of less than 450 mm, insufficient for dryland cropping. Before 1909 that land was used for grazing sheep. Today, consistent with that use, areas adjacent to the MIA remain

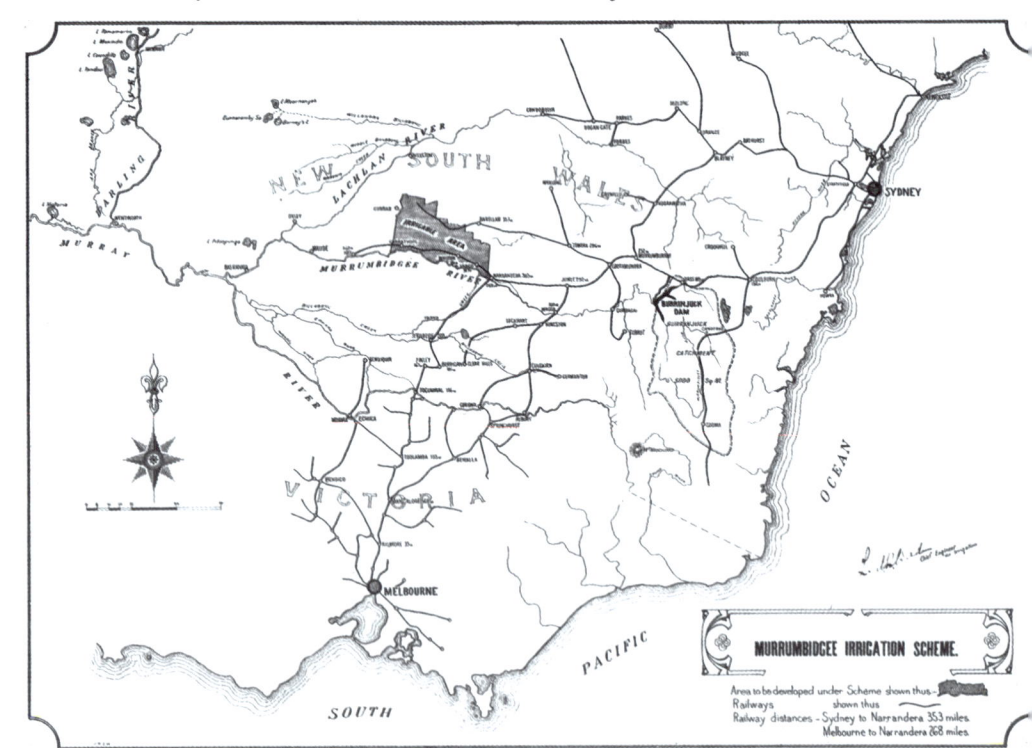

Figure 5-6. Murrumbidgee Irrigation Scheme 1908. State Archives of NSW

sheep-grazing pastoral properties. During a severe drought, lack of water forces those adjacent properties to remove livestock or suffer savage losses from thirst. The consequence was that, with the exception of land around dams, vegetative cover was preserved to some extent. This meant that prior to the MIA the land had reasonable vegetation cover, even during the worst drought, because destocking was a necessary farm management policy.

Even today, pastoral properties with no water allocation will have a problem with watering stock and consequently adopt a more aggressive destocking policy. Reducing stock numbers not only reduces losses but also allows the land to regenerate.

On the other hand, farmers with land within the MIA, rather than prepare for a drought, will prepare a seed bed. This is because they can commonly rely on a water entitlement to irrigate crops or to water stock. A water entitlement creates an assumption that even if rain is not forecast, the water allocation will be sufficient to get through a normal or slightly dry summer, so resting the land (with vegetative cover intact) or destocking is not necessary. Additionally, as conserving plant available water (PAW) over the summer is not as essential, MIA farmers tend to use tillage for weed control, rather than leaving stubble standing, particularly on share farms or leased paddocks.

Similarly, dryland farmers cannot afford the risk of loss of Financial Capital from seed bed preparation if rain does not eventuate, therefore they also tend to plant later, using direct tilling to avoid seed bed preparation. Hence, many farmers who have a water license, prepare a heavily tilled seed bed on the off-chance they will get a water allocation. Furthermore, paddocks are overall smaller in irrigated systems and so conversion of tractors and motorised seeders for GPS 'controlled traffic' is less likely. Such a practice also leaves stubble and typically requires less tillage.

Controlled traffic is a technique used by farmers which is part of a suite known as Precision Agriculture. Controlled traffic is ensuring all agricultural tractors and implements have the same wheel base. This means that, when utilised with GPS, control can ensure that the same track or path is used each and every time. This ensures compaction by wheels is limited to the same path and loss of yield and soil biome via wheel compaction is limited in the paddock. Precision agriculture also allows seeds to be accurately placed in rows and rows accurately placed offset from the previous year's crop by at least 100 mm. This ensures root fungal diseases are minimised and nutrient and plant-available water maximised. When Precision Agriculture is practised with a plant rotational system to promote fertility, reduce disease, reduce herbicide-resistant weeds, break up plough pans and increase carbon, it is known as Conservation Agriculture.

If water is not allocated and the season becomes an extended drought, the land remains uncovered and the soil is baked hot, turning crumbly. With no cover, erosion is assured. Almost all solar radiation is converted to sensible heat. With air temperatures above these paddocks likely to reach 50 to 60° C, heating the air which is pushed southward by the northerly wind generated by the superheated land, massive infra-red radiation release in the evening is assured too.[157] The hot dry strong wind so created then exacerbates any fire started in central and eastern Victoria, turning a local fire to a regional fire.

The perverse outcome of the MIA project is that the availability of irrigation itself has led to further, but different, poor land management practices, compounding the already unintended consequence of irrigation degrading soil fertility.

Early colonial land management practices from about the early 19th century onwards, mined the soil making it unfit for cropping. Potential cropping land was then sought in undeveloped semi-arid land that could be irrigated and so the MIA was developed. Though a great short-term agricultural boom occurred, we have shown that the MIA scheme has potentially enabled practices that compound the soil security issue, further degrading the land and reducing the small water cycle. The result has led to bare and exposed ground during prolonged low rainfall periods, and the consequent effect of an increase in sensible heat during these dangerous periods, more heat waves and their resultant hot dry winds. Scarily, the foundations of desertification and bushfires.

What other practices are there?

The common practices to replace Excess Till has been the farming practice of No Till (or minimum till) and the less commonly practised permaculture and biodynamics. Is No Till without adverse consequences?

At the same time of the emergence of No Till was the practice of organic farming. Organic farming *per se* is not necessarily No Till, as organic farming often continues the use of excessive till for weed control and thereby may still be mining carbon and not necessarily be sustainable. The farm practice of all ancient civilisations was organic but degradation and desertification still occurred. Organic farming without the benefits of modern science and technology is certainly not sustainable.

No Till was trialled throughout the 1970s, and gained momentum with early adopters in the 1980s. Although increasingly common, it is still not widely adopted in cropping regions that depend on irrigation, as is apparent in Figure 5-1, Figure 5-2 and Figure 5-4. No Till involves the use of herbicides to control weeds prior to sowing (pre-emergence) and during the growth of the crop (post-emergence). Initially, the most commonly used pre-emergence herbicide was glyphosate. For over 25 years glyphosate did not appear to infer resistance to its effects in any weeds in the field.[158] As a result its use in weed control in all settings increased tenfold in the decade after 1995.[159] The unexpected consequence of glyphosate's effectiveness is that, not only did it allow No Till to occur, but rotational systems of crops effectively ceased beyond those of the most commercial of crops. The limited commercial crops in rotation were typically wheat and canola or cotton in Australia, and the government-subsidised wheat, corn or cotton in the US. Rotation of herbicides in many instances did cease. Glyphosate came to dominate herbicide use.

These heavily used crops not only created a farm system having a heavy reliance on glyphosphate but also a dependency on synthetic fertilisers, devastating impacts on soil function, thereby decreasing soil security. Not the least of the impacts of glyphosate dominance is impact on the cost of running a farm. Governments, banks and suppliers in countries with modern agricultural industries encouraged farmers 'to get big or get out' if pursuing 'modern' industrial agriculture practice. Compliant farmers did not realise that effectively profit (Financial Capital) was being transferred from farmers to agribusinesses, businesses which will not be around when Natural and Financial Capital are run down.

Following this heavy period of glyphosate use, throughout the first two decades of the 21st century, farmers and farming communities in Australia started to note unusual associations:

- bird numbers dropped and bird species changed
- field mushrooms appeared less frequently
- insect numbers (except flies) at dusk were diminishing—less squashed bugs on windscreens
- with the exception of kangaroos and emus, native wildlife was diminishing or becoming locally extinct
- hot days and droughts became more frequent
- willy willies [dust devils] were more numerous, lasted longer and were stronger and more destructive;
- light winter rain, fogs, mists and summer thunderstorms, previously the norm, disappeared until 2020, a La Nina year.

If there was a battle against Nature, in which many thought farming was winning, it was not 'all quiet' on the Western Front. Local, regional and continental based changes appeared to be happening. Not only was the landscape being altered to the detriment of Nature, but the rapid return of droughts of longer duration and severity was causing disquiet in the bush.

Evidently, No Till farming was and is not sustainable. However, as explained in the next chapters, there are other farming and land management practices that are succeeding in restoring soil security, and in turn terrestrial health.

Chapter 6

The Emergence of Regenerative Agriculture

A potential solution?

Existing and past agricultural practices have failed to stop the gradual loss of the small water cycle and concomitant loss of vegetative cover, leading to increased heat. If Australia is truly committed to limiting global warming, it must consider how to secure our soils to reverse climate change through widespread adoption of different or new land-management practices.

There are already two systems capable of reversing climate change by sequestering carbon. Both practices are 'regenerative' and require accelerated adoption and ongoing advancement to responsive development practices. We can unpack Aboriginal land management knowledge to apply to our systems to increase sustainability. In European terms, the Aboriginal landscape management system would be seen as 'regenerative agriculture', a name and a series of innovative practices which is gaining momentum to give hope for securing the health of our soils. Soil security is being achieved through some types of conservation agriculture, biodynamic farming and the regenerative farming movement. The terms 'regenerative farming' and 'regenerative agriculture', can be used interchangeably, and are rapidly becoming rural buzz words.

'Regenerative agriculture' is a form of agriculture in which farmers go beyond seeking to be just sustainable, and work to regenerate terrestrial ecosystems. The focus on repairing the land aligns with the notion of farmers being custodians of the Earth. This focus, whether by intent or accident, is to eliminate adverse off-farm impacts that detrimentally impact our water, air and climate. Unfortunately, because regenerative, sustainable and conservative land-management practices are all perceived as different, regenerative agriculture has a perception problem. The distinction is a matter of degree and requires specialised knowledge. This is analogous to making bread, underpinned by science but overlayed with the art of practitioners. The science behind regenerative agriculture is understandable, but there is a critical lack of experienced landscape-management practitioners familiar with the science behind the art. Most scientists are trained to solve single-issue problems and the broad, systematic approach necessary to resolve landscape problems is beyond their training, with the result that many of them regard regenerative agriculture as 'alternative', untested and non-scientific.

The type of landscape management used, determines whether organic matter is mined by it, with carbon leaving the farm as agricultural products, or exported to the air as CO_2, or sequestered. For example, soil loss from conventionally tilled land exceeds the rate of soil formation from the bottom up, by more than two orders of magnitude.[160] Regenerative practices that increase rainfall, vegetative litter and charge will increase organic matter, and in so doing remove CO_2 from the air and build soil from the top down.

On the Western Plains of NSW, farmers have observed that some farms receive more rainfall than adjoining farms. They are always 'the lucky ones' to get the summer thunderstorms and are considered blessed that 'square' clouds occur over their land; that is, the rain is reserved for them. Square clouds seem to occur more frequently over farms greater than 1000 ha where regenerative farming methods are practised, although they may occur on farms as small as 90 ha.

One the world's leading sugar-cane farmers, Robert Quirk, who has a farm in Northern NSW, has been experimenting with innovative practices for over 30 years and in the last 15 years has focused on improving the soil biome and carbon sequestration. He said that on his small farm of less than 100 ha, in the last five years he has noticed that river mists form over his farm but not over adjoining farms; and when mist is present over the whole valley, it persists longer over his farm. These mists reduce large diurnal temperature change, raising predawn minimums and increase precipitation. This notion of increased mists and square clouds supports the previous explanation of the small water cycle being maintained and even increased by improving soil security through the maintenance of vegetation cover and the increase of organic carbon in soil.

Essentially, regenerative agricultural practices are designed to build or regenerate soil health through maintaining or improving soil organic matter. This may be achieved through the application of several different methods applied together, including: minimum tillage; controlled traffic; standing stubble; crop rotation; cover crops; green manures; composting and mulching; wide tree breaks on large areas (to propagate rain and increase biodiversity); perennial crops; and mob grazing. In addition to these practices, reducing or eliminating the use of herbicides and most acidic fertilisers is also practised. All three different farm practices that meet these criteria: conservation agriculture, biodynamic farming, and regenerative farming, have been developed along the same scientific principles, but were arrived at via different pathways.

The key principles of regenerative farming practices are set out on the next page in Figure 6-1.

	Science	Activity	Notes
1	Reduce sensible heat	Maintain vegetative cover—No bare ground. Conservation agriculture/no-till agriculture. Consider stubble residue as ground cover	Regenerative farming and conservation agriculture differ in approach over plant-available water during summer in winter crop region (>300 mm rainfall)
2	Build system resilience—build soil charge, increase organic matter, avoid monoculture	1. Promote rotational systems and soil biome for fertiliser reduction and reduction of herbicides and diseases. 2. Use perennial grain crops if possible 3. Build multiple income sources via different profit centres 4. In some environments (low charge) consider controlled but infrequent use of fire 5. Monitor soil phosphate carefully and replace as necessary but minimise or eliminate salts of acids	If cropping only, need advice from regen-ag/cons-ag consulting agronomist (unlikely to be found at agrichemical produce merchants)
3	Increase air turbulence and lower boundary layer	Plant ecosystem corridor >50 m wide. Use where possible both native food and timber trees. Non-native production trees can also be used but less desirable. Also use crops of varying heights in the same season	Needs to be > 50 m for insectivorous birds and to create air turbulence and a range of other benefits. How high and how thick the vegetative break has to be to influence air turbulence and therefore rainfall is not yet resolved for many areas.
4	Systems approach—shifting the definition of 'success' away from yield to cost reduction, profit and co-benefits (increase of native species, streamflow etc)	Reduce input costs by crop rotation and build-up of OM. Use manures, composts and inoculum (e.g. Biodynamic 500, as well as probiotic seed coatings to get PO_4 from rocks) wherever possible; recharge alluvium	Create other measures of successful system performance other than yield. Use also work-life balance and soil security and basal stream flow

Science	Activity	Notes
5 Use animals (or manures for cropping systems) to lift fertility. Croppers can use animals during crop manure stage. Animals can be sourced on agistment or trade opportunity	1 Must use mob (cell or rotational) grazing; 5 ha mini paddocks: 200 m to nearest water point. 2 Rotation according to soil fertility as well as pasture management. 3 Back-load animal manures from stock yards and feedlots 4 In some environments (low charge) controlled but infrequent use of fire	Animal manures contain phosphate but when comparatively fresh also provide inoculum. It takes up to four days (depending on the animal) for grass to pass, therefore move animal from P-rich bed rock to P-poor soil over 1 to 3 days.

Definitions

Conservation agriculture: Includes all of:
No-Till + controlled traffic + rigorous rotational system + complete ground cover (not necessarily living) minus routine use of acidic fertilisers and herbicides.
Regenerative farming:
As above, but incorporating animals, plus increased multiple profit centres by use of increased diversity of crops and fruiting trees and a greater use of perennials and rare use of chemicals.

Figure 6-1. Key principles of practices to build Natural Capital and resilience as well as Financial Capital, while reversing agriculture-derived climate change

Organic farming may be regenerative but often it is not as wholesome for the land as its name might imply. Organic farming may not be sequestering organic matter, so organic matter can decrease as readily in organic farming as via conventional farming, particularly if phosphate lost in products exported from the farm is not replaced.

Though existing longer than regenerative agriculture as a farming practice, permaculture is considered a subset of regenerative agriculture. In our opinion biodynamics is the only other form of organic farming that is definitively regenerative; providing phosphate released by the biome plus imported phosphate balances the phosphate exported from the system, but comes with a philosophy that is not palatable for every modern family or appropriate for corporate farming. In most environments biodynamics and organic farming will have to be augmented by external source of phosphate to be defined as regenerative, that is sequestering carbon. Studies on biodynamic dairies have not demonstrated increased concentrations of soil organic carbon compared to conventionally managed dairies, but whether soil organic carbon increased with time for dairies compared to non-dairy farms in the study was not stated.[161]

Although soil security is not often expressly addressed, there is much literature about regenerative agriculture generally, including from pioneers and leaders of the movement such as Allan Savory,[162] Wes Jackson,[163] Joel Salatin,[164] Gabe Brown,[165] Mark Shepard,[166] James Rebanks[167] and Charles Massy[168]. Not to discount any one of those authors, the summary of their collective commentary is that regenerative farming sequesters organic carbon, restores the ecosystem—and provides for truly sustainable production.

In his book *Call of the Reed Warbler*, Charles Massy calls on his own personal experience and that of dozens of other farmers, to evocatively describe the history of land degradation in Australia, and he urges Australian farmers to switch to regenerative land practices. In some ways, Massy is the farmers' face of the emerging regenerative agriculture movement in Australia and his book may be regarded as a call to arms, but a widespread uptake of regenerative farming practices is yet to occur.

Case studies of many innovators have also been put together by Soils For Life Foundation in a report available on their website, *Innovators for Regenerative Landscape Management*.[169] The scientific principles adopted by these innovators are consistent with the principles set out in Figure 6-1. Regardless of what productive system is adopted to sequester carbon into the soil, all systems require nitrogen-fixing plants and, in Australia, phosphate sourced from offsite.

Lack of uptake of regenerative systems is partly due to farmers not wanting to significantly deviate from the norms of the district because of the lack of peer support,[170] and because it has always been done that way, coupled with the notion that regenerative farming cannot be done profitably. Nevertheless, financial success continues to be demonstrated by farmers practising regenerative farming and two examples that have received news media attention are Ian and Di Haggerty near

Wyalkatchem WA,[171] and the Dunnicliff family at Beetaloo Station in the Northern Territory.[172]

To achieve the rapid change necessary to reverse the impacts of destructive land management practices, government policy must provide education for farmers and change farming incentives to drive uptake of regenerative agricultural practices.

Australia is unique globally in its combination of climate, soil type, vegetation and the integration of fire into its agricultural cycles. Quickly finding the right system—which will vary with location, rainfall, soil charge and desired cultural practice—and ensuring its prompt and extensive uptake, should be the focus of every government.

Interdependence of natural capital, measured as soil security and financial capital

Increasing soil security (measured via organic matter) increases profit, Financial Capital. Maintaining soil security has many advantages, not the least maximising both Natural and Financial Capital. Consequentially, soil security (using organic matter as an analogue) and profit are related and this relationship can be used as a means to classify, not just farm performance, but future farm viability.

Whether a farm can be managed without degrading Natural Capital depends not only on current organic matter but also the Financial Capital available to the farm management team. In our opinion currently less than 2 per cent of farmers are maintaining and increasing Natural Capital. Most are degrading Natural Capital either slowly or rapidly. With appropriate training, advice and support, this can be reversed without a change of ownership for over 73 per cent of farms. The remaining farms do not have the financial strength and should be encouraged to leave the industry or at least not be supported in remaining as farm managers.

Social, environmental and economic imperatives

To reverse the loss of soil carbon and increase soil security requires managing the soil and the land as an integrated system to promote soil security over carbon mining. When a farm is financially constrained, this is difficult because farmers are not then in a position to address the degradation of Natural Capital of their land. Figure 6-2 plots the theoretical relationship between sustainable profit, five-year average profit, versus soil security measured indirectly by the percentage of OM, organic matter.

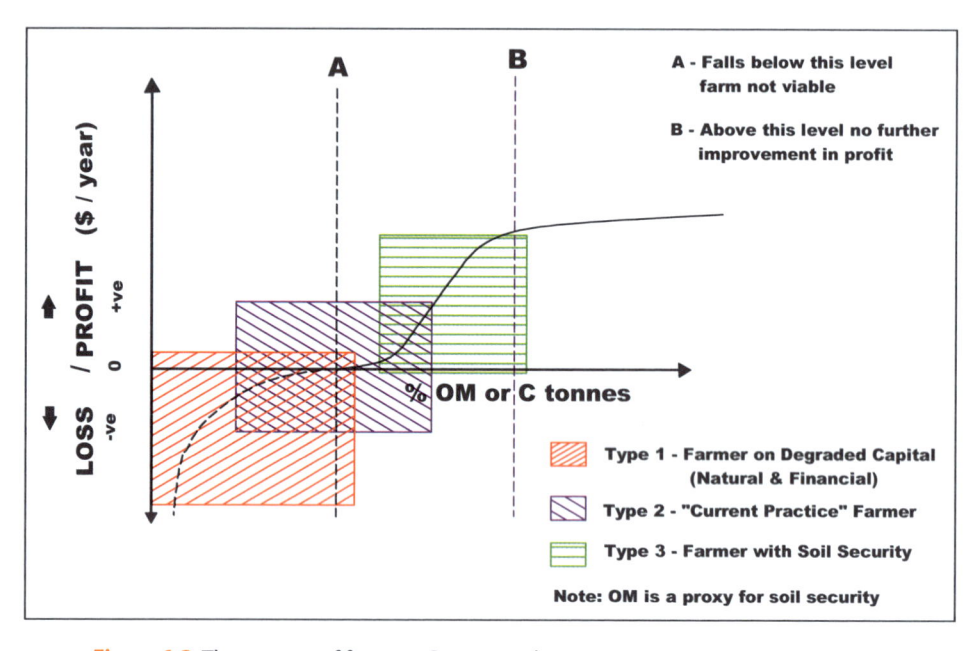

Figure 6-2. Three types of farmers. Source: carboncount.com

Figure 6-2 considers that Australian farmers in general fall into three pools:

Type 1: These are farmers whose capital, both Natural and Financial, is so degraded their activities are constrained and for fear of financial failure they cannot risk a change. They receive rainfall from medium to large falls from continental systems, as well as, more frosts, hail and days over 40° C. They have no revenue during drought years and only make a profit during the exceptionally good seasons, but this profit does not compensate for the losses during the average and bad seasons. They rely on off-farm income which includes drought relief and social security. Consequently, as their Natural Capital declines, and in turn their Financial Capital, they often reduce their land by selling portions. This cohort potentially represents 25 per cent of family farms.

Type 2: Most of these farmers have limited capital but are not so constrained that change cannot be made. Cultural practices, management systems and a lack of clear guidance may all apply but their situation is not degraded enough to be a catalyst for change. These farms barely make a profit during the average season, but make a good profit during a good season, while during a drought they may suffer a loss but retain some revenue. Except for drought years these enterprises do not need off-farm income to make a living, though they are on a steady decline. They receive small amounts of rain from the small water cycle, including local summer storms and light winter rain from continental systems as well as the heavy rain from the continental systems. They represent about 73 per cent of farms.

Type 3. This group are neither capital or environmentally constrained. They operate either conservation agriculture, biodynamics or regenerative practices, but in all cases, they are innovative and manage the farm as part of a long cycle integrated into the ecological system. Typically, over 20 per cent of the farm is devoted to ecological corridors, organic matter is high and the land has vegetative cover (either living or dead plants) over more than 90 per cent of the time for greater than 90 per cent of the area. This encourages 'square clouds', summer thunderstorms, light local winter rain, and light, medium and heavy rain from continental systems, with fewer frosts and days over 40° C. The farms are profitable in all seasons, although in a good season, while the yields may be less than the Type 2 farmers, costs are significantly less, so profit is often greater. They never require government assistance or off-farm income and are generally able to increase their holdings. They represent less than 2 per cent of farmers.

Looking simplistically at what Type 1 and 2 farmers practise in comparison with Type 3 farmers, it is obvious that regenerative farming models offer a long-term financially viable solution.

As has been the case since the 1880s, most Australian family farms are currently capital constrained and cannot take the risk of innovation or new techniques because they cannot afford—financially, mentally or physiologically—to fail. It is a perverse outcome that farmers have to run Natural Capital down to build enough Financial Capital to achieve the change necessary to build Natural Capital up. The sad reality is, during long drought years the stress becomes unbearable and suicide rates rise.

Corporate farms, being run for a profit, are financially better managed than most family farms. Their focus is on return on investment for shareholders. In the short term this can be at the cost of Natural Capital, which is commonly ignored unless it directly impacts Financial Capital. Consequently, and for a variety of factors not relevant to this discussion, corporate farms are rarely Type 3 farms but typically are successful Type 2 farms.

Generally, innovation in agriculture does not come from government departments or university laboratories. In Australia innovators and industry have historically worked together to improve practice, while academic researchers mostly only validate any innovations for uptake by the majority of farmers. Although the innovation for repairing the soil is coming from behind the farm gate, as we said, it takes about 30 years between innovators demonstrating an improved technology and industry uptake. This period must be reduced and this is where science comes in with research focussing on understanding why some areas succeed and how that success can transfer to a wider industry uptake. Going forward such research has to move from being one-dimensional to systems-based.

Chapter 7

Carbon Sequestration in Soil

Building soil organic matter, building soil security

The process of capturing and storing atmospheric CO_2 is called 'carbon sequestration'. It occurs both naturally and as a result of human activities. The main natural carbon sinks are soil and rocks, plants, and the ocean. The main artificial CO_2 sinks are landfills, geological sequestration and carbon capture and storage processes (such as 'clean coal' and timber as a mass construction material replacement for steel and concrete).

Many people believe mitigating carbon emissions is not as effective as not emitting CO_2 in the first place. If greenhouse gas emissions were the main cause of climate change, we would agree. However, mitigating CO_2 emissions through sequestering it in soil may be even more important. Most of the civilisations which collapsed did so as a result of climate change caused by agriculture, not greenhouse gas emissions.

Our thesis is that the way we practise agriculture degrades soil security and destroys the small water cycle. In turn, it is a significant cause of the rise of global mean temperature, increasing the frequency of extremely hot days, droughts and fires. Consequently, if sequestering CO_2 in soil achieves a reduction in atmospheric CO_2, it will have a greater impact on climate change because at the same time it increases soil security and assists the return of the small water cycle.

Substantial uptake of soil carbon in sequestration, called 'carbon farming', augmented by other landscape practices necessary for returning the small water cycle, is as vital to stopping and reversing climate change as the vaccination for COVID-19 is to the world travel industry. The fact that sequestering carbon in soil simultaneously builds soil security while drawing down CO_2 from the air is an exciting opportunity for reversing climate change. It is a mutually inclusive solution. As carbon sequestration improves soil security, aiding in reducing sensible heat and improving the small water cycle, it is much more important than merely ceasing emissions of greenhouse gases from industry.

Sequestering carbon is essential for soil security and a key component to achieving the return of the small water cycle. Any mechanism that promotes sequestration is on the pathway to reversing climate change in Australia, but more, much more, needs to be done.

Australian regulation – the Carbon Farming Initiative

'Carbon farming' is farming in a way that reduces CO_2 emissions and/or captures and holds CO_2 in vegetation and soils, also commonly known as 'soil sequestration'. The Carbon Farming Initiative allows farmers and land managers to earn carbon credits by sequestering soil as a source of greenhouse gas abatement.

Soil carbon is already being sequestered by farmers and sold as offsets, and it is proving successful but slow in uptake. The first soil carbon sale occurred in Australia in 2019 using the Australian Government Legislation of 2018. It was recently reported, in what was likely the first inter country soil carbon credit sale, that Microsoft (USA) had purchased around half a million dollars of carbon credits from NSW cattle farmers Wilmot Cattle Co.[173] Though there has been many scientists criticising the efficacy of the process used in this instance,[174] it heralds international trade of soil carbon. Building up soil carbon is one type of carbon farming practised in Australia. Savannah burning practices, partial destocking, increased growth of trees on farms are all practices considered as carbon farming. Carbon farming remains new and novel but is increasingly popular. Farmers, like the Henderson family of Colodan in Central Queensland, tell of how establishing carbon farming not only enabled their land to become more resilient to major climate events such as drought and extreme rainfall events but also affords them greater financial security through reliable carbon cash flow in the business.[175] While carbon farming remains a new industry, soil carbon sequestration is embryonic having evolved out of the Paris Agreement, ratified in 2016.

At the United Nations Framework Convention on Climate Change (UNFCCC) Conference of the Parties 2021 (COP 21) in Paris, almost all nations of the world agreed to a landmark international accord in the effort to combat global climate change: the Paris Agreement.[176] Central to the agreement is a low carbon future achieved through objective targets and interim assessment of Parties 'nationally determined contributions'. The key goal is keeping a global temperature rise this century to well below 2° C above pre-industrial levels and to pursue efforts to limit the temperature increase even further to 1.5° C.

On Earth Day, 22 April 2016, the Paris Agreement was opened for signature. On 10 November 2016, Australia ratified the Paris Agreement, as a signatory to which Australia is committed to reducing its 2005 emissions by 26–28 per cent by 2030. Sitting behind the Paris Agreement, is Australia's voluntary commitment to the '4 per 1000' initiative.

This promising initiative is the crown jewel of the Paris Agreement. It complements GHG reduction efforts, facilitates the vital role of improving soil carbon stocks in topsoil *and* significantly reduces CO_2 concentration in the atmosphere.

The 4 per 1000 initiative is based on the concept that if emissions are stopped, the existing elevated CO_2 in the atmosphere can be drawn down into the soil. Given it is our thesis that stopping and removing CO_2 emissions from the atmosphere without addressing soil security will not stop climate change, the 4 per 1000 initiative is the most important Paris Agreement initiative, as it can only be achieved by agricultural practices that promote soil security. The 4 per 1000 initiative will be more impactful than carbon farming practices that just focus on vegetation or mitigating uncontrolled fires.

Despite the Australian government's commitments as a signatory to the Paris Agreement, and its voluntary commitments to the 4 per 1000 initiative, we are are likely to fall short of our 2030 Paris Agreement targets. As hailed leaders in the carbon farming space, it might prove embarrassing. Knowing the connection between soil and climate change, and understanding soil security is our greatest defence against climate change, we are now empowered afresh and must choose to act.

Ongoing legislative and regulatory reform and understanding what informed it in the first place is critical to meaningful development. To many people our former Prime Minister Tony Abbott is seen as a pariah of the climate change debate, foremost among climate deniers. However, as part of the process of dismantling Australia's carbon market, the Abbott government created emissions-reduction legislation. This legislation, *Carbon Credits (Carbon Farming Initiative) Act 2011* (Carbon Credits Act), set up a process of offsetting carbon emissions to landscape. This reform from the Abbott government was before the French launched the 4 per 1000 initiative. In 2021 Australia had the first and most successful scheme for mitigating carbon by offsetting activities that reduce carbon emissions or sequestering carbon to soil—the Emissions Reduction Fund (ERF), a Commonwealth initiative administered by the Clean Energy Regulator. This scheme, acknowledged by many countries as making a significant contribution to the 4 per 1000 initiative, is being increasingly evaluated and starting to be copied by other nations. Reduced clearing of mulga vegetation, tree planting and managed savanna burns are part of the methods for offsetting carbon to land, known collectively as 'carbon farming'. An industry has developed to manage, record and audit those activities to provide certainty that the carbon *was* offset and engender confidence in the scheme. Regardless of people's views of the politics of the past two decades on climate change, this piece of legislation and its supporting regulations initiated by Abbott's government set up a process of offsetting carbon emissions that also has the capacity to create soil security.

In 2021 section 160 of the Carbon Credits Act, the *Carbon Credits (Carbon Farming Initiative—Estimation of Soil Organic Carbon Sequestration Using Measurement and Models) Methodology Determination 2021* (Soil Carbon Methodology Determination), facilitated a methodology to sequester soil carbon effectively covering all agricultural activities, which replaced an earlier 2018 and 2015 method of limited application. This methodology is currently undergoing review.

The infrastructure—the soil samplers, farm advisors and laboratory capability—as well as auditable processes, is still under development, and currently less than 100 farms across Australia are being approved under this carbon-sequestration methodology and less than five have demonstrated tradeable carbon from soil sequestration.[xiv] The Federal Government has offered farmers a $5,000 subsidy to measure carbon for soil sequestration to accelerate uptake and to assist Australia in meeting its Paris Targets. Additionally, on 2 October 2020, the Minister for Energy and Emissions Reduction, Angus Taylor, announced that the Clean Energy Regulator would lead development of Emissions Reduction Fund methods, as well as continuing to administer the scheme; ostensibly to accelerate development. This accords with the Minister's announcement on 22 September 2020 that the government would deliver a new soil carbon method, effectively an upgrade of the 2018 method, within 12 months.

Most recently, in the 11 May 2021 Federal Budget the government announced $102 million over two years from 2021–22 to incentivise farmers to increase soil testing, and enhance the National Soil Resources Information System by feeding in new and existing data. How effectively this money is deployed is yet to be seen …

It is exciting and commendable that Australia is investing in pioneering methods to sequester carbon to land. But, while the $5,000

---

xiv <80 farms at the time of publication, August 2021.

subsidy scheme is a great start, the uptake will continue to be slow as the technology and frameworks are expensive, and farmers remain uncertain of the value or are unable to source the advice to make it viable. Again, the most recent budget announcement has directed some funding to improve this issue, but it is not enough. The government is exploring technology and administrative barriers to greater farmer participation. However, significant departures from the principles of the current regulations for carbon sequestration to soil are not expected.

Before undertaking an 'eligible management activity' that is proven to sequester carbon, the Soil Carbon Methodology Determination currently requires a soil-carbon project be registered and for each carbon estimation area to have a baseline of soil carbon and farm greenhouse emissions.[177] The Soil Carbon Methodology Determination lists 13 land management activities proven to sequester carbon:

- applying nutrients to the land in the form of a synthetic or non-synthetic fertiliser to address a material deficiency;
- applying lime or other ameliorants to remediate acid soils;
- applying gypsum to manage sodic or magnesic soils;
- undertaking new irrigation;
- re-establishing or rejuvenating a pasture by seeding or pasture cropping;
- establishing, and permanently maintaining, a pasture where there was previously no or limited pasture, such as on cropland or bare fallow;
- altering the stocking rate, duration or intensity of grazing (or any combination of such activities) to promote soil vegetation cover or improve soil health, or both;
- retaining stubble after a crop is harvested;
- converting from intensive tillage practices to reduced or no tillage practices;
- modifying landscape or landform features to remediate land;
- using mechanical means to add or redistribute soil through the soil profile;

- using legume species in cropping or pasture systems;
- using a cover crop to promote soil vegetation cover or improve soil health, or both

Under the Soil Carbon Methodology Determination an improvement on the land management activities during the baseline period occurs when at least one of the land-management activities is new or materially different from existing practices and more carbon can reasonably be expected to be sequestered in that system as a result of carrying out that land management activity (the newness test).[178] Currently, rotations that include legumes and pulses and use of crops to break plough pans—the compacted layer at 15 cm, or other hard pans—rather than mechanical tilling are not considered, and nor are the practices of biodynamics or permaculture, all of which are proven carbon sequesters, and all of which should be incorporated into the scheme and promoted for their landscape and ecosystem benefits. Based on the 'newness test', any farm that converted to regeneration practices previously but is still yet to achieve the full carbon sequestration potential is unfortunately not considered. Consequently, existing good behaviours and some anticipated future practice are not being rewarded. Most of the regenerative farming pioneers are excluded from participating unless they can add one of the 13 practices listed above. Although conceptually the scheme is largely applaudable, operationally it is still navigating teething issues.

The current regulations require a large amount of adminstration and compliance. Similarly confirmation of the management plan by an independent agronomist and auditor to confirm compliance, adds significant costs to the process of proving carbon sequestration for the 4 per 1000 initiative. Without government support for automating registration, measurement and auditing, the sale of carbon will not exceed the costs of measurement and compliance for a 1000 ha farm until carbon costs exceed roughly $25/tonne of CO_2. Fortunately the price exceeded this level in mid-2021 and continues to rise. Nevertheless, the increased soil security and resultant mean five-year profit of the farm, greatly exceeds the cost of administration, measurement and compliance. Carbon farming to sell carbon sequestration is the icing on the cake, which comes from the improved profit and recovery of ecosystem services that result from a management system that is less reliant on chemical inputs and that promotes soil security.

In this regard, Graeme Samuel recommended greater alignment between the carbon and biodiversity markets as part of his recommendations on environmental offsets policy. On 28 January 2021, the Minister for the Environment Susan Ley released Professor Samuel's review of Australia's environmental laws: the Final Report of the Independent Review of the EPBC Act (Final Report). In these concluding words, Samuel commented 'offsets are ecologically feasible and deliver genuine protection and restoration in areas of highest priority'. While we agree with this statement, his recommendation for environmental offset policies and its implementation is centred on his proposed National Environmental Standards. For obvious reasons, we have and will continue to have reservations about the merits of this suggestion until soil is identified and captured as a critical environmental function within the EPBC Act (or a subsequent new Act) and incorporated into the proposed National Environmental Standards.

Apart from measurement, the government is not doing enough to encourage widespread uptake of regenerative land practices, which are more effective in mitigating the effects of human accelerated climate change than decarbonisation. Currently the Australian government is exploring other mechanisms to encourage the uptake of regenerative practices.

The science of soil security and carbon sequestration

Maximising soil sequstration while maintaining agricultural production is difficult.

Essentially the soil biome converts leaf stem litter and redundant roots to organic matter. Unfortunately modern agricultural practices do not favour the development of the right biome to do this. The key factors controlling the rate and amount of carbon sequestration are:

- water
- heat (which differs depending on latitude)
- the amount of soil charge, including cation exchange capacity
- the soil biome, particularly the comparitive amount of fungi to bacteria in the soil
- the availability in certain ratios of carbon; nitrogen; phosphorus; and sulfur (C/N/P/S)

Previously we discussed the importance of an appropriate distribution of soil pores to ensure rapid infiltration and ample water storage before drainage. This secures sufficient water and air for the plant root to maximize production of organic matter. Keeping the soil shaded or covered with either vegetation or plants is essential to prevent the surface of the soil heating up, and drying out. These are physical attributes that need to be maintained in good soil. Ensuring that at least fungi exceed bacteria in total numbers was discussed. The importance of pH (acidity and alkinity) and soil charge also. But what is often ignored when people try to optimise the sequestration of soil carbon is achieving the right ratios of C/N/P/S.

All life on Earth requires a particular ratio of these elements for cell function and this varies depending on the function of the compound and the function of the cell. Plant structural matter such as lignin, the tough stuff that produces strong stalks and stems, and trees contains a greater amount of carbon relative to nitrogen and phosphorus than what is required by microbes. Lignin is the main constituent of wood, so nitrogen is required to convert wood to organic matter. For plant growth, the ideal C/N/P/S ratio is typically 100 C: 8 N: 2 P: 1 S. Though the C/N ratio can push out to 20:1 with regard to microbes, and lignin to 30:1.

Agriculture typically removes the nitrogen and phosphorus into the produce and fibre sent to market. Without nitrogen and phosporus available in the right ratio, dead plant matter is mineralised, and not converted to organic matter. But if nitrogen and phosphate are introduced as manufactured fertilisers, particularly as salts of acids, organic matter can be sequestered up until the time the pH drops below 5.5. In most Australian soils this causes the charge to drop. The loss in charge results in the loss of glues that hold aggregates and organic matter together and ultimately the loss of stored organic matter. Therefore, although nitrogen and phosphate can be introduced occasionally as manufactured fertiliser to soil dominated by pH variable charge, it cannot be added frequently without loss of soil security. Other ways of more frequent addition of plant-available nitrogen and phosphorus are required.

Maximum conversion to organic matter is achieved by the introduction of nitrogen by manures or microbial-mediated means. Though there are free-living nitrogen-fixing microbes, most fixation undertaken in soil is done by *Ryzobium* bacteria, which require a plant host, as they live in nodules on plant roots. Typically, in agricultural settings this includes legumes and pulses in pasture and crops, but also acacias and casaurinas. Hence, to optimise carbon sequestration, crop rotation and pasture require inclusion of legumes and pulses.

Phosphorus is not so readily addressed. The natural options are limited, particularly in regions and countries with old soil from which any rock phosphate, the common form of phosphorus, has been leached. Unrefined phosphate can be sourced from rock rich in phosphate (aptite), volcanic rocks, or animal manures (including guano). The amount of phosphate removed in cropping is significant. Roughly only half the phosphate applied is used by the crop in that season; about a quarter is lost to groundwater and surface runoff, either dissolved or attached to fine sediment. The other quarter is stored in the mineral phase and, subject to the right pH and microbial conditions, this can be released. Of the 50 per cent uptake by the crop, 80 per cent of that, 40 per cent of the applied tonnage, is stored as protein in the grain and removed with the crop.

To sequester carbon, microbes have to access the stored portion of phosphate or have phosphate added to achieve optimum sequestation. Addition of slow-release nonacidic phosphate is best achieved by the use of animal manure, either by directly using sheep or cattle fresh from grazing over phosphate-rich soil, shown in Figure 7-1. It is

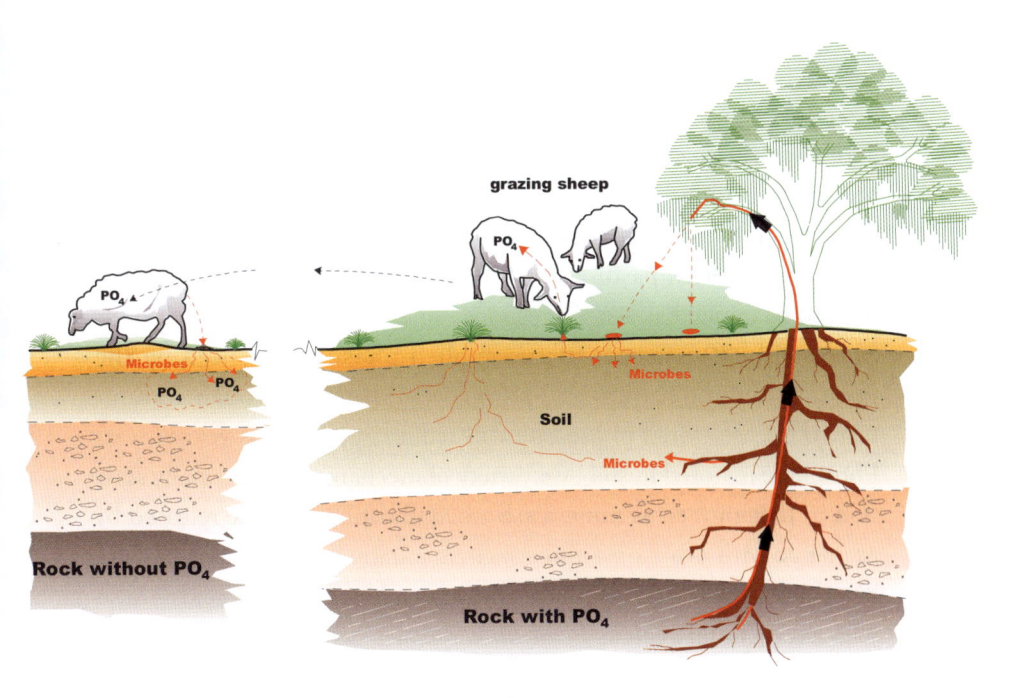

Figure 7-1. Movement of phosphate in the landscape by stock animals

similar to how kangaroos had been suggested to be moved around by patch or corridor burning by the Aboriginals in Figure 2-12 on page 67. Or achieved indirectly by adding animal manure or compost. Ecologist Allan Savory advocates a similar idea through his holistic farm management and planned grazing method.

The problem is, for grain production, a lot of phosphate is required. For example, the 2018 season was a great season for the WA wheatbelt, roughly 12 million tonnes of wheat was harvested, but that 12 million tonnes exported took 150 000 tonnes of phosphate from the district, and given the losses of phosphate to storage and the environment, requires 375 000 tonnes of phosphate to replace it, that is, about 450 000 tonnes of Mono-Ammonium Phosphate (MAP). This is equivalent to 31 million tonnes of cow manure or 12.5 million tonnes of chicken manure, as cattle and chicken manure have about 1.2 and 3 per cent phosphate respectively. Ignoring the logistical nightmare, there is simply insufficient manure in WA for the task.

There are non-acid phosphate fertilisers in liquid form but they are not yet universally available. These are known as polyphosphate and its use in Australia is increasing, but it is clear that if Australia is to achieve high productivity and sequester carbon, phosphate has to be added and in the absence of sufficient manures from stock grazing on phosphate-rich pasture or from feedlots, phosphate fertiliser will have to be applied as a rapid response solution.

As only 40 per cent of the applied phosphate is used by the plant, better application and stimulation of the microbial community to release stored phosphate will reduce applications year on year. Phosphate is stored in soil by a variety of mechanisms, principally sorbtion or precipitated as minerals. Sorbed phosphate can be released by exchange with other oxyanions such as sulfate. Exchange can be facilitated by organic acid exudates from microbes. Stronger acids – also released by fungi such as *Penicillium bilaiae* – break down phosphate minerals, making stored phosphate available to plants or preventing phosphate mineral precipitates. Promoting or allowing a complex rhizosphere or soil biome to develop can promote more efficient use of any applied phosphate, as well as releasing stored phosphate, reducing either the frequency and/or the quantity of phosphate that needs to be applied to counteract the phosphate removed by agricultural activities. Phosphate and nitrogen must be replaced by the production system if carbon is going to be sequestered. Unlike nitrogen, phosphate will require off-farm sources to counteract this loss.[xv]

---

xv Noting, the addition of crushed rock phosphate and basalt inoculated with *Penicillium bilaiae* is being trialled as a replacement for synthetic acid phosphate salts.

Chapter 8

Australia in Focus

Long time coming, but looking up

The focus remains on addressing how landscape change adversely impacts climate and how to mitigate that while maintaining productivity. Here we touch on previous soil policies, and propose a way forward to encourage and support our farmers.

For brevity and as agriculture has in our opinion a far greater impact on anthropogenic climate change, national parks are not covered, but more active management of national parks is needed, particularly with regard to reducing the density of trees. In this regard, we concur with Kate Dooley from the Australian-German Climate and Energy College, that 'protecting primary and intact forest ecosystems is a critical part of any climate mitigation strategy, to maintain the world's existing terrestrial carbon stock, its biodiversity hotspots and the climatic regulation that primary forests provide. Planting trees is no substitute for protecting and restoring natural forest ecosystems.'[179] But we note this also means restoring forest densities to the pre-1770 densities, not allowing unfettered revegetation.

The same general principle applies to land clearing. We go further by suggesting that all land within Australia, including forests and wild areas, consistent with Bill Gammage's thesis, requires management, and removing active management by humans from any landscape in Australia is detrimental for both humanity and the environment.[180]

The history of soil as an asset worth protecting

The challenge of soil security has been fermenting in the Australian consciousness for some time. There is increasing disquiet with current conventional agricultural practice as more farmers are noting the degradation of the landscape and the number of Type 1 farmers is increasing: see Figure 6-2 on page 148. Not discounting any work undertaken in the past, the actions detailed below demonstrate the slow emergence of soil security as a national policy issue.

Although, soil and land conservation have been legislated in some states and territories since 1938,[181] the first large-scale study on the extent and impact of land degradation in Australia was not undertaken until 1971, by the Australian Standing Committee on Soil Conservation. It was then estimated that the cost of controlling soil erosion with structural measures in non-arid regions of Australia would be approximately $350 million in 1970 prices (or approximately $4.2 billion today).[182]

In 1974 the Federal Parliament passed an Act to provide financial assistance to the states for purposes connected with soil conservation: *The States Grants (Soil Conservation) Act 1974* (Cth).

In 1978 the State Collaborative Soil Conservation Study published a report on the cost of land degradation which estimated that nationally 51 per cent of rural land used for agriculture required treatment for erosion or vegetation degradation. Essentially, the report proposed simple improved land management practices as the solution to land degradation, at an estimated cost of $2 billion, approximately $11.1 billion today.[183] Since the report did not consider acidification or soil structure decline or land-induced climate change, this was a conservative estimate.

In recognition of the serious challenges land degradation presented, the first National Soil Conservation program was established in 1983.

In May 1985, to stimulate increased action from the states relating to soil conservation, the Federal Parliament passed the *Soil*

Conservation (Financial Assistance) Act 1985. It also established a fund, the National Soil Conservation Program Fund, for this purpose, and the Soil Conservation Advisory Committee to make recommendations with respect to funding.

In late 1989 the Government's Standing Committee on Environment, Recreation and the Arts published a report entitled *The Effectiveness of Land Degradation Policies and Programs.* This report speaks of how land degradation had long been recognised as a serious but unresolved problem: 'The seriousness of the land degradation problem facing Australia is so great that it is difficult to comprehend, but there should be no doubt that if the trend is not reversed it could have serious consequences for the economy and the environment.' The paper commented that a large number of reports over many years had called for a national land use policy, intended to provide an overall framework for land use, and resource and environmental management at the national level. It also detailed support for the establishment of a Commonwealth State Co-ordinating Council to plan and implement such a policy.

Some action did result from this committee's work. Landcare was set up in July 1989 as a national programme with funding announced for the 'Decade of Landcare Plan'. With the Hawke Government committing $320 million to fund the program. The focus of which was initially on community action programs using reforestation to stabilise erosion-prone land and for protection of the riparian zone, the interface between land and a river or stream. As the program started to focus more directly on soil health after 2005, funding in Landcare decreased, particularly over the last decade: soil is not as visible or as valued as trees. Without first having a landscape management plan, maximum benefit from planting trees, although satisfying, is not often effective in sustainable landscape recovery.

In 1994, as a consequence of a recommendation from the United Nations Earth Summit held in Rio de Janeiro in 1992, the International Convention to Combat Desertification in those Countries Experiencing Serious Drought and/or Desertification (UNCCD) was adopted. Australia became a signatory on 14 October 1994 and ratified the

Convention on 15 May 2000.[184] Stemming from wide adoption of the UNCCD, in early 1995, the United Nations General Assembly passed a resolution proclaiming 17 June as "World Day to Combat Desertification and Drought". The UNCCD remains the sole legally binding international agreement linking environment and development to sustainable land management. The UNCCD and Australia's signatory to same, signalled a shift in thinking in which desertification and drought, along with the interrelated issues of land, agriculture and rural development were viewed as interdependent and critical to achieving sustainable development.

In 1997 the Heads of Agreement on Commonwealth and state roles and responsibilities for the environment considered the prevention of land and water degradation a matter of national environmental significance. It recognised 'that it is vital to develop and continue land use programs and co-operative arrangements to achieve sustainable land use and to conserve and improve Australia's biota, and soil and water resources which are basic to the maintenance of essential ecological processes and the production of food, fibre and shelter'.

The 1997 Heads of Agreement preceded the *Environment Protection and Biodiversity Conservation Act 1999* (EPBC Act). However, for reasons not apparent to the authors, though it featured in the Heads of Agreement, soil management and its key aspect of landscape resilience and function was not addressed in the EPBC Act. This is an *extraordinary* omission. As the above history demonstrates, securing healthy soils had been an ongoing environmental concern of national significance and for which Australia now has a variety of obligations under a range of international agreements. Furthermore, soil fundamentally underpins landscape resilience and is the key component to land restoration and land sustainability; functions which underpin ecological sustainability.

In June 2014 the Federal Government, released the nation's first National Soil Research, Development and Extension Strategy (2014 Soil RD&E Strategy).[185] This strategy listed and elaborated on a number of key challenges and drivers for soil research and development and identified 'terrestrial life of the Earth is ultimately dependent upon soil for its survival'.

A national soil carbon map, co-ordinated by the CSIRO, and funded by the Federal Government was completed in 2014 to complement the then still-being-developed soil carbon-sequestration regulations (the Soil Carbon Methodology Determination).

More recently, on 18 July 2019 Prime Minister Scott Morrison, in his address to the *Daily Telegraph* Bush Summit, recalled to service our first National Soils Advocate, the late Major General Philip Jeffery.[186]

When speaking at the National Drought Summit in October 2018, Prime Minister Scott Morrison said that the voice of the former National Soils advocate had 'stuck in his head'. He quoted Major General Jeffrey's end-of-term advice to government in 2017: 'Australian farmers can improve their profitability and the resilience of their farming systems, even in the face of more frequent and extreme droughts, and climate change, if they are supported in nurturing their soils … Excellent soil management increases water storage, builds carbon, slows rates of soil acidification and minimises soil lost through wind and soil erosion.'

Almost three years since then, the Australian government has called for comment on the development of our 'first' national soil strategy. Undoubtedly publication of Australia's first national soil strategy is a commendable step, but if the current government's response and rate of action continues, 60 years since declaring the problem urgent, it may be too slow to prevent further land degradation, soil security and climate problems.

In August 2020 the government started stakeholder engagement through public surveys and a series of workshops on the proposed first national soils strategy. In support of that initiative, the Commonwealth Department of Agriculture, Water and the Environment released a discussion paper: *Developing a National Soil Strategy Discussion Paper*. In this discussion paper the Government identified that, while responsibility for soil management lies predominantly with state and territory governments, there is a need for greater national Federal Government coordination and leadership.

We couldn't agree more, the irony being however, that there is also a need for greater coordination and collaboration within government itself. By way of explanation, in the discussion paper, the government identifies and admits that it has obligations in relation to soil through a variety of commitments under a range of international agreements, including the United Nations Framework Convention on Climate Change, the Convention on Biological Diversity, the Convention to Combat Desertification and Drought, and the United Nations Sustainable Development Goals—we would also add the Revised World Soil Charter and the Paris Agreement. A key component from Paris was the international agreement that soil was a key reservoir for mitigating atmospheric CO_2 (the four per thousand initiative). This is really important, as the EPBC Act could be the legislative vehicle by which Australia implements its responsibilities concerning soil under those international agreements. It is therefore perplexing that, notwithstanding the government having identified its obligations under those international agreements, it has not acted to reform the EPBC Act, or to enact other responsive legislation to include protections for our soil.

While we commend the Government on releasing its first national policy on soil in May 2021, the National Soil Strategy does not go far enough. It does not comment on law reform or regulation to put their policies into action.

It is evident that in Australia land degradation and soil conservation has been widely recognised, and clearly demonstrated as a serious problem for a long time. In addition, climate change is undoubtedly commonly understood as the defining issue of our lifetime. However, the connection between the two, and the causal link to soil security that we have discussed, is not yet widely known.

History has demonstrated desertification decimates bread baskets and can lead to the collapse of civilisations. President Roosevelt cautioned us. It is therefore perplexing that once again through soil degradation we may well chronicle our demise. We must act now to rapidly achieve maximum soil security on all our managed lands. Our very being depends on it.

Chapter 9

Environmental Law in Australia

First, it is important to understand the framework from which environmental regulatory powers are derived under Australian law. Under our federal system of government, there is a dual regulatory approach; that is, responsibility for environmental regulation is carried concurrently by the Commonwealth government and state and territory governments. The Australian Constitution does not explicitly provide the Federal Parliament with power to make laws for the environment. The Federal Parliament's responsibilities are principally established as a result of the foreign affairs power under the Constitution and the Commonwealth government enacting Australia's responsibilities under international agreements on environmental protection. Recent history has demonstrated that the lack of an express constitutional power for the Federal Parliament to address environmental matters does not prohibit it exercising its power to meet complex international obligations.[xvi]

[xvi] *Murphyores Inc Pty Ltd v Commonwealth* (1976), 136 CLR 1; *Commonwealth v Tasmania* (1983) 158 CLR 1; *Richardson v Forestry Commission* (1988) 164 CLR 261 and *Queensland v Commonwealth* (1989) 167 CLR 232.

Political Action

State and Territory Action

The 1992 Council of Australian Governments' (COAG) Intergovernmental Agreement on the Environment (IGAE) established a framework for intergovernmental action on environmental issues. Under the IGAE, the Australian government and all state and territory governments agreed to integrate environmental considerations into their decision making and pursue the principles of ecologically sustainable development (ESD).

There *is* some evidence of greater state and territory government action on matters concerning soil. For brevity, we set out only a few examples:

Western Australia
In WA land mapping by the Department of Primary Industries and Regional Development began as early as the mid-1980s and involved identifying and then attributing land qualities, land characteristics and land capability to conventional land resource survey maps. (Although not uniform, mapping continues to occur to varying degrees in all of the states and territories.)[187] WA has arguably recently been the forerunner for implementing educational and mitigatory initiatives, including: the West Australia Soil and Land Conservation Council, the Western Australian Department of Agriculture Regenerative Agriculture Round Table, the Ministerial Soil Advisory Committee, and the Conservation and Land Management Executive Body. The state also has some very active community-led groups, notable examples being the Western Australia No-Till Farming Association (WANTFA) and Regen WA. Burning in WA also occurs under the auspices of the Savanna Burning Project.

Northern Territory
Through its Department of Environment, Parks and Water Security, the NT has commenced its 'Mapping the Future' initiative which involves

surveying and mapping land capability, water availability and biodiversity assets. In addition, the Aboriginal Carbon Industry Strategy establishes the government's approach to supporting the continuation and development of greenhouse gas emissions abatement and carbon sequestration activities on Aboriginal land. A well-known example being the West Arnhem Land Fire Abatement (WALFA) Project.

In relation to the WALFA Project in the Northern Territory and the Savanna Burning Project in Western Australia, as discussed in Chapter 4, burning as a land management tool is complex and more recently the merits of carbon abatement schemes are being called into question as too frequent or mistimed burning may be having a perverse effect on the ecology of those areas.[188]

Victoria
In the relatively new amendments passed in the *Environment Protection Amendment Act 2018* (VIC), Victoria has implemented a bold 'General Environmental Duty' (GED). The amendments reflect a policy shift requiring all Victorians to accept responsibility to prevent and minimise environmental harm as far as reasonably practicable. Also, the objective of the Environmental Protection Authority is to protect human health and the environment by reducing the harmful effects of pollution and waste. Implementation of the GED has an initial four-year transition period and so the effect of the provision in practice is yet to be tested. Arguably the current wording of the GED is too narrow to meaningfully mandate soil security or landscape management responsibilities, as the objective is to reduce 'risks of harm to human health and the environment *from pollution or waste.*'

New South Wales
An outcome of the NSW *Soil Conservation Act* which passed in 1938 is the Soil Conservation Service, an entity that still exists today within the Department of Primary Industries. In 2005 the NSW Natural Resources Commission set a key natural resource management target of 'an improvement in soil condition by 2015.' To help achieve this target, in 2008 a program to establish a baseline for soil condition and land

capability called Monitoring, Evaluation and Reporting (MER) was implemented. To measure soil health over time, the program adopted eight soil condition indicators: sheet, wind and gully erosion; soil acidity; organic carbon; structure and salinity; and acid sulfate soils oxidation status.[189]

Notwithstanding the above state and territory actions, at the state and territory level efforts to combat soil and landscape degradation have continued to weaken. Soil conservation services have been wound back, as have soil science advisory units and research within state agricultural departments. For example, the WA Council of Soil and Land Conservation does not have one soil scientist member and auditings of pastoral leasehold land has declined. In October 2017, the WA Auditor General released a report which found Western Australia's rangelands cover 87 per cent of the state, of which 39 per cent (87 million hectares) is under pastoral lease. Since 2009 the scale of lease monitoring of the pastoral estate declined from 15 per cent of all leases inspected each year to less than 3 per cent.[190]

Similarly, the Climate Council in its 2018 paper *Land Clearing & Climate Change: Risks & opportunities in the Sunshine State* illustrates the acceleration of deforestation and land clearing in recent decades in Queensland. Figure 9-1 clearly demonstrates the correlation between regulatory change in land clearing and poor environmental outcomes.[191] While the timescale is narrower, arguably in NSW the *Biodiversity Conservation Act 2016* is having a similar effect.[192]

This point is picked up by Kate Dooley from the Australian-German Climate and Energy College in her 2020 essay *Climate of stagnation: The EU seizes the green agenda*. Dooley says: 'relaxing state-based regulations has significantly increased Australia's land-clearing rate, with almost half a million hectares of vegetation cleared in a single year (2015–16) in Queensland alone, contributing 80 per cent of Australia's land-use change emissions. Effective climate mitigation in Australia would require significantly reducing land clearing and deforestation, which means that overhauling land-clearing regulation

Environmental Law in Australia   173

HISTORY OF VEGETATION CLEARING IN QUEENSLAND

Feb 1996 - Jun 1998
Liberal National Party

Jun 1998 - Mar 2012
Labor Party

Mar 2012 - Feb 2015
Liberal National Party

2000: *Vegetation Management Act 1999* comes into force

2006: Ban on broadside vegetation clearing

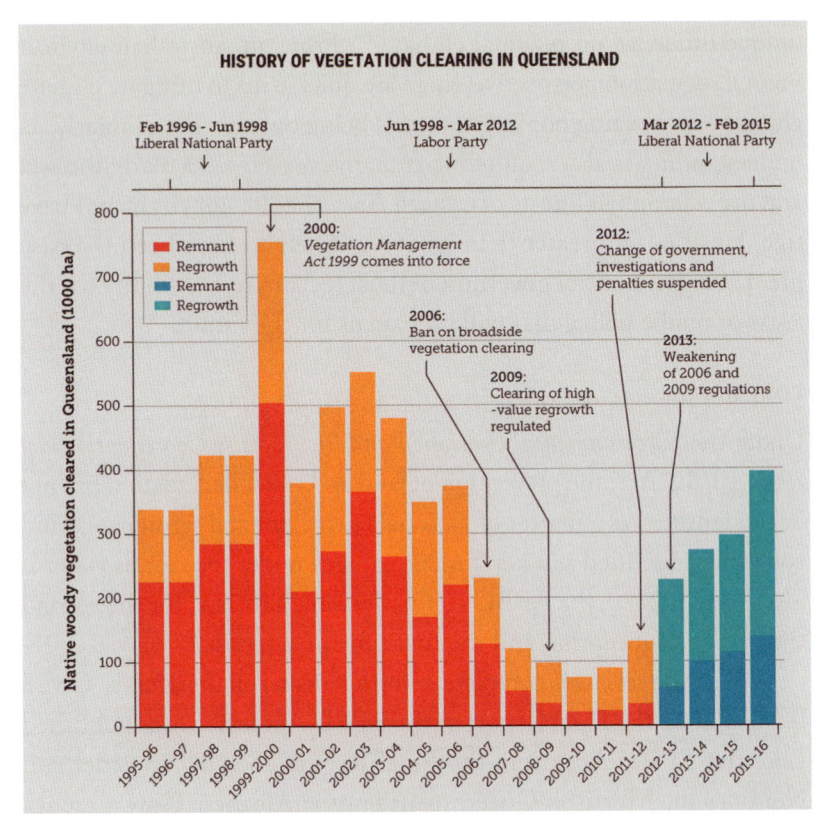

2009: Clearing of high-value regrowth regulated

2012: Change of government, investigations and penalties suspended

2013: Weakening of 2006 and 2009 regulations

Figure 9-1. History of vegetation clearing in Queensland. From 'Land Clearing and Climate Change: Risks and Opportunities in the Sunshine State,' Will Steffen and Annika Dean (Climate Council of Australia).[236]

and biodiversity protection laws is needed for greater protection of native vegetation.'[193]

Clearly environmental policy and in turn legislation can significantly impact environmental outcomes and it is apparent that national coordination and leadership are urgently required. In this regard, it would be remiss of us not to briefly mention one of Australia's great environmental regulatory shames, insufficient protection of virgin or old-growth areas, including the Tarkine Forest (particularly given Tasmania's distinct soil profile compared to the mainland). As explained by Peter Wohllenben in his compelling work *The Hidden Life of Trees*, the soil and small-water-cycles in primary forests have a strong and unique influence on regional climate.[xvii] From an Australian environmental regulation perspective, there are quick wins to mitigate climate change—protecting our virgin forests being but one. But similarly, an understanding is also required that many forests, particularly the wet and dry sclerophyll forests of eastern Australia, are not virgin and have tree densities far greater than what was likely to have been the case pre-1700. The Federal government must reclaim responsibility for the areas of public policy that will prepare us for the future.

EPBC Act review—a once-in-a-decade opportunity

Under the *Environmental Protection and Biodiversity Conservation Act 1999* (EPBC Act) the prevention of land and water degradation has not been identified as a matter of national environmental significance and soil is not identified as a key 'functional' area under the Act, as water is. However, in 2020, the EPBC Act underwent a review; for the second time since its inception and the first time in a decade.[194]

While the review is complete, reform remains on the agenda. On 28 January 2021 the Final Report of the EPBC Act review was published. Like the EPBC Act itself, the Final Report does *not* consider soil. Nor does the Morrison Government's or the Albanese Government's substantive response (respectively '*A pathway for reforming national environmental law*' published June 2021 and '*Nature Positive Plan: better for the environment, better for business*' published December 2022).

Given the land degradation and resultant climatic problems we have identified above, whether the EPBC Act is the best vehicle to manage, monitor and regulate soil in the national interest or not is an issue that should have been discussed in the 2020 review of the EPBC Act.

Under the EPBC Act the Commonwealth is responsible for protecting and conserving the environment in the national interest.

[xvii] Wohllenben's work focuses primarily on primeval forests in Germany and more broadly Europe. As with soils influence on climate, more research is required to understand the interconnectedness of regional ecosystems in Australia.

This expressly includes a number of matters under the Act referred to as 'Matters of National Environmental Significance' or MNES. MNES include World and National Heritage sites, internationally important wetlands, migratory species, threatened species and ecological communities, as well as the environment of Commonwealth areas and actions by the Commonwealth (including Commonwealth responsibilities to the UN Sustainable Development Goals). Many of these MNES require soil to deliver all functions expected to achieve landscape resilience, and thereby achieve the Act's objective to provide for the protection and conservation of the environment through ecological sustainable development (ESD).

With an estimated value of $3,860 billion, Australia's greatest natural asset is its soil, accounting for 80 percent of all of Australia's natural assets.[195] Some 45 percent of the nation's soil is used for agricultural production, with 84 percent of this used for grazing, 8 percent for cropping and the remaining for forestry and other practices,[196] resulting in an annual output of $37 billion.[197] This is a 2.7 percent share of all national industry, employing over 320 000 people, without accounting for indirect contributions to other industries such as tourism, health and wellbeing and the cost of climate-related disasters.

It is obvious that securing Australia's soils is a matter of national environmental significance and should be captured as such under the EPBC Act. Currently soil security is only regulated under the EPBC Act in so far as it is broadly captured by a MNES; including through the Environmental Impact Assessment Process described in Chapter 4 of the EPBC Act. Given the environmental impact assessment process established by the Act, this is particularly important at present, as it is the principal point of interaction between the EPBC Act and the agriculture sector.[198]

As detailed in the recent 2018 Craik Report, agriculture accounts for 58 percent of Australia's land use,[199] of which 90 percent occurs on leasehold land. Notwithstanding the size of the industry and the affect agriculture has on the environment and climate change, agricultural referrals through the environment impact assessment process in the EPBC Act have accounted for only 2.7 percent or 156 of the 6002 referrals since the inception of the EPBC Act in 2000.[200] This is because the process relies on self-referral.[201]

Self-referral, and the issue of duplication with state and territory environmental regulatory frameworks for development assessment and approval, is to an extent demonstrated in the case of *The Environment Centre Northern Territory v the Northern Territory Environment Protection Authority and Anor*.[202] That case concerned the application to clear vegetation from 237.95 km^2 of land at Maryfield Station, located two hours south east of Katherine. In this case the decision was administrative in nature and did not address the grounds of challenge in relation to climate change. Notwithstanding the outcome, the case was important in sparking debate. Recent legislative changes to the Territory's environmental regulation means the new Northern Territory *Environmental Protection Act 2019* now mandates that 'climate change' be considered as part of the Northern Territory's environmental impact assessment process (s42(b)(v)). The 'impacts of a changing climate' should always capture land clearing, soil security and landscape management. The need for Federal legislation is critical to establishing clear, consistent and equitable rules and regulation for industries across Australia.

Although the express inclusion of soil security in the EPBC Act, when considering the MNES framework, is not immediately obvious, it is easily integrated when considering the objectives of the Act. The key objective of the EPBC Act, environmental protection and conservation, cannot be achieved without nurturing and securing Australia's soils. Furthermore, the inclusion of soil security is starkly necessary if Graeme Samuel's long-term recommendation for a comprehensive redrafting of the EPBC Act, or a new set of related Acts, is adopted.

This discussion can probably best be summarised by thinking about the extent to which water is regulated, that is drinking water, water courses, water flow, water pollution. Water is protected under numerous pieces of state and Commonwealth legislation, and the *Commonwealth Water Act 2007* section 88 mandates triennial review. And yet soil, which similarly underpins our very existence, for which the health of water and our planet is dynamically intertwined and indivisibly connected, is barely considered, let alone protected.

While not beyond salvage, to date the government's reform efforts in response to the Final Report have failed to demonstrate real commitment to protect and restore our environment. On or about 11 February 2021, the Government's proposed Interim National Environmental Standards were leaked.[203] Those standards were subsequently introduced into Federal Parliament as part of the *Environment Protection and Biodiversity Conservation Amendment (Standards and Assurance) Bill 2021* (the 2021 Bill).[xviii] The 2021 Bill provides a framework for national environmental standards to underpin bilateral agreements between the Commonwealth and states and territories, and the establishment of an Environment Assurance Commissioner to oversee the devolution of environmental decision-making powers to the states and territories. The Bill claims to adopt the central recommendation of the Final Report, however, there is a significant disjunct between Graeme Samuel's proposed standards and what the government is proposing in its Bill. The proposed standards in the Bill reflect the current requirements of the EPBC Act, and devolution of responsibility was not a recommendation of the Final Report.

Four developed standards are suggested by Graeme Samuel in Appendix B to the Final Report. The intent of Graeme Samuel's proposal is laudable: standards 'to define clear outcomes for matters of national environmental significance (MNES), and for important processes, to set the legal benchmark for protecting the environment and provide the ability to measure the outcomes of decisions'. Their practical implementation to all 'actions, decisions, plans, policies and other pressures' — application at all levels of the environmental regulatory process and

---

[xviii] The Standards and Assurance Bill was referred by the Senate to the Environment and Communications Legislation Committee on 25 February 2021. Submissions to the Committee on the Standards and Assurance Bill closed on 25 March 2021. The Committee is due to conclude its inquiry and report on the Standards and Assurance Bill by 1 June 2021. At the time of publication the Bill remained before the House of Representatives.

at both an ecosystem and project scale — requires careful consideration and clear articulation. It is imperative as a community we hold the government to implementing the ambitious national environmental standards proposed in the Final Report.

The panel also suggest the national environmental standards mandate actions be taken to prevent detrimental cumulative impacts or exacerbation of key threatening processes.[204] Cumulative impacts here being the collective impacts from all actions, decisions, plans, policies and other pressures, measured against a stipulated baseline.

Assessing cumulative impacts aligns with our commentary and vision for Landscape Regeneration Plans as presented in Chapter 11. As discussed by the Full Federal Court in *Tarkine National Coalition v Minister for the Environment*, the EPBC Act in its present form only requires consideration of cumulative impacts that have some relationship with the project being assessed: direct or indirect (substantially causative) consequences.[205] However, this approach while easier to regulate, fails to recognise our integrated landscapes. As argued above and much like with urban development, active management of the environment should be strategic and extend consideration to all reasonably foreseeable cumulative impacts. Then, in accordance with the principles of ESD, an informed decision can be made as to whether on balance those environmental risks and impacts are acceptable.

During the 2020 Black Summer bushfires Prime Minister Morrison effectively tested the limits of constitutionally-defined roles and responsibilities between the Commonwealth and the states and territories by using his initiative to align with what he believed was 'clear community expectation' by providing troop support ahead of a formal request from state governments.

Black Summer was quickly followed by a second national emergency, the COVID-19 pandemic. Prime Minister Morrison again exercised novel initiative by deviating from the standing dogma on debt and deficits to provide record amounts of financial assistance to the multitudes.

Arguably the insidious effects of Australia's environmental decline, including soil health, land management and climate change, could be seen as an equally pressing emergency requiring immediate expenditure of significant national funds to protect the future economy. Considering the recent cumulative effects of drought, flood and fire, and the consequent loss of biodiversity and viable arable land, such an investment is comparably tiny.

Soil security and climate change in Australia, most of which is due to landscape practices, is having and will continue to have significant economic consequences — not to mention environmental, health and social ones — and yet little of substance gets done. It is unacceptable that under the government's current proposed timeline for EPBC Act reforms that national environmental standards will still be being developed into 2024.[206] An initial investment of $12.2 million is not enough, and worse still is that soil is not identified as a critical priority to draw any of that immediate funding. The political system will not restore public confidence without a more responsive government. And the economy won't stabilise and be sustainable, without more active federal government involvement in securing our environment.

If the Prime Minister is truly committed to 'climate action now',[207] then greater consideration must be given to restoring and protecting Australia's soils through increased funding, and a more robust legislative and policy framework.

One silver lining of COVID-19 is the action of putting public health ahead of our economy. We should keep that vision as we look to secure our soils; a function of life that contributes to the clean water we drink, the food that we eat and the air we breathe.

Chapter 10

Economic Imperative

Climate Change as Risk

C limate change is a foreseeable and material financial risk.
The economy, the landscape, the climate and our wellbeing are intertwined and interdependent on healthy soil. Government for landscape management is increasingly important and urgent.

The Intergovernmental Panel on Climate Change Report estimates that:

- Each USD invested into land restoration can have social returns of about 3 to 6 USD over a 30-year period
- Most Sustainable Land Management practices can become financially profitable within three to 10 years.[208]

Bennet *et al* state: 'Australia is the fifth largest country by area, covering some five per cent of the world's land area. The capital value of the world's soil stock is equal to $325 trillion, suggesting that Australia's contribution is $16 trillion. The annual value of ecosystem services contributed by soil is estimated at $11.4 trillion, suggesting that soil provides $570 billion to Australia's ecosystem services annually.'[209]

The economic ramifications of the capital value of soil to Australia are important and diverse: including less weather and climate variation, more viably profitable farms, tourism, export markets and healthier citizens—less climate-impacted stress-related illnesses such as heat stroke and respiratory issues and/or death. Greater climate stability equates to improved planning, funding and financing.

Pioneering developments in this space by greening the desert and sustainable management of arid lands, will provide unprecedented advantage for Australia's economic position globally. Israel has demonstrated this potential with the Yatir Forest as an example of a manufactured carbon sink. From modest beginnings in 1964, conifers and broadleaf trees were planted over 30 km^2 of semi-arid land with annual rainfall of 300 to 360 mm. It halted desertification around Beersheba, trapped CO_2 and reduced evaporation.

The National Soil Strategy Discussion Paper estimated that in 2011 the investment and activities carried out by all governments in Australia into soil research was worth only $124 million per annum; about 8 per cent of the total investment in primary industry. That same paper also noted that the estimated economic cost of the dust storm that swept over Australia's east coast in 2009 to NSW alone was more than double that, $299 million. This dust storm serves as an example of the cost of a single environmental disaster and also demonstrates that current investment in mitigation or prevention is not realistic.

The 2019–20 Black Summer bushfires serve as another example. These fires were unprecedented in their extent and intensity. Over the course of approximately six weeks at least 8.4 million hectares across the country was burnt, or approximately 1.1 per cent of Australia's land area, costing about $100 billion: not to mention lost lives, and the impact on health, homes, livelihoods and wildlife. By way of comparison, the annual production revenue from the MIA is about $5 billion.[210]

Graeme Samuel in the Final Report, quoting Ward & Lassen, says the predicted shortfall in restoration funding in Australia is $10 billion annually.[211] As reported by the IPCC above, investing in restoration can have significant socioeconomic returns—presenting a huge economic opportunity for Australia. While Professor Samuel is correct in saying it is unrealistic to expect government, the tax payer, to fund this level of investment, the government must lead the way.

In this regard, the 7 October 2020 Federal Budget offer to fund research and industry, though welcome, was insufficient and not directed to landscape management and repair. However, we saw some improvements in the 11 May 2021 Federal Budget. Extensive lobbying from three strongly aligned groups, Soil Science Australia, the University of Sydney and the Soil Carbon Industry Group, has resulted in soil management getting a renewed focus in the budget to support the National Soil Strategy. Notably the following funding indicates consideration of landscape solutions:

- $102 million over two years from 2021–22 to incentivise farmers to increase soil testing, and enhance the National Soil Resources Information System by feeding in data
- $20.9 million over four years from 2021–22 to implement a National Soils Science Challenge to advance understanding of Australia's soils
- $18 million over two years from 2021–22 for Soils Extension Services to assist farmers understand the benefits of soil testing and help interpret and act on soil test results. The cost of this component will be met from within the existing resources of the Department of Agriculture, Water and the Environment
- $5.9 million over four years from 2021–22 (and $1.5 million ongoing) to implement and coordinate programs in support of the National Soils Strategy
- $1.1 million over two years from 2021–22 to develop and roll out an accreditation standard to enhance soil education and expertise

Additionally: $565.8 million was allocated for international technology partnerships/initiatives and co-funding research and demonstration projects. Of which, $263.7 million will support the development of carbon capture, use and storage projects. $316.7 million is earmarked to help industry and businesses reduce their emissions through voluntary action and adopting low emissions technology.

In relation to biodiversity:

- $22.3 million to deliver a pilot biodiversity stewardship program
- $5.4 million to implement an Australian farm biodiversity certification scheme
- $4.4 million to establish a Biodiversity Trading Platform

Though it is a great start and an improvement, as identified above, this level of funding is not enough to make any meaningful impact in the immediate to short term. The $10 billion annual predicted shortfall in restoration funding in Australia detailed in the EPBC Review Final Report likely doesn't even account for soil.[212]

It is illuminating to compare this funding with funding allocated to climate disaster response and climate adaptation. By way of example, the government allocated $600 million in a new program of disaster preparation and mitigation, managed by the new National Recovery and Resilience Agency. That is $600 million compared to the $147.9 million allocated to support the National Soil Strategy; the latter being a strategy that likely will have far greater impact. Climate mitigation and adaptation are both important, but funding should arguably be balanced in favour of mitigation. More specifically, mitigating climate change through securing our soils.

The National Soil Strategy does not go far enough towards maximising soil security, mitigating climate change and promoting landscape sustainability. It does not provide enough incentive for farmers to change, to risk sliding into the red financially. Without significant incentives that would be repaid from later increased profit and rewards from increased landscape values and externalities to farm production, which are not currently monetised, such as ecosystem management and water production, significant uptake by farmers of methods such as regenerative agriculture will not occur.

It is pertinent to note here that the Australian government's $34 million over four years (2018–19 to June 2023) Agriculture Stewardship Package, inclusive of the Australian Farm Biodiversity Certification

Scheme, an evolution of the Biodiversity Fund announced in 2012, is a step in the right direction. Although still in its infancy, the scheme is poorly defined.[213] Notwithstanding, we commend the government for recognising that a certification system is required, a certificate recognised by the Commonwealth, banks and financial institutions, one in which the certification could be used to demonstrate 'clean and green' provenance and thereby build a social licence to operate.[214]

On the other hand, we note that State and Federal governments failed to act on a proposed $4 billion over four years post-pandemic stimulus package suggested by a coalition of more than 80 land-care, environmental, farming and conservation groups. The proposed package was for job creation through high quality conservation and land management programs directed to rehabilitating landscapes and infrastructure damaged by recent drought and bushfires.[215] The economic feasibility of such a program was confirmed in Ernst & Young's 25 June 2020 report for the Conservation Council of South Australia titled *Delivering economic stimulus through the conservation and land management sector*.[216] While we disagree with the proposed focus and execution of the program as set out, the report does illustrate the varied and strong economic benefits the conservation and land management sector can provide to the Australian economy.

The government has, however, supported the industry led Ag2030 initiative, Australian Agriculture's Plan for a $100 billion industry by 2030.[217] And while the Australian government's report on delivering Ag2030 included delivery of the National Soil Strategy by June 2021 and soils work supported through the National Soils Advocate, both the Commonwealth and National Farmers Federation reports on delivering Ag2030 are somewhat concerning for their lack of content on soil conservation, and landscape repair and management.

The National Farmers Federation report notes agricultural businesses manage 51 per cent of Australia's landmass. Although they claim that 94 per cent already actively undertake some form of natural resource management,[218] land used for farming in Australia has declined from 500 million hectares, 65 per cent of the country's landmass in 1973, to 406 million hectares, 53 per cent of the total landmass in 2015.[219] Industry's aim is to 'maintain Australia's total farmed area at 2018 levels', but the actionable items identified to achieve this objective are limited. Future growth of the sector cannot be sustained by incremental productivity improvements alone without structural change.

In the last decade, but particularly in the last two years, there has been an industry-wide understanding that the way we practise most land management in Australia through agricultural management is broken.[220] The cost of externalities of agricultural production and national park management now exceeds all other measures of income, particularly when externalities, including climate change, are considered.

Leaving aside the problem of national park management, the key question in the agricultural sector is how do you avoid going broke when transitioning from conventional agriculture to regenerative agriculture practice? How do you move from soil carbon mining to soil carbon sequestration and stay in the black?

Chapter 11

Acid Sulfate Soils

A successful example of control of off-farm impacts

The history of acid sulfate soils in Australia provides a template for approaching other landscape issues that have a range of causes spread over a wide area with multiple diffuse impacts.

Acid sulfate soils are naturally occurring soils formed under waterlogged conditions. Around 100 000 km² of Australia's coastal land is impacted,[221] and over 200 wetlands in the Murray Darling River Basin. Acid sulfate soils are safe and harmless until they are disturbed and come into contact with oxygen in the air. Then a process occurs resulting in sulfuric acid, which is toxic.

Between 1989 and 1992 there were numerous fish kills in the waterways of the north coast of NSW, resulting in the decimation of stocks for commercial fishers and oyster farmers. Testing revealed the cause was *not* illegal dumping of pollution, but a natural process that was exacerbated by the extension of farm drains using mechanical excavation equipment in the 1950s and 1960s. Rather than remove flood-water, for which farm drains were installed, over-digging to a greater depth meant these drains also removed groundwater and lowered the water table, exposing natural sulfide minerals, which in the presence of oxygen produced sulfuric acid. Also, these changes induced de-oxygenation of waterways. This outcome is known as Acid Sulfate Soils, or ASS. Soil not yet dewatered is known as Potential Acid Sulfate Soil, or PASS.

What began as a small local conference on soil at Tweed Heads NSW in 1992 quickly morphed into the first National Acid Sulfate Soil Conference. Farmers, commercial fishers, scientists, state and local planners and developers attended, but it soon became apparent that the scientists had no idea how to define the problem; even basic things like what to measure and what measurement to use were not known. The safe threshold for levels of sulfides in the environment, or in exposed soil, had not previously been contemplated. The fishers blamed the farmers, and everyone blamed the scientists and government planners. The anger in the room was palpable.

Figure 11-1. Lacustrine ASS sediments showing a highly ferruginous oxidised zone underlain by the black sulfuric muds (sour clay). Photo: Robert Fitzpatrick.

Although the main drains were put in by the government and the farm drains under government advice, the drains alone were not the cause, but the combined management of the land *and* the drains.

Figure 11-2. Acidic drainage of groundwater from acid sulfate soil of the farm being drained to the estuary, an example of adverse externalities of farm production on this flood plain. The pH of the water is around 4.5. The orange precipitate of iron minerals is from discharge of iron-rich groundwater. Both the low pH and iron precipitate have an adverse effect on the downstream ecosystem. Photo: Robert Fitzpatrick.

Put simply, modern digging equipment meant it was easy to excavate the drain to greater depth. Previously, hand-dug drains stopped when diggers struck the sticky sulfidic muds known as 'sour clays' because of difficult digging conditions. The results were wide, shallow drains. But modern mechanical excavators had no trouble digging into sour clays, resulting in narrow deep drains. Mechanical diggers became widely used to dig drains on most farms on the flood plain for over three decades. Exposing sulfidic mud banks and draining shallow groundwater both brought the drained soil into contact with oxygen, producing sulfuric acid. It took some decades for full oxidation to occur and acid drainage was worse after floods, particularly the first flood after a dry spell, making every farm a source of sulfuric acid contamination.

The sulfuric acid was caused by diffuse source pollution. As such, it was both a community and government problem, which had to be identified, delineated and solutions put in place at regional scale through the planning system. Work began in the mid-1990s when the NSW government produced risk maps which were followed by planning guidelines. The risk maps indicated the likelihood of occurrence of PASS and the nature of investigation required. The accompanying guidelines specified the standard conditions for activities on land, including agriculture, for assessment, management and farming on acid sulfate soils. Separate guidelines for planning authorities defined standard conditions for permitted activities. These risk maps and planning guidelines placed restrictions on what could be done on the land according to zoning.

This was followed by identification of priority areas—those with the greatest production of acid export, known as 'Hot Spots'—for which government assistance was prioritised. These solutions were replicated in each state. During the 2009 drought acid sulfate soils again emerged as a significant issue, particularly the new category of inland acid sulfate soils, and further work was done, culminating with the release of the National Guidelines in 2015.

Since 1992 there have been many conferences on understanding the science of acid sulfate soils and the impact on the ecology, as well as conferences dedicated to developing regulations for use of land on acid sulfate soils to mitigate against further polluting events, whether it be urban developments, motorway tunnels, large sugar-cane plantations or cattle farms. Though the problem remains, it is now managed as part of the planning, development and land title process in every state. As a result, fish kills in coastal rivers from ASS have drastically diminished. Some land which was too damaged by acidification was purchased by governments and returned to managed wetlands. Farm practices across all coastal catchments and wetland management along inland rivers has been altered to prevent offsite migration of acid. Australia has exported these solutions to our Asian neighbours.

ASS to PASS is the first case of successful management and restoration of landscape damage occurring outside farms but caused by regional farm practices. Diffuse source impacts require multi-disciplinary systems analysis involving open dialogue between all stakeholders. Twenty-five years passed between recognising the problem and being certain the regulatory system and community could manage the impacted landscape for production and other land-uses without off-site impacts. During that time methods, criteria, guidelines, specialist training, education (including education of the community), development of a new profession, and developing a national management system with new legislation, regulation and compliance, have all successfully been implemented and continue to operate.

Given that this was the first time such a program had been undertaken, considerable investment from the government was required, as well as goodwill and time by all in the affected communities.

Palpable anger has now mellowed to normal business relations and landscape operations. Research identification and regulation were aligned early to inform management and correction. As it was a divisive issue for two decades in communities, broad nationwide stakeholder engagement was continually and consistently prioritised. The response to acid sulfate soils in Australia provides a template for approaching new landscape issues with multiple diffuse sources generating adverse offsite impacts, a lesson for successful landscape management.

Chapter 12

A Solution

We've got a plan

We've established how land use and land management have a huge impact on heat (temperature) and the small water cycle (precipitation). And, we've explained how changes to land use, principally from agriculture—by mining organic matter from our soils—have at least as significant an effect on climate change as carbon emissions. So what can *we* do?

There is hope—in this chapter we present a range of solutions:

- **A blue-print for getting started on solutions**—our historical national response to acid sulfate soils (ASS) (discussed in Chapter 11) demonstrates all tiers of government can work together to deliver a new approach to land management in Australia
- **Strategic Rural, Regional and Remote (RRR) planning**—learn from the ASS framework to develop a National Landscape Regeneration Plan, complemented by a national agriculture strategy and food security plan
- **Professional development**—develop and fund new skilled and accredited workforces—Landscape Science, Landscape Engineering and Regional Planning

- **Turn the dirt we've cultivated back into soil**—Defend and monopolise our carbon treasury by making our farms profitable, diverse and sustainable. Boost soil organic matter through reduced bare ground, holding water at source, elimination of monoculture and increased bush corridors—and in turn, cool the continent by restoring the small water cycle
- **Incentivise and support our farmers**—subsidies, including concessional loans, for environmental (Natural Capital) and community outcomes, such as landscape management training to farmers and RRR councils, and land-use adjustments
- **Connect consumers to country**—champion the Australian Government to provide subsidies for funding of chain of custody certification and the equivalent of a Defence Force gap year for on land experience
- **Law reform**—review land clearing laws and incorporate soil into reform of the *Environmental Protection and Biodiversity Conservation Act 1999*, or any consequent new Act. Additionally, expand the *Agriculture Biodiversity Stewardship Market Bill 2022*, replacing biodiversity with Natural Capital and include sections on landscape water management
- **Research and Modelling**—account for sensible to latent heat ratios and precipitation in future climate modelling and boost research into the phosphate problem by finding alternatives to salts of acids. Design and incorporate Natural Capital measurement and trading schemes
- **What you can do**—every little bit helps; advocate for each of the above points, particularly become a champion for covering bare ground and be a proactive consumer
- **Secure our future**—we will have plans that fail, so plan, enact, measure, replan, and remain hopeful

These solutions emphasise that we must address both the heat source (sensible heat) and the blanket (greenhouse gases). As climatic events continue to escalate, in both frequency and intensity, our land remains our greatest asset. We must engage with the science and collectively take active steps to nurture, protect, and enhance our land.

Acid sulfate soils: a blue-print for getting started on solutions

Soil security must be managed, monitored and regulated in the national interest. In simple terms land must have greater than 90 per cent vegetative cover more than 90 per cent of the time, and carbon sequestered as organic matter in soils. The landscape needs air turbulence, which requires wide, multi-storied eco-corridors. Together, these simple measures will return the small water cycle.

To achieve this, all tiers of government must work together to deliver a new approach to rural land management in Australia—the counterpart and complement to urban planning—and it must start at the federal level.

Fortunately, in response to ASS we previously developed a national strategy for a land use crisis, that also had many contributors to regional impact. Australia's nationwide response to ASS is a blue-print for getting started on developing and implementing a National Landscape Regeneration Plan.

When ASS first became known as a problem, Geographical Information Systems or GIS were embryonic. There is now a national framework and strategy for ASS, which is regulated using detailed local strategies or risk maps. As such the proposed framework is not novel, but the use of modern IT tools to facilitate the proposed national landscape regeneration framework is.

The outcome will be a national strategy with the granularity of local application. Central to its success is the premise that increasing farmer Financial Capital is tied to increasing regional Natural Capital, and thereby regional, state and national soil, landscape and climate restoration.

As we learned from responding to ASS, correcting those areas that produce the greatest adverse externalities (i.e. drought, more rapid floods, dust storms, heat waves) should be funded regardless of where blame lies. Doing so restores the regional environment and climate faster and for the benefit of the community at large, as well as the private landholder. Waiting until the landholder can afford correction measures may result in countless further years of preventable damage. As such, we suggest work commence at the earliest opportunity to implement the framework set out below.

The following process to facilitate long-term training support programs has been adopted from the experience gained from ASS prevention:

- develop ranked nationwide landscape recovery mapping inclusive of landscape/ecology capability mapping, that sets out planning zones and priority areas, and that considers all the linkages in a landscape
- running parallel to the mapping program, preliminary systems analysis of what works in what regions
- practice and planning guidelines to support regulations

Given that technology has advanced, and the current Draft National Soil Action Plan, we expect the above points, principally the mapping and setup of research and training programs, could be achieved in eighteen months. To achieve this timeframe requires a considered structure and proper resourcing.

Though they have a role to play, research or research project management organisations like the CSIRO, Grains Research and Development Corporation and Meat and Livestock Australia should not lead any research efforts. Organisational bias or competitiveness could sabotage cooperative efforts and a fast response. These organisations might lead long-term research efforts, but they do not have the broader skills required to efficiently and effectively deliver a structure that can facilitate landscape management change.

To succeed in producing a National Landscape Regeneration Plan, with supporting guidelines, draft permit conditions and priority ratings, requires a special-purpose vehicle — private-public-partnership or statutory organisation—to deliver this outcome. We suggest that, whatever form it takes, it will require three teams:

- mapping
- land unit processes
- Practice guidelines

Project managers will be required in each team with supporting administration and appropriate professional contractors or staff or individuals with experience in:

- GIS
- fauna
- avian fauna
- feral management
- ecologists
- forestry
- national parks management
- fire management
- soil science
- regolith geologists
- agronomic systems
- hydrologists
- hydrogeologists
- meteorologists and climate modelling

The three projects be managed by a technical team coordinated by a lead project manager and CEO. The CEO will report to a national board of 10–12 members monthly. The board be comprised of a representative from the Australian Government and each state and territory government. And the chairman come from business and have experience in science, farming and landscape knowledge with an understanding of product development and regulatory processes.

Further, we suggest that four advisory committees should be established to provide:

- financial supervision
- farming industry advice and community liaison
- scientific collaboration and advice

- Indigenous and Torres Strait Islander advice and community liaison

Ideally, each advisory committee would meet quarterly and each convenor would be a member of the national board. Each advisory committee would have the ability, consistent with best practice, to establish industry advisory groups comprised of private-and public-sector members. Additionally, we suggest the financial supervision advisory committee be convened by representatives from theAustralian Government and the farming industry, and advice for committee members should be sourced from innovative farmers from different industries, not just association representatives. We believe that all of the above will best assist trained professionals and lead farmers in guiding the community through the change period.

These technical teams and committees would then be able to fulfill the final role of informing content for draft bills and regulations. Their input will be invaluable to ensure regional landscape management plans and delivery are incorporated into national and state and territory environment and planning frameworks.

To accelerate delivery and enhance stakeholder and community engagement a single point of coordination and information should be established.

We anticipate that sometime between five and ten years from commencement, the special purpose vehicle will become redundant as administration of the respective roles will become the responsibility of the three tiers of government in accordance with enacted legislation.

The process of gearing up the teaching institutions and preparing agricultural landscape officers and farmers for a new farming process will take time. However, there are some measures that can be undertaken to help farmers in the short term that will assist in reversing climate change immediately. These short-term recommendations are provided with the following caveats:

- the number of experienced professional advisors is limited;
- giving national guidance across different latitudes, rainfall zones,

soil type and aspect would be too broad to have any more meaning than what has previously been done.

Evidently, there is much to consider in the development of a National Landscape Regeneration Plan. To best inform the process, we recommend a desktop study be undertaken of environmental and planning regulation and legislation internationally. If Australia is to develop best practice solutions to soil security, we need to understand what has been successful in other parts of the world.

National Landscape Regeneration Plan

The objective of landscape recovery is determined by identifying and ranking priority landscapes through a mapping program. To successfully reverse climate change and restore ecosystems, a landcare framework for the National Landscape Regeneration Plan must be both regional and national. We suggest government sponsored, community agreed, Natural Capital development strategies based on regional landscape planning maps and region-specific regenerative farming management practices. These could commence immediately, and concurrently with the proposed landscape mapping exercise discussed below. The principal objectives would be to delineate ecosystem corridors, wind turbulence creation zones, land capability zones, groundwater recharge and soil security protection zones. The data obtained through the mapping exercise would subsequently be used to fine-tune capital development strategies and regional priorities.

In 2019, in a paper titled Soil Security for Australia, some of Australia's eminent soil scientists proposed the development of an Australian Soil Security framework (National Soils Framework). Bennett et al describe the National Soils Framework as holistic, multi-dimensional and multidisciplinary: an integrated framework identifying the economic value of our soils for multiple uses and provides a systematic way of guiding land-use and management decisions well beyond our current compartmentalized systems'.

Bennett *et al* describe the National Soils Framework as holistic, multi-dimensional and multidisciplinary: an integrated framework identifying the economic value of our soils for multiple uses and provides a systematic way of guiding land-use and management decisions well beyond our current compartmentalized systems'.[222] Deploying a market-based approach, relying particularly on incentives, will drive adoption of good land management practice.

The proposed National Soils Framework has two main interconnected components:

- a National Soil Capability Statement and a
- changed land management culture based on shared responsibility

Although we commend their work, these strategies alone and funding of them, are insufficient. We have expanded their concepts and include them in our proposed National Landscape Regeneration Plan.

Analogously, the IPCC Report discusses what it has termed 'Sustainable Land Management' or 'SLM': 'the stewardship and use of land resources, including soils, water, animals and plants, to meet changing human needs while simultaneously assuring the long-term productive potential of these resources and the maintenance of their environmental functions, and includes ecological, technological and governance aspects. The choice of SLM strategy is a function of regional context and land-use types, with high agreement on (a combination of) choices such as agroecology (including agroforestry), conservation agriculture and forestry practices, crop and forest species diversity, appropriate crop and forest rotations, organic farming, integrated pest management, the preservation and protection of pollination services, rainwater harvesting, range and pasture management, and precision agriculture systems.'[223]

We agree and recommend that this approach be adopted, as the success of any strategy turns on its ability to be both locally and regionally, contextually responsive.

Understanding the condition of the soil against its potential is critical to making land-use decisions in a systematic fashion and maximizing production capacity, while conserving the environment. Bennett *et al* 2019, propose that a National Soil Capability Statement be prepared through the collection of agreed mandatory data, such as soil carbon, pH, microbial diversity, bulk density and salinity. In some ways, this is similar to the Monitoring, Evaluation and Reporting (MER) program in NSW, but both schemes focus on unintegrated symptoms of poor soil function, which fails to distinguish and address that it is agriculture that has degraded the land.

It is critical to include an emphasis on a systems approach in the Bennett *et al* National Soils Framework. That is, evaluation of the landscape system, and the interaction of system components, not just soil mapping. Evaluating the landscape systems is important to understanding why innovative farm businesses of any practice are successful. For the mapping to be effective, it must be targeted to landscape management and identifying priority areas. As well as mapping soil functionality and vulnerability, a mapping program should include land capability (vegetation type including diversity, volume and coverage), best placed location of eco-corridors for optimising bird habitat, and location of height differences for systems analysis of air turbulence, wind protection and linkage of bush reserves etc. As such, we suggest it is not so much a National Soil Capability Statement as a National Landscape Regeneration Plan that is required, and one developed in conjunction with a national agriculture strategy and food security plan—as the policy objectives of each are interdependent.

Implicit in any mapping exercise, and underpinning any effective solution, are comprehensive geographical information systems, or GIS. Consideration should be given to whether Digital Earth Australia, a platform developed by Geoscience Australia from Federal funding may be suitable. In the 2018–19 budget the government committed $224.9 million over four years for improved Global Positioning Systems. Digital Earth Australia is a platform that uses spatial data and images recorded by satellites to detect physical changes across Australia in unprecedented detail. Although the data already includes crop health and ground cover, thought should be given as to whether some of the other metrics suggested above can be incorporated into the existing software. Furthermore understanding what converts data to knowledge should underpin any data management scheme. Collating a central repository of soil health data (as currently being undertaken) without being tagged to farm practise is not overly useful for extrapolating systems management to other areas.

Under the National Landscape Regeneration Plan, land use would be informed by economic, environmental and social standards driven by the second mechanism of the Bennett *et al* National Soil Framework: decommoditisation and provenance. Each region could be measured against a suite of regional sustainability factors that become the measure of their provenance.

In this regard, we make the following observation: understanding and reversing the link between adverse climate change and agricultural practices can be achieved by using the above mapping to evaluate the landscape system, and in turn suggest a process by which to transition to secure soils for any type of farm (broadacre, dairy and mixed farming) uniquely suited for any given area of Australia. The *suitability* of proposed changes to the specific locality is critical to succeeding in securing our soils and thereby our climate.

Essentially, establishing the framework must include selection of mandatory reporting data. To avoid unintended consequences, a feedback loop should be established to ensure that, on balance, soil security and ecological sustainable development is continually achieved and all farms of the region are compliant with regional plans and objectives. The regulatory tools are available for confirming compliance in the urban environment, and such tools, including remote sensing, can be readily applied through existing government departments and compliance mechanisms.

One way to make regional plans enforceable is through landscape co-ops or corporations similar to body corporates for a block of flats or Pasture Protection Boards (acknowledging that some are toothless tigers, a better example may be animal disease and quarantine protection). Environmental quality parameters for the district should be considered similar to the way common property is administered by the body corporate. Compliance with certain regulations in regard to achieving climate stability and maximising rainfall is required. Activities can be banned or only available at certain times depending on the Regional Landscape Management Plan e.g. fire-ban days. Limitations on species planted, rotations, and land set aside for eco corridors will be required to be undertaken for the good of all in the district. The benefits of soil security and increased latent heat, such as increased profit together with income from carbon trading and land stewardship mostly will exceed any loss or costs associated with land removed from production, as well as the loss of unfettered land use.

Without pre-empting what an in-depth regional landscape study may reveal, in relation to irrigation districts regional planning and regulatory compliance will be essential to ensure regional agricultural viability and community cohesion, by ensuring downstream off-district impacts are minimised.

We may also have to rethink some land tenure issues. Much of northern Australia is Crown Land held under state and territory pastoral leases. Pastoral leases commonly prevent pastoralists from readily diversifying beyond the stated 'use', that is, 'pastoral purposes' which are generally restricted to running sheep or cattle.[224] The primary agricultural activity on pastoral leases in Western Australia is effectively the same now as it was when leases were first granted in the 1850s, grazing stock on native vegetation. Further, the nature of pastoral leases precludes them from the security afforded in freehold title, which means a lessee's ability to secure investment is diminished. Similarly, greater land use and planning restrictions will be needed to minimise external, off-farm, impacts of farming. Considerable public consultation will be required and considered government subsidies, subsidies that could be offset by the concomitant reduction in broadly applied drought resilience support schemes.

Further, clear-cut prohibition of urban encroachment and active management for all non-urban land is aligned with developing the National Landscape Regeneration Plan. As Bennett *et al* record, it is imperative to saving some of Australia's highest-producing horticultural soil regions. Land-banking of peri-urban land and allowing weeds, fire hazard, feral animals and land degradation to accrue, should be an offence.

Consideration should be given to the subdivision of arable land. Hobby-farming is not uncommon, and consideration should be given as to whether it is in the national interest, and aligned with the National Landscape Regeneration Plan. By way of example, the Foxhill homestead near Braidwood was recently advertised for sale. It is situated on 194.25 hectares, but a selling point is that the land could be subdivided into 40-hectare blocks. Owning a hobby farm must come with the same obligations of owning any farm. The banking of land without active management should be prohibited, no matter if it is in the peri-urban zone or marginal agricultural land; land is a shared commodity.

While minimum regional standards and land-use planning restrictions are necessary, unless there are good reasons for the community as a whole to constrain private choices, such as farm management which creates adverse external impacts or regional directives for group benefit, landholders should be free to use their land as they judge best *for themselves*. To this end, the majority of our proposed solutions leverage off the market economy, with initial government assistance and subsidies as the catalyst. Restrictions should be seen as akin to existing urban environmental restrictions on land use.

Regional landscape planning should be just as much a part of planning for the future of regional areas as town planning is to urban development. Regional planning should be directed to considering, what are the values we want from a landscape, what are the system connections, and how do we protect both. All the while allowing appropriate productive use of the land for both private and social benefits. All positive externalities should be allowed outside boundaries, consistent with a duty of care to the environment, as well as, your neighbours.

Introducing such a radical concept with the rural land holder having similar but different restrictions on land use as the urban dweller will require careful consideration. Stimulus programs will be needed, not just for planning, but also for education programs for the community, farmers and government service providers. Stakeholder engagement and consultation will be critical to the success of any proposed response. A National Landscape Regeneration Plan developed in conjunction with a national agriculture strategy and food security plan will provide for Australia's future prosperity.

Integrated Landscape Management

How can a farmer prevent the externalities of agriculture impacting their neighbour, their catchment or all of Australia? Maximise soil security. To do so requires management to be greater than just a farm by farm production system but an integrated landscape system. This can be achieved systematically in all regions, through management of:

- Systems balance
- Economic sustainability
- Environmental recovery
- Social and cultural resilience

To be successful, each of these factors require parameters that can be measured.

System balance starts with recovering the small water cycle through management of vegetation, vegetative litter and soil organic matter, as well as, landscape roughness and holding water naturally (i.e. not in engineered structures) from precipitation at or close to where rainfall occurred. Success in recovering the small water cycle can be measured by soil organic matter, basal stream flow and the nature of rainfall.

We recommend that farmers look to harness technology to monitor the return of the small water cycle. In Australia most farms have rainfall records, often spanning fifty years, but the nature of rainfall is not recorded. Though the years of 2021 and 2022 have been unusually wet, many farmers intuitively know that a portion of the small water cycle has been lost. However, farm rainfall records do not record the observation of rainfall intensity, duration, and dominant type of raindrop. Laser measurements of rain drop size and intensity are available and can assist in measuring landscape/climate interaction. Though expensive, the price is falling. It is with this measurement that floods can be seen as abnormal or a combination of heavy rain cycle coupled with land practice induced accelerated runoff. This is one way of monitoring the return of the small water cycle and it is recommended that farmers begin doing so.

Soil organic matter has not historically been monitored in a meaningful way, being seen either as a non-essential component of the production system or as being unlimited. Mapping of soil organic matter economically has only just become available as a useful farm management tool but practices to achieve soil organic matter build up and observational skills necessary to facilitate improvement is yet to be disseminated. Observational tools are necessary as whole-farm carbon testing is too expensive to perform more than once every several years.

Along with soil organic matter, vegetation also makes up the vegetative layer. Maintaining 100 percent vegetative cover of the entire landscape (farm), 100 percent of the time, is the optimum goal and is readily measurable via remote sensing or on farm surveys. Though living plants are best at maximising the small water cycle, residual standing straw stalks are preferable to bare ground. If soil organic matter is maximised and the small water cycle returned, maintaining vegetative cover via green manure crops, crops grown to be dug back into the soil, may not result in as much loss of plant available water as thought, as more effective rainfall occurs and infiltrates with green manure crop, compared to bare ground.

The last imperative element to achieving systems balance, is holding water where it falls, at source. The recovery of the small water cycle and increased soil organic matter causes more rain to fall and infiltrate, leading to elevated groundwater and increased period of streamflow or increase base flow of permanent streams. It also leads to slower moving and lower flood levels due to much greater infiltration of rainfall (less runoff). Lifting stream beds with wetlands, more frequent flooding of alluvium soils and use of Yeoman ploughs or similar to disperse gully runoff water along contoured sub-drains, known as Keyline drains, all assist in holding water at its source by increased infiltration, which in turn reduces floods and dry periods—less dry river beds.

To accelerate adoption of and outcomes from an integrated landscape management approach, the Government should also consider subsidising off-farm co-benefits, such as:

- Cultural Burns—Infield char generation > 5 years, to increase the CEC for low charged soil
- Eco-corridor maintenance, to increase wind turbulence and thereby summer thunderstorms
- Wetland, water meadow and stream base flow restoration, to recharge river bed alluvium and slow floods
- Macrophytes (aquatic plants growing in or near water) salinity scald restoration

How to define and measure change

What constitutes a successful farm or other productive enterprise in a landscape and how can we best measure it? In implementing the National Landscape Regeneration Plan we must assist farmers to create sufficient profit in a stress-minimised, balanced lifestyle, operating within a functioning and connected ecosystem.

This definition recognises that profit is both a necessary part of a balanced lifestyle, and understands that in order to accrue Natural Capital a farm has to have Financial Capital. Farms without Financial Capital, those that rely on outside income, without drastic change and support will never achieve this objective and impact on the district, thus preventing a sustainable landscape. Such farmers should be assisted to change or encouraged to leave the industry. We understand that with this change many corporate farms as well as many small family farmers will be disadvantaged and a compensation scheme will need to be evaluated. For corporate farms, though a regional measure of success is still relevant, a farm-specific measure should prioritise regional and environmental Natural Capital outcomes ahead of Financial Capital performance.

Economic Sustainability is not just of the farm but the district and can be measured via community responses such as:

- increased sports, social and community clubs in towns
- increased small businesses in town (as a result of increased farm profit across the district, not just a few farms)
- reduced suicides
- increased classrooms in the primary schools (life balance attracting young families)

Social and cultural resilience is reflected in the increased activities, diversity and frequency of social, sporting, religious and volunteering organisations in the district. A healthy community needs the young, and the young at heart, to support these essential services within our farming communities. Volunteer fire brigades, CWA, and the SES are essential mechanism to support communities during times of distress. The size and integration of these volunteer service providers is the key factor in community recovery from natural disasters. The fact that maximising soil security and the small water cycle not only diminishes the return time and intensity of extreme events (which in Australia, no matter how strong the small water cycle is, natural disasters will always occur) but accelerates community recovery is a good reason for communities to adopt these practices together.

Farming innovators and early adopters (comprising 1 and 20 per cent of farmers respectively) can be profitable all the time. However, a sustainable community requires the majority of its farmers to be profitable, the majority of the time, including during bad seasons. To achieve economic sustainability of the district, the whole community must adopt system management techniques.

Environmental recovery is largely achieved by managing the farm ecosystem in collaboration and cooperation with the district and minimising the use of manufactured chemicals within the farm rotational system. Doing so will achieve system balance and economic sustainability. Though not a part of this discussion, the environmental benefits of these two factors results in increased small insectiferous birds, beneficial insects, flora and macrofauna diversity. Though the primary function of multi-storeyed vegetation corridors is to increase flora and macrofauna diversity, as they function as wildlife corridors connecting reserves through farm land, the impacts on production profitability are manyfold, principally:

- increase wind turbulence to create clouds and more rainfall
- maintenance of baseline streamflow
- increase pollination of crops
- fungal bank and increased fungal diversity (lignin degraders—white wood rot fungi)
- reduce wind and frost damage
- provide shade for stock and a cool summer breeze
- allow long runs for efficient cropping

Increasing wind turbulence is essential for the return of the small water cycle and maximising its function. A model farm of the future is shown in Figure 12-1. It has eco-corridors over 50m wide, running perpendicular to the prevailing wind, comprised of diverse multi-story species.

Changing how we perceive and judge success in the way suggested

Figure 12-1. A model farm of the future.

above will take time, but the emphasis ought to remain on the fact that cultivating Natural Capital and Financial Capital go hand-in-hand.

A new skilled and accredited landscape sciences workforce

A skilled and accredited workforce will be required to service the above proposed solutions, but there are too few consulting agronomists or agriculture scientists and soil scientists who have the systems knowledge to guide farmers in making the change to regenerative agriculture. Though there are more innovators with local practical knowledge, their knowledge is often constrained to their specific location or those areas with similar latitude, rainfall and soil.

Before the late 1970s, the process and the professions of Environmental Planning, Environmental Sciences and Environmental Engineering did not exist. These professions emerged from social, cultural, policy and legislative changes in response to harmful development impacts on the environment; from point-source activities. How to restore those environmental impacts and to consider incremental multiple-point-source or diffuse-source impacts has, over the last decade, become an emerging science.

In a similar manner to how the environmental professions emerged in the late 1970s, aggregated diffuse impacts on land and restoration of the accumulation of below threshold point-sources is emerging as a separate field of knowledge. To service this new science requires a new suite of professions: Landscape Science, Landscape Engineering and Regional Planning.

For these new professions, new qualifications are required: a specific university post-graduate degree in landscape science and/or landscape engineering. To our knowledge there is no course anywhere in the world for landscape management, let alone landscape restoration or landscape planning.[xix] To capture incremental diffuse-source

---

[xix] Although we do note and applaud Southern Cross University for introducing a regenerative agriculture major Bachelor of Science (Regenerative Agriculture)—a step in the right direction.

environmental impacts, landscape science would be a multidisciplinary production and ecologically focused accreditation. Additionally, a new regional planning accreditation is required to consider the interconnections of human activities, ecological activities and climate. We propose government or industry cadetships subsidise the fees for these accreditations.

Most people view landscape in terms of ecosystems, or human activity in the landscape such as the built environment or mining. These are not the structure of the landscape, and a key aspect of landscape resilience is its structure, which mostly comes from soil. Landscape function is dependent on the soil. The fact that so many landscapes are degraded is directly related to the fact that the soil has been degraded so it cannot deliver its primary function to maintain landscape health, which supports the ecosystem.

In broad terms environmental science courses have minimal regard to landscape structure. They tend to focus on ecosystem function resilience, with a focus on flora and fauna. Environmental engineering focuses on waste disposal to landscape and impacts on human health. Physical geography has insufficient depth in earth sciences and production systems. Landscape use tends to be limited to agriculture and earth-science courses, with a focus on productive (Financial Capital) landscapes. Interdisciplinary teaching is rare and so there is a gap between agriculture and geology, as essentially one course deals with the top metre of the landscape and the other with solid rock below the surface. The in-between zone, known as the regolith, is not captured. Nor are aggregate diffuse and multi-functional impacts on land in a broad geographical area and its connection with climate. A good example is that no-one teaches how landscape change adversely impacts climate and how to mitigate that while maintaining productivity.

Additionally, until very recently, enrolment in agricultural science or agricultural engineering courses over the last two decades have experienced significant decline as there was little interest from fee-paying overseas students. As a result, many of the separate agricultural and geological university faculties have become too small to sustain an independent faculty and so have been rolled into the science faculty, to the detriment of the discipline.

Though geology and geography students may also take soil science as an elective, the responsibility of maintaining teaching staff, research farms and laboratories rests with the former agriculture faculties whose future is now uncertain. The schools or departments of agriculture continue to have one of the most successful postgraduate and research teams of any of the nonmedical sciences. Just as the need is now drastic and starting to be understood, the capacity to understand the science of what the innovators have done is critically diminished and is a major limitation to achieving anthropogenic climate change mitigation and reversal.

A major part of the job of landscape management professionals will be to work with practitioners. Much landscape degradation and loss of ecosystem diversity has occurred as a result of people seeking a living—often acting on the best advice of the time. In this light, we would also advocate for ongoing professional development for farm owners, managers and corporate boards. To bridge the gap while formal courses are being designed, we suggest a series of short courses in which land management advances are taught to farmers by qualified professionals in conjunction with the relevant regional government department. This is essential and as such should be subsidised or incentivised by government. To keep costs low, the program could be delivered via a video conferencing platform. Videoconferencing has the added benefit of facilitating readily accessible and ongoing group mentoring, as required. Such meetings would also provide an opportunity for input from local stakeholders on regional plans and sharing of industry knowledge as it develops.

We must also seek assistance from traditional owners of country. Their connection to country should be upheld as we need advice from those with traditional practice knowledge on how to best manage the landscape. Culture permitting, we should seek to understand the science behind their stories, songlines and methods of land management in a respectful, mutually beneficial framework.

Funding is required immediately, both to improve industry knowledge, research, and development, and to implement programs to collect data, map and record, and make accessible the existing state of our landscapes. We need innovation in land-use and landscape management. It is imperative to design productive landscapes to deliver multiple environmental benefits, sustain natural capital, and reverse anthropogenic climate change in the immediate future.

We are all in this together

Australian farmers are some of the least subsidised in the world. A lot could be gained from a little more strategic support for the stewards of our land. Direct farm support should be provided through professional development and a regenerative farming landscape management transition loan.

To incentivise and assist farmers to transition to regenerative practice and participate in the regional National Landscape Regeneration Plan, advocates for change have proposed a HECS-HELP-like based approach to retrain over a three-year period via a subsidised TAFE-like mature-age, apprenticeship scheme. Once farm profits have returned, the cost of the training, less any subsidy, is deducted as increased tax by the government.

Initially the government, or better still corporates with an environmental, social and governance impact investing or legacy mindset, through corporate social-responsibility pressure from shareholders or otherwise, should consider rewarding farmers for practices which improve their land's Natural Capital, social outcomes or other co-benefits, providing further incentive for farms to participate in local and regional National Landscape Regeneration Plans.[225]

Similarly, to drive momentum toward improved Natural Capital, towns should be acknowledged for their adoption and support of landscape management practices. To this end, akin to the concept of tidy towns from the 1950s to 80s, Local Council or State Government should consider funding a national Sustainable Landscape (District) competition. Measured by an absence of adverse externalities in the region and sustainability datasets. Those that live in rural centres which provide services to farms are colloquially known as "townies". There is some rivalry between Townies and Farmers. But landscape management requires both to work together—a spin on the old concept of civic pride.

Other community projects, that promote sustainability and could be subsidised, include:

- campaigns to educate the community about landscape management and its benefits (including, whole of community benefits);
- Best Practice Field Days (underway);
- funds to reward co-benefits such as ecological and social outcomes;
- funds for community programs to restore the small water cycle and eco-corridors (undertaken by the likes of NRMs and Landcare);
- regional urban green waste compost programs and school programs such as Food Scrap Friday;[226]
- regional organic waste trading or brokers; and
- programs for dryland salinity restoration, providing subsidised halophytes (salt tolerant plants).

Additionally, the Government could implement an on farm gap year similar to the Australian Defence Force funded gap year. It would provide young Australians with 12 months paid on farm experience. An opportunity for them to gain invaluable skills, work experience, and a connection to country.

Demand side solutions to climate mitigation

The second component of the National Soil Framework is shifting the land management culture to one of shared responsibility by elevating food from the normal, basic and banal. Bennett *et al* propose this can be achieved through decommoditisation of food, principally using product provenance. Bennett *et al* rightly contend there is a growing spatial disconnect between regions of production (farmers) and urban centres (consumers). The majority of consumers do not understand where and how our food is produced. They argue that provenance and decommoditisation is a way of assuring quality and sustainability of agricultural products and thereby creating social operating licenses. Of course, the success of any proposed solution is underpinned by communication; building, consolidating and disseminating knowledge—starting with the consumer. Bennett *et al* say the connection of people to soil is key to shrinking the gap between production and consumption. Consumers must have a choice to buy produce that sustains the land and reverses climate change. The introduction of QR codes to produce is starting to make this feasible.[227]

A way to measure product provenance to the region and even to the farm, is the accreditation system for carbon sequestration. Soil carbon measurement data is already collected by the government for reporting on international conventions in regard to climate change; initially the Kyoto agreement and then the Paris Agreement. Though embryonic, this data could be easily incorporated into an indelible blockchain-like confirmation system for produce quality and/or quality of land management, and a sustainability tracking system for consumers (think chain-of-custody tracking such as FSC Certification). A trial using soil carbon and other measures of natural capital is already being researched and market tested by a number of Australian research Institutions working collaboratively. Similar research has been occurring in a number of countries including the USA and the UK. Such a market system would likely increase confidence for consumers, producers, business and government.

In this regard lessons can be learned from the Australian Farm Biodiversity Certification Scheme. In particular, regard to the recommendations of the report commissioned for the National Farmers' Federation by the Australian Farm Institute, *Recognising On-farm Biodiversity Management*. The Australian Farm Institute were tasked with undertaking 'desktop and consultative research into existing verification or certification schemes, sustainability frameworks and best management practices, both domestically and internationally, to determine their applicability in Australian agricultural systems.'[228]

Technology is enabling processes to reduce the disconnect between producers and consumers, but we must accelerate development and coordinate a regulated standard.

Commonwealth legislative reform—review of the EPBC Act

As we have stated, soil security requires a national coordinated approach, making it a Commonwealth responsibility, and a good place to start would be for soil security to be considered as part of the future proposed reforms to the EPBC Act, particularly inclusion in the proposed national environmental standards. The Final Report contains no recommendation for soil, and little commentary of substance in this regard. The Australian government must consider substantive reform of the EPBC Act to capture and regulate soil security. Time is critical.

The EPBC Act Final Report states 'active mechanisms are required to restore areas of degraded or lost habitat to achieve the net gain for the environment that is needed.'

We believe successful landscape management can be achieved by creating a 'landscape management' functional area within the EPBC Act, with specific national environmental standards and its own expert, independent, specialised committee to form part of the proposed 'Ecologically Sustainable Development Committee'.

If not the EPBC Act, or a new set of related Acts as suggested by the Final Report, new Commonwealth legislation must be enacted to give the Australian Government a larger role in environmental regulation. As the Final Report of the EPBC Act Reform identifies, this should include greater collaboration with the states and territories and greater dialogue with Aboriginal and Torres Strait Islander people. Any such reform should also consider how it might complement any future national food security plan and national agriculture strategy.

Additionally, we suggest the *Agriculture Biodiversity Stewardship Market Bill 2022* be expanded to address Natural Capital.

Notwithstanding the progress being made through regenerative farming practices and in implementing the National Soil Strategy, other solutions for preventing and reversing land degradation and restoration of our soils must be explored.

Climate change modelling

As already laboured, and set out in the Appendix, our societies over reliance on erroneous or misleading climate modelling is contributing to misinformation about climate change. Precipitation provides a more accurate regional model compared to global average temperature rise as a measure of climate change. Mankind has now significantly influenced about 70% of Earth's terrestrial surface and that change must be accounted for if we are to truly mitigate climate change. Landscape practices and associated data points are absent from assumptions and sensitivity analysis underpinning current climate change modelling and that absence is expressed through inaccurate predictions. Climate model projections of precipitation must be carried out that account for soil and vegetation variability with time, not just inter-seasonal variability.

Further, research into solar radiation under different agricultural practices is yet to occur. Only in the last two years have flux towers been engaged over agricultural land, though with a focus on GHG emissions over solar radiation and heat. Sensitivity analysis on these missing parameters is also essential, particularly impact of agricultural areas on adjoining forests.[229]

What you can do

Your actions can substantively affect how quickly we adopt and transition through the above proposed solutions and we encourage you to champion change and be a steward of our land in the following ways.

Champion change:

- consume conscientiously by buying products from farms which use regenerative practices

- educate people about sensible and latent heat, and the small water cycle
- support considered government subsidies for farmers
- advocate for policy change, write to your local Member for Parliament
- share this work

In your own backyard and community:

- reduce bare ground, not with concrete, tiles or artificial turf but with vegetation or vegetative litter
- input eco-corridors
- advocate for planning changes which adopt the National Landscape Regeneration Plan to deliver functioning and connected ecosystems

Collectively we are empowered to shape our future for the better.

Chapter 13

Land Management for Climate Change

Our children's future

The catalyst for this book was informed by the despair of extreme natural disasters in 2020–21 and the fatalistic and disempowering reporting of those events. As we close, we continue to feel hope but more than ever we feel emotionally charged. The writing process has intensified the upsetting reality that humanity is causing more frequent, extended and intense extreme climatic events. Though such natural disasters may be expressed in different ways, relative to latitude and topography, they are universally caused by anthropogenic altered land use. Particularly when the land use change leads to loss of vegetation, leading to loss of soil security, and in turn loss of the small water cycle.

When we started writing, massive flooding was occurring across parts of Europe, particularly Germany—an event environmental scientist Michal Kravik predicted in 2007. He warned that, due to the loss of the small water cycle in the lowlands, increased precipitation in the highland areas would cause massive floods. As we were revising this second edition of Ground Breaking, floods in Pakistan occurred in 2022 that met the circumstances of the flood events predicted by

Michal Kravik. It is heartbreaking to understand both that we caused this problem and we were empowered to prevent it—but didn't. It is time we paid heed to *all* climate science.

The volume of extreme climatic events globally is near debilitating. Savage cold snaps are occurring on the Steppes of Mongolia, wiping out nomadic herds. Again, through effective land management practices, the cold snaps are preventable. Since the collapse of Soviet communism in the early 1900s stocking rates have soared, increasing 300 percent. The increased stocking rate removed the grass cover, lowered the soil organic matter and dropped the water table. The vegetative layer, including the soil organic matter, is no longer able to buffer the relative humidity in the atmosphere and consequently the cold snaps are more extreme. Elsewhere, forest fires burn in areas downwind from substantial cropping land. While we are familiar with this kind of event in Australia, in 2021, this also occurred in Russia, the Western USA, and Canada.

Countless examples lead us to conclude that, universally, agricultural-induced landscape change, when measured by precipitation or repeat occurrence of extreme events, is the leading precursor to climate change. And as we explained in Chapter 5, agricultural-induced climate change is not new. Plato recorded it happening in the Neolithic period, well before GHGs had begun to rise.

There is no doubt that the climate change we are experiencing is human induced. Mounting evidence demonstrates that agricultural practices are the principal changers of landscape and are a major contributor, if not the leading cause, of climate change. The need for change in how we manage the land is clear, essential and urgent.

Reducing GHG emissions by investing in solar energy or the hydrogen economy is important, but decarbonisation alone will not stop anthropogenic climate change in Australia. GHGs are just a part of what is regulating the Earth's temperature. The greenhouse effect requires two components: a heat source and a blanket. The impact of GHGs, acting as the blanket, is significant, but land management is crucial as it leads to increased sensible heat at the expense of latent heat.

The state of our land changes how heat is absorbed, processed and emitted, and consequently how heat effects atmospheric processes, particularly where, when and how much precipitation occurs.

Climate science is nuanced. Terrestrial systems and atmospheric processes are interdependent, and individually and collectively complicated. Focusing almost exclusively on emissions of carbon dioxide and other greenhouse gases is self-sabotage. To mitigate or reverse anthropogenic climate change, we must have broad and robust discussions. The beauty of science is that it is an ongoing conversation, learning from the past and present to problem solve for our future. It is within our power to create a better future.

Through regenerative farming practices, farmers have demonstrated what can work to secure our soils, return the small water cycle and reverse climate change—to heal our country. And through our national response to acid sulfate soils we have a framework to inform our immediate regulatory response. We need to mobilise technology, industry, labour, regulatory reform, and, critically, finance. Our choice and implementation of legislation will determine the future quality of our land and our climate.

Ensuring the centrality of our soil in policy is essential to achieving soil security, which in turn will mitigate climate change, and regenerate our land. For a world looking to bounce back from the COVID-19 pandemic and its impact on the economy, there is no other cause that will have as profound a long term effect. Boosting our Natural Capital will create a great many jobs and secure sustainable economies—landscape management is the currency of the coming decades.

While the science is complicated and requires further investigation and interrogation, the principles for mitigating anthropogenic climate change through landscape science are clear. We must:

- Actively manage the landscape
- Sequester organic matter in soil
- Reduce bare ground
- Increase multi-functional ecology corridors

We must work with nature.

Right now we face a decision, here in Australia and around the world, do we wish to continue down the path of making the world's bread baskets deserts by 2039? Resulting in more heat waves, floods, plagues, warfare and societal collapse, and potentially, leading to a new mostly dark age plagued by extreme climatic events? Or do we wish to positively manage our landscapes to ensure the well-being of the custodians of our country, and ultimately humankind?

We must act now. There is hope for the future, but we must break new ground.

Appendix

Role and problem of models

It was reported in January 2021 that many scientists have the view that climate change will stop quickly once emissions are brought to zero and under this scenario the climate will stabilise within a decade or two.[237] This is the opinion of Dr Joeri Rogelj, a lead author of the next major climate assessment from the Intergovernmental Panel on Climate Change (IPCC). But Dr Rogelj assumes that the most significant contributor to climate change is greenhouse gases led principally by emissions of CO_2.

Reinforced by the IPCC's newly released Sixth Assessment Report, the world's entire strategy for stopping climate change is based on this consensus view. The IPCC announced: 'the report shows that emissions of greenhouse gases from human activities are responsible for approximately 1.1° C of warming since 1850–1900, and finds that averaged over the next 20 years, global temperature is expected to reach or exceed 1.5° C of warming'. This assessment is based on improved observational datasets to assess historical warming, as well progress in *scientific understanding of the response of the climate system to human-caused greenhouse gas emissions*.

This conclusion is underpinned by the premise that climate change is caused by carbon dioxide emissions and stopping these emissions will reverse climate change and models accurately predict climate change.

Models are predictive tools not forecasters of future events. They are commonly not accurate. Nonetheless, they are useful: in reducing a range of uncertainty in complex problems; as management tools for the scale of the problem; and indicating the variability expected.

They can also be used to define important factors impacting the problem. All models are based on the same foundations, a conceptual model, the assumptions used in the equations, and the size of the smallest area seen as constant—known as cells. All physical environmental models are based on an equation known as the Laplace Equation in which flow (heat, water, gas, electricity) is from high gradient to low gradient. In its simplest form, steady state flow of a physical characteristic, the equation is a function of the properties of the medium and the change in gradient in three dimensions, over time.

To increase certainty on parameters chosen for the model that have not been measured, but assumed or estimated, a process called 'sensitivity analysis' is undertaken. This is the process by which the values chosen for any variable are tested at values significantly greater and smaller than the value chosen or even reversed. Climate modelling is hugely complex and involves several mediums that are anisotropic with time, direction and change in physical characteristics. It also potentially involves change agents known as 'forcers' that may not yet considered. Therefore, sensitivity analysis is essential.

Sensitivity analysis is about questioning and testing the data that informs climate modelling and its creation objective. Presently we are not thoroughly testing whether other factors contribute to anthropogenic climate change. If we do not understand what other terrestrial and atmospheric processes impact climate change, impact the heat that is regulating our earth's temperature, and if we haven't ruled out all other key environmental functions, then how can we be sure that zero emissions will reverse climate change?

Parameters chosen for sensitivity analysis are the key to proving a model. A correlation with one parameter is insufficient to say the model is a useful predictive tool. As discussed in relation to Figure 3-8 and Figure 3-9, even the most conservative climate models were unable to predict the reduction in rainfall and dam inflow that was measured. This means that the parameters chosen were incorrect, not subject to appropriate sensitivity analysis, or a real process has been omitted, that is the conceptual model is incorrect.

All models improve over time as new information allows both better estimates of constants—assumptions—and improvement in the processes involved in the conceptual model. The latest IPCC set of reports, August 2021, has a greater discussion on natural variability and effects of clouds. The former was not even considered in the previous reports. The modelling is effectively considered so poor that the average of many models compares better with actual measurements than any individual model. Most models have not predicted that the rate of climate change as measured by temperature is worse than that modelled overall. Some other forcer of climate change (parameter) may not be considered or just be missing altogether.

If a key parameter that can be made variable or reversed remains constant with time, the model becomes insensitive to actual changes in the parameter and underestimates both rate of change and rate of recovery. This could be the problem with the current climate change models which are reportedly underpredicting the climate change occurring and have been doing so since modelling was first seen as a primary evidence line. Are we missing a process in our models? Why does the rate of change appear to be worse than expected? As discussed earlier in citing the opinion of Dr Joeri Rogelj, if emissions are reversed, will temperature and rainfall changes revert? No, not if the conceptual model is wrong. It appears that a major characteristic of landscape has not been subject to sensitivity analysis, or, worse, is not included in the conceptual model.

Now it is clear that anthropogenic climate change is occurring, the IPCC in the latest report publicly recognise models are problematic: 'unlike in previous assessments, climate models are not considered a line of evidence in their own right in the IPCC Sixth Assessment Report'.

What happens to climate models if vegetative cover and organic matter are increased progressively with time, both in concentration and extent? We know that sensible heat is reduced and the small water cycle returns. Thereby it is logical that if infrared radiation is diminished, the radiated heat by the GHGs are also diminished. If solutions are being modelled surely this is just as important, if not more important, to model than GHG emission fluctuation.

Models to be useful need to do sensitive analysis on all parameters. Based on information we have read as at August 2021 this is still yet to be done.

Acknowledgements

Three Scientists, Pawel Strzelecki, Roger Pielke Senior, a meteorologist, and Michael Kravcík, a hydrologist, who we have not met, have blazed a trail without which this book would not have been possible. We acknowledge them in particular, but also thank and pay homage to the many scientists, explorers and aboriginal elders whose published work we have relied upon. Special mention also to my colleagues at University of Sydney, particular Alex McBratney, for their ongoing work in championing and advocating for soil security and carbon farming.

A sterling job of converting my thumbnail scratches to legible figures and the numerous revisions I insisted upon was patiently and superbly undertaken by Trevor Jones who has been doing illustrations and drafting for me for almost 40 years. Thanks to Terry Gould who provided valuable GIS manipulation for some of the figures.

Thanks to those who were great hosts and provided the aerial inspection of the MIA.

Special thanks to early supporters Sharon Carleton, Brendan 'Bird' Parnell, Andy Ball, Peter McInerney, Godwin Bradbeer, and Gerry Nolan for guidance, feedback and initial editing. Thanks too to Amelia de Bie who provided some initial editing. We also thank the many others who provided feedback and encouragement along the way.

Wrestling a manuscript of dense science and regulatory review in the emotionally charged atmosphere of climate change to a more readable text was a gargantuan task ably achieved by John Kerr. He and Paul Taylder, typesetting and layout, guided us to the finish line of publication. Heartfelt thanks.

Finally, we thank our partners Allison and Stefan for understanding and helping, and tolerating us while we were writing and lost in thought.

Endnotes

1. Finkel, A, 'Getting to Zero' *Quarterly Essay*, March 2021, p 26.
2. Loeb N, Johnson G, Thorsen T, Lyman J, Rose F and Kato S, 2021 'Satellite and Ocean Data Reveal Marked Increase in Earth's Heating Rate,' *Geophysical Research Letter* 15 June 2021; https://doi.org/10.1029/2021GL093047
3. Ing. Michal Kravcík M *et al*, *Water for the Recovery of the Climate - A New Water Paradigm*, Municipalia a.s. and TORY Consulting a.s.2007; English translation by David McLean and Jonathan Gresty. Available from: http://www.waterparadigm.org/download/Water_for_the_Recovery_of_the_Climate_A_New_Water_Paradigm.pdf [Date accessed: 29 October 2020].
   See also Lowdermilk W C, *Conquest of the land through seven thousand years*, US Government Printing Office 1953; Hillel D, 1992—*Out of the Earth, Civilisation and the Life of Soil*, University of California Press; Montgomery D, *Dirt: The Erosion of Civilisation*, University of California Press 2012.
   See also Lyons T, Smith R and Xinmei H, 'The impact of clearing for agriculture on the surface energy budget, *International Journal of Climatology* Vol 16, 551-558, 1996.
   See also Nair, U S, Y. Wu, J. Kala, T. J. Lyons, R. A. Pielke Sr., and J. M. Hacker, 'The role of land use change on the development and evolution of the west coast trough, convective clouds, and precipitation in southwest Australia', *J. Geophys. Res.*, 116, D07103, doi:10.1029/2010JD014950 2011.
   See also Esau I and Lyons T, 'Effect of sharp vegetation boundary on the convective atmospheric boundary layer,' *Agricultural and Forest Meteorology* 114 (2002) 3-13.
   See also Ray D, Nair U, Welch R, Su W and Kikuchi T, 2001, 'Influence of land use on the regional climate of SW Australia'. See also Pielke Sr. R, 2001, 'Influence of the spatial distribution of vegetation and soils on the prediction of Cumulus convective rainfall', *Review of Geophysics*, 39, 2, May 2001, p151-177.
   See also Pielke R Sr, Adegoke J, Chase T, Marshall C, Matsui T, Niyopi D, 2007, 'A new paradigm for assessing the role of agriculture in the climate system and in climate change'; *Agricultural and Forest Meteorology*, p 234-254
4. Yue, C *et al*, 'Contribution of land use to the interannual variability of the land carbon cycle', *Nature Communications* 11, 3170 (2020). Available from: https://doi.org/10.1038/s41467-020-16953- [Accessed 24/07/2021].
5. John McLean Bennett *et al*, 'Soil Security for Australia', *Sustainability* 2019, 3416, 4.
6. See 3 above.
7. The term 'Soil Security', was coined by Professor Alex McBratney, Director–Sydney Institute of Agriculture, Professor of Digital Agriculture & Soil Science of the University of Sydney.
8. John McLean Bennett *et al*, 'Soil Security for Australia', Sustainability 2019, 3416, 2.
9. Lowdermilk W C, *Conquest of the land through seven thousand years*, US Government Printing Office 1953; Hillel D, *Out of the Earth, Civilisation and the Life of Soil*, University of California Press 1992; Montgomery D, *Dirt: The Erosion of Civilisation*, University of California Press 2012.
10. El-Baz F and Hassan M, *Physics of Desertification*, Dordrecht, Netherlands 1986.
11. Klein Goldewijk K and Ramankutty N, 'Land use during the past 300 years in Landuse, Landcover and Soil Science', Vol 1 UNESCO EOLSS-online 2005.

12 Poulter B, Frank D, Ciais P, Myneni R, Andela N, Bi J, Broquet G, Canadell J Chevallier F, Lui Y, Running S, Sitch S and van der Werf G, 'Contribution of semi-arid ecosystems to interannual variability of the global carbon cycle' *Nature* Volume 509, pp 600–3 (2014).
13 Gilligan I, *Agriculture and Aboriginal Australia: Why Not?* Bulletin of the Indo Pacific Pre-History Association Vol 30 2010, p 145-155. Denham T *et al Horticultural Experimentation in Northern Australia Reconsidered*, 83 Antiquity 2009, 634-648..
14 Sturt C, *Two Expeditions into the interior of Southern Australia during the years 1828, 1829, 1830 and 1831 with observations on the soil, climate and general resources of the colony of New South Wales*, Vol 1 Smith Elder and Co. London 1833.
15 Strzelecki P, *Physical description of NSW and Van Diemen's Land*, London: Longman, Brown, Green, 1845.
16 Griffin E, Hoyle F and Murphy D (2013). 'Soil organic carbon', Report card on sustainable natural resource use in agriculture, Department of Agriculture and Food, Western Australia. Available from: https://www.agric.wa.gov.au/sites/gateway/files/2.4%20 Soil%20organic%20carbon.pdf [16 November 2020].
17 Kravcík M, Pokorný J, Kohutiar J, Kovác M, Tóth E, *Water for the Recovery of the Climate—A New Water Paradigm*, ENKI 2007.
18 ABC *Science Show* Radio National 15 May 2021- Smarter irrigation keeps Adelaide's parks greener and cooler.
19 Kravcík M, Pokorný J, Kohutiar J, Kovác M, Tóth E, *Water for the Recovery of the Climate—A New Water Paradigm*, ENKI 2007.
20 Lyons T, Smith R and Xinmei H, 'The impact of clearing for agriculture on the surface energy budget', *International Journal of Climatology* Vol 16, 551–558, 1996: https://www.semanticscholar.org/paper/THE-IMPACT-OF-CLEARING-FOR-AGRICULTURE-ON-THE-Austmlia-G./071924212a18dd71b53d3980b1f81ff4a2d 20e69.
21 Nair, U. S., Y. Wu, J. Kala, T. J. Lyons, R. A. Pielke Sr., and J. M. Hacker, *The role of land use change on the development and evolution of the west coast trough, convective clouds, and precipitation in southwest Australia*, Journal of Geophysics. Res., 116, D07103, doi:10.1029/2010JD014950 2011.
22 Nair, U S, Y. Wu, J. Kala, T. J. Lyons, R. A. Pielke Sr, and J. M. Hacker, 'The role of land use change on the development and evolution of the west coast trough, convective clouds, and precipitation in southwest Australia', *J. Geophys. Res.*, 116, D07103, doi:10.1029/2010JD014950 2011.
23 WA Dept of Agriculture, 'Climate Change: impacts and adaptations' *WA. Bulletin* No 4870, 2016
24 Lyons T, Smith R and Xinmei H, (1996), 'The impact of clearing for agriculture on the surface energy budget,' *International Journal of Climatology* Vol 16, 551-558.
25 Nair, U S, Y. Wu, J. Kala, T. J. Lyons, R. A. Pielke Sr, and J. M. Hacker, 'The role of land use change on the development and evolution of the west coast trough, convective clouds, and precipitation in southwest Australia', *J. Geophys. Res.*, 116, D07103, doi:10.1029/2010JD014950 2011.
26 Pielke R Snr, Adegoke J, Chase T, Marshall C, Matsui T and Niyogi D, 2007, 'A new Paradigm for assessing the role of agriculture in the climate system and in climate change', *Agricultural and Forest Meteorology* 142 (2007) 234-254

27 Pielke R Sr, Adegoke J, Chase T, Marshall C, Matsui T, Niyopi D, (2007), 'A new paradigm for assessing the role of agriculture in the climate system and in climate change', *Agricultural and Forest Meteorology*, 234–54.
28 Intergovernmental Panel on Climate Change *Annual Report* 5 2014, pp 4–5.
29 The Special Report on climate change, desertification, land degradation, sustainable land management, food security, and GHG fluxes in terrestrial ecosystems (SRCCL), p 44. Jia, G, E Shevliakova, P Artaxo, N De Noblet-Ducoudré, R Houghton, J House, K Kitajima, C Lennard, A Popp, A Sirin, R Sukumar, L Verchot, 2019: Land–climate interactions. *Climate Change and Land: an IPCC special report on climate change, desertification, land degradation, sustainable land management, food security, and greenhouse gas fluxes in terrestrial ecosystems* [P R Shukla, J Skea, E Calvo Buendia, V Masson-Delmotte, H-O. Pörtner, D C Roberts, P Zhai, R Slade, S Connors, R van Diemen, M Ferrat, E Haughey, S Luz, S Neogi, M Pathak, J Petzold, J Portugal Pereira, P Vyas, E Huntley, K Kissick, M Belkacemi, J Malley, (eds). In press, Box-2.1 - Figure 1
30 Poulter *et al* 2014, *Nature* Volume 509, pages 600–603.
31 Poulter *et al* 2014, *Nature* Volume 509, pages 600–603; and Yue *et al* (2020)11:3179, doi.org/10/1038/s41467-020-16953-8.
32 Yue *et al* (2020) 11:3179, doi.org/10/1038/s41467-020-16953-8.
33 Yue *et al* (2020) 11:3179, doi.org/10/1038/s41467-020-16953-8.
34 Kravcík M *et al*, *Water for the Recovery of the Climate—A New Water Paradigm*, Municipalia a.s. and TORY Consulting a.s. 2007 and also Makarieva and Gorshkov (2007), *Hydrology and Earth System Science*, 11, 1013-1033.
35 Makarieva and Gorshkov 2007, *Biotic pump of atmospheric moisture as driver of the hydrological cycle on land*; Hydrology and Earth System Science, 11, 1013-1033.
36 Makarieva and Gorshkov 2007, *Biotic pump of atmospheric moisture as driver of the hydrological cycle on land*; Hydrology and Earth System Science, 11, 1013-1033.
37 Kravcik, M *et al*, 'Water for the Recovery of the Climate – A new Water Paradigm', 2007, p 71
38 Kravcík M *et al*, *Water for the Recovery of the Climate - A New Water Paradigm*, Municipalia a.s. and TORY Consulting a.s. 2007.
39 Kravcík M et al *Water for the Recovery of the Climate - A New Water Paradigm*, Municipalia a.s. and TORY Consulting a.s. 2007; Makarieva and Gorshkov 2007, *Hydrology and Earth System Science*, 11, 1013-1033.
40 Van Heerwarden *et al*, 'Understanding the Daily Cycle of Evapotranspiration: A Method to Quantify the Influence of Forcings and Feedbacks', *Journal of Hydrometeorology* 11 (6): 1405–1422, 2010.
41 Faleiros G, and Andreoni M, 'Agro-suicide: Amazon deforestation hits Brazil's soy producers' Dialogo Chino 2020. Available from: https://dialogochino.net/en/agriculture/37887-agri-suicide-amazon-deforestation-hits-rain-brazils-soy-producers/ [Accessed 02/11/2020].
42 Lyons T, Smith R and Xinmei H, 'The impact of clearing for agriculture on the surface energy budget' *International Journal of Climatology* Vol 16, 551-558, 1996.
43 Nair U, Wu Y, Kala J, Lyons T, Pielke R Sr. and Hacker J *et al* (2011), 'The role of landuse change on the development and evolution of the west coast trough, convective clouds and precipitation in southwest Australia,' *Journal of Geophysical Research*, Vol 116, DO7103, doi:10.1029/2010JD014950, 2011

44 McAlpine C *et al* 2010, Climate change and land clearing: a short note; *Australian Zoologist*; Jan 2010 Mahmood *et al* 2010, Impacts of landuse/land cover change on climate and future research priorities; *Bulletin of the American Meteorological society*, Vol 91, Issue 1 (Jan 2010) p37–46

45 Peterson T, Saft M, Peel M, John A, 'Watersheds may not recover from droughts' *Science* 14 May 2021, Vol 372 Issue 6543 pp 745–9.

46 Intergovernmental Panel on Climate Change (2019), *The Special Report on climate change, desertification, land degradation, sustainable land management, food security, and greenhouse gas fluxes in terrestrial ecosystems*, P R Shukla, J Skea & anor, p 50.

47 James Atkinson, *An Account of the State of Agriculture and Grazing in NSW*, 1826, J Cross London.

48 Anthony Scott, 'Water Erosion in the Murray-Darling Basin: Learning from the Past', CSIRO Land and Water, Canberra, Technical Report 43/01, November 2001: http://www.clw.csiro.au/publications/technical2001/tr43-01.pdf (accessed 29 October 2020).

49 Gray J, Bishop T and Wilson B, 'Factors controlling soil organic carbon stocks with depth in Eastern Australia', 2015, *Soil Sci. Soc. Am. J.* 79:1741-1751, doi:10.2136/sssaj2015.06.0224.

50 Viscarra Rossel R, Webster R, Bui E, Baldock J, 'Baseline map of organic carbon in Australian soil to support national carbon accounting and monitoring under climate change', *Glob Chang Biol*. 2014 Sep; 20(9):2953-70. doi: 10.1111/gcb.12569. Epub 2014 Apr 28.

51 Scott, Anthony, *Water erosion in the Murray-Darling Basin: Learning from the past*; CSIRO Land and Water, Canberra, Technical Report 43/01 November 2001.

52 Pawel Strzelecki, *Physical Description of New South Wales and Van Diemen's Land*, Longman; Brown; Green; London 1845, p224–227 and p239.

53 Victor Seffenson, *Fire Country*, Hardie Grant, Melbourne, 2019.

54 Pascoe, Bruce, Introduction, Comments in Panel discussion, 'Bushfires, Indigenous land management and carbon farming,' Part 2, Wednesday, 26 May 2021; Norton Rose, Fulbright, Brisbane, Australia.

55 Mariani, M et al 'Disruption of cultural burning promotes shrub encroachment and unprecedented wildfires' *Frontiers in Ecology & Environment* 2022; DOI;10, 1002/FEE.2395

56 Mariani, M et al 'Disruption of cultural burning promotes shrub encroachment and unprecedented wildfires' *Frontiers in Ecology & Environment* 2022; DOI;10, 1002/FEE.2395

57 Bill Gammage, *The Biggest Estate on Earth: How Aborigines Made Australia* Allen and Unwin Sydney, 2012.

58 Tindal N, *Aboriginal tribes of Australia: their terrain, environmental controls, distribution, limits, and proper names*, ANU Press, Canberra, 1974.

59 Ampt P, 'Grasses for Grain and Indigenous Food Landscape,' Conference Notes, Growing Sustainable Communities, Sydney Institute of Agriculture, 6 July 2018.

60 Allen H, (1974) *The Bagundji of the Darling Basin: Cereal Gatherers in an Uncertain Environment*, World Archaeology 5(3): 309-322.

61 Oxley J (1820) *Journal of 2 expeditions into the interior of NSW: Undertaken by the order of British Government in the years 1817-18*.

62 Broome, Richard *Aboriginal Australians*, Allen and Unwin Sydney, 2002.

63 Flannery, Tim, *Future eaters – an ecological history of the Australasian lands and people*; Reed Books, Sydney, 1994.

64   Harari, Yuval Noah, *Sapiens: a brief history of Humankind* Harper Collins, 2015; Victor Seffenson, *Fire Country*, Hardie Grant, Melbourne, 2019; and Seminar *Bushfires, Indigenous Land Management and Carbon Farming*; Norton Rose Fulbright, Melbourne 14 October 2020.
65   The University of Melbourne, 'Mysteries of megafauna extinction unlocked' (webpage, 18 May 2020) https://about.unimelb.edu.au/newsroom/news/2020/may/mysteries-of-megafauna-extinction-unlocked [Accessed 11/02/2021]
66   Koch A, Brierley C, Maslin M, Lewis S, 'Earth system impacts of the European arrival and Great Dying in the Americas after 1492,' *Quaternary Science Reviews* 207 (2019) pp 13–36
67   Victor Seffenson, *Fire Country*, Hardie Grant, Melbourne, 2019, and *Trading Lightly* by K Sveiby and T Skuthorpe, Allen and Unwin, Sydney, 2006.
68   Gammage, Bill, *The Biggest Estate on Earth: How Aborigines Made Australia* Allen and Unwin, Sydney, 2012; Koch A, Brierley C, Maslin M, Lewis S, 'Earth system impacts of the European arrival and Great Dying in the Americas after 1492,' *Quaternary Science Reviews* 207 (2019) 13-36.
69   James Atkinson, *An Account of the State of Agriculture and Grazing in NSW*, 1826, J Cross London.
70   Allen H, (1974), 'The Bagundji of the Darling Basin: Cereal Gatherers in an Uncertain Environment,' *World Archaeology* 5(3): 309–22.
71   Gammage, Bill *The Biggest Estate on Earth: How Aborigines Made Australia* Allen and Unwin, 2012; Pascoe B, *Dark Emu, Black Seeds: Agriculture or Accident?* Magabala Books 2014.
72   Sturt, Charles 'Two Expeditions into the Interior of Southern Australia during the years 1828-1831' Vol 1 Smith Elder & Co 1833 Cambridge Library Edition]
73   ABC *Australia Wide* 'Fighting fire with fire: has burning in the Kimberley gone too far?' Alex Hyman 10 June 2021. Available at: https://www.abc.net.au/radio/programs/australia-wide/australia-wide/13372998 [accessed 1 July 2021] ; Greg Miles, *Flame of Convenience: Early Dry Season Burning on Trial in Kakadu and the Western Top End of the Northern Territory* Green Hill, Adelaide, 2020.
74   Gilligan I, 'Agriculture in Aboriginal Australia: Why Not' *Bulletin of the Indo-Pacific Prehistory Association* Vol 30, 2010, p 145-55
75   Sveiby, Karl-Erik and Tex Skuthorpe *Treading Lightly: The Hidden Wisdom of the World's Oldest People*, Allen & Unwin, Sydney, 2006.
76   johnhollander.net
77   https://www.climate.gov/news-features/understanding-climate/climate-change-atmospheric-carbon-dioxide (Accessed 30/06/22).
78   https://www.climate.gov/news-features/understanding-climate/climate-change-atmospheric-carbon-dioxide (Accessed 10/06/21).
79   Coates L, Haynes K, O'Brien J, McAneney J, and Dimer de Oliveira F, 'Exploring 167 years of vulnerability: An examination of extreme heat events in Australia 1844–2010,' *Environmental Science and Policy* 12, 2014, pp 33-44.
80   IOCI Stage 3 (2012), 'Western Australia's Weather and Climate: A synthesis of the Indian Ocean Climate Initiative', Stage 3 Research, CSIRO and BoM Australia
81   Griffith-Taylor T, *A study in warm environments and their effects on British settlements*. Methuen London, 1940, p 68; Curlewis E, 'The Climate of Western Australia in Results

82. Indian Ocean Climate Initiative, 'Climate variability and change in south west Western Australia,' Dept of Environment Water and Catchment Protection, Western Australia, 2002.
of rainfall observations made in Western Australia' in Hunt H (ed), Government Printer Melbourne 1929; and Gentilli J, *Climates of Australia and New Zealand*, Elseveir, 1972
83. Indian Ocean Climate Initiative 'Western Australia's Weather and Climate: A Synthesis of Indian Ocean Climate Initiative Stage 3 Research.' CSIRO and BoM, Australia. Editors: Bryson Bates, Carsten Frederiksen and Janice Wormworth, (2012).
84. Indian Ocean Climate Initiative (2002) Climate variability and change in south west Western Australia.
85. Smith I and Power S, 'Past and future changes to inflows into Perth (Western Australia) dams' *Journal of Hydrogeology: Regional studies* 2, 2014 84-96
86. Intergovernmental Panel on Climate Change (2002) Climate variability and change in south west Western Australia.
87. Intergovernmental Panel on Climate Change (2002) Climate variability and change in south west Western Australia.
88. Smith I and Power S 2014, Past and future inflows into Perth, SA, dams; *Journal of Hydrogeology*: Regional studies 2 (2014) 84-96.
89. Loeb N, Johnson G, Thorsen T, Lyman J, Rose F and Kato S, 'Satellite and Ocean Data Reveal Marked Increase in Earth's Heating Rate', *Geophysical Research*, letter 15 June 2021; https://doi.org/10.1029/2021GL093047; and Yue, C et al, 'Contribution of land use to the interannual variability of the land carbon cycle', *Nature Communications* 11, 3170 (2020): https://doi.org/10.1038/s41467-020-16953- [Accessed 24/07/2021].
90. Peterson T, Saft M, Peel M, John A, 'Watersheds may not recover from droughts,' *Science* 14 May 2021 • Vol 372 Issue 6543 pp 745–9
91. Loeb N, Johnson G, Thorsen T, Lyman J, Rose F and Kato S, 'Satellite and Ocean Data Reveal Marked Increase in Earth's Heating Rate', *Geophysical Research*, letter 15 June 2021; https://doi.org/10.1029/2021GL093047
92. Lowdermilk W C, *Conquest of the land through seven thousand years*, US Government Printing Office 1953; Hillel D, *Out of the Earth, Civilisation and the Life of Soil*, University of California Press 1992; Montgomery D, *Dirt: The Erosion of Civilisation*, University of California Press 2012
93. Faleiros G, and Andreoni M, 'Agro-suicide: Amazon deforestation hits Brazil's soy producers' Dialogo Chino 2020. Available from: https://dialogochino.net/en/agri-culture/37887-agri-suicide-amazon-deforestation-hits-rain-brazils-soy-producers/ [Accessed 2 November 2020].
94. Friedlingstein *et al*, 'Global Climate Budget', Earth System Science Data, 12, 3269-3340, 2020
95. Goldewidj K, Dekker S and van Zanden J, 'Per-capita estimation of long-term historical land use and the consequence for global change research', *Journal of Land Use Science*, Vol 12, No 5 pp 313–37, 2017
96. Box, G E P and Draper, N. R. (1987), *Empirical Model-Building and Response Surfaces*, John Wiley, Hoboken NJ, 1987 and https://medium.data4sci.com/epidemic-modeling-102-all-covid-19-models-are-wrong-but-some-are-useful-c81202cc6ee9.
97. http://dhmontgomery.com/portfolio/all/2019/01/land-use-visualization/
98. BoM, *State of the Climate*, Government of Australia, 2020; and IOCI Stage 3, 'Western Australia's Weather and Climate: a Synthesis of the Indian Ocean Climate Initiative', CSIRO and BoM, 2012

99   BoM, *State of the Climate*, Government of Australia, 2020.
100 O'Connell M and Molloy K, 2001, Farming and woodland dynamics in Ireland during the Neolithic, Biology and Environment Proceedings of the Royal Irish Academy Vol 101B No1-2, 99-120 and UNESCO, "The Céide Fields and North West Mayo Boglands" UNESCO. [Accessed 7 July 2022].
101 Goring-Morris A and Belfer-cohen A, Neolithization Processes in the Levant: The outer envelope; Current Anthropology 2011 Vol 52, No S4 pp S195-S208, and Baird et al, Agricultural Origins on the Anatolian Plateau 2018; PNAS, Vol 115, No 14, E3077-E3086.
102 Denham et al Horticultural experimentation in Northern Australia reconsidered 2015 Antiquity 83 (DO 10.1017/S0003598X00098884).
103 Stanley Graham Brade-Birks, Good Soil: Teach Yourself Farming, Hodder & Stoughton 1944.
104 Laffan et al *Some Properties of Soils on Sandstone, Granite, Dolerite in relation to dry and wet Eucalypt forest types in Northern Tasmania* Tas Forests Vol 10 1998, 49-58.
105 O'Connell M and Molloy K, Farming and woodland dynamics in Ireland during the Neolithic, Biology and Environment Proceedings of the Royal Irish Academy 2001 Vol 101B No1-2, 99-120 and UNESCO, "The Céide Fields and North West Mayo Boglands". *whc.unesco.org*. UNESCO. Retrieved 7 July 2022.
106 Ibid.
107 Ibid.
108 McGosh, FWJ *Boussingault Chemist and Agriculturalist* 1984 Reidel Publishing Company.
109 Sir Humphrey Davy, *Elements of Agricultural Chemistry 1813* – 6th edition 1839.
110 Ibid, page 282.
111 McGosh, FWJ *Boussingault Chemist and Agriculturalist* 1984 Reidel Publishing Company.
112 Ibid, page 81.
113 Ibid.
114 Denham et al *Horticultural experimentation in Northern Australia reconsidered* 2015 Antiquity 83 (DO 10.1017/S0003598X00098884).
115 David Collins, An Account of the English Colony in New South Wales 1910 edition edited by James Collier Published by Whitcombe and Tombs Ltd.
116 Ibid and Charles Sturt Two expeditions into the Interior of Southern Australia 1833.
117 John Oxley, Journals of Two Expeditions Into the Interior of New South Wales London, 1820.
118 Charles Sturt, Two expeditions into the Interior of Southern Australia 1833 page liv-lv Volume 1.
119 Atkinson *Account of the State of Agriculture and Grazing in New South Wales* London 1826.
120 Ibid.
121 Ibid and Pawel Strzelecki Physical Description of New South Wales and Van Diemen's Land Longman; Brown; Green; and Longmans; London 1845.
122 Strzelecki, Ibid.
123 Strzelecki, Ibid p 348 and 340.
124 Parliamentary Papers of the Legislative Council of New South Wales 5 October 1853, Cited in Strzelecki *The Discovery of Gold and Silver in Australia* London 1856 printed by Spottinswoode& Co., New-Street-Squre. Available from https://nla.gov.au/nla.obj-70909594/view?partId=nla.obj-70912746#page/n5/mode/1up [Accessed 5 July 2022].
125 'Report by Count Streleski. Appendix C in Despatch from Sir G. Gipps . . . to the

Secretary for the Colonies..', Great Britain & Ireland Parliament, House of Commons paper 120, 9 March 1841 as cited by Organ, Michael K.: W.B. Clarke as Scientific Journalist 1992: https://ro.uow.edu.au/asdpapers/99.

126 Strezelecki *The Discovery of Gold and Silver in Australia* London 1856 printed by Spottiswoode& Co., New-Street-Square. Available from https://nla.gov.au/nla.obj-70909594/view?partId=nla.obj-70912746#page/n5/mode/1up [Accessed 5 July 2022].

127 Charley Tarra By Keith Vincent Smith 1 November 2017, Eora People, https://www.eorapeople.com.au/uncategorized/charlie-tarra/ [Accessed 01 July 2022]

128 Gray J, Bishop T and Wilson B, 'Factors controlling soil organic carbon stocks with depth in Eastern Australia', 2015, Soil Sci. Soc. Am. J. 79:1741-1751, doi:10.2136/sssaj2015.06.0224.

129 Pawel Strzelecki Physical Description of New South Wales and Van Diemen's Land Longman; Brown; Green; and Longmans; London 1845, p 215. []

130 Ibid, p 219.

131 Ibid, p 227.

132 Ibid, p226.

133 Ibid, p 258.

134 Ibid, p 361.

135 Ibid, p 431-432.

136 Ibid, p 433.

137 Ibid, p 226 and 433.

138 Ibid, p 435.

139 Ibid, p 226.

140 Beresford Q, 2021, Wounded Country: The Murray-Darling Basin, a contested history, New South Publishing, Sydney, Australia.

141 Ibid

142 Soils and Soil Management by A F Gustafson, 1941, Publ McGraw Hill; Farm Soils; Their management and fertilisation Worthen E 1927 Wiley Farm Series; The study of the soil in the field Clarke G1936, Oxford University Press; The rape of the earth: a world survey of soil erosion Jacks G and Whyte R 1939 Faber and Faber, Stanley Graham Brade-Birks, Good Soil: Teach Yourself Farming, Hodder & Stoughton 1944

143 G.V. Jacks and R.O. Whyte, Rape of the Earth: A world survey of soil erosion Faber 1944.

144 Lowdermilk W C *Conquest of land through 7000 years*, US Government Printing Office 1953.

145 Professor Hillel *Out of the Earth: Civilisation and the life of the soil* University of California Press 1992.

146 Pielke Sr. R, 2001, 'Influence of the spatial distribution of vegetation and soils on the prediction of Cumulus convective rainfall', Review of Geophysics, 39, 2, May 2001, p151-177 and Ing. Michal Kravčík M et al, Water for the Recovery of the Climate - A New Water Paradigm, Municipalia a.s. and TORY Consulting a.s.2007; English translation by David McLean and Jonathan Gresty. Available from: http://www.waterparadigm.org/download/Water_for_the_Recovery_of_the_Climate_A_New_Water_Paradigm.pdf [Date accessed: 29 October 2020]

147 McAlpine C et al, Climate change and land clearing: a short note, Australian Zoologist Vol 35 (2) 2010.
148 Mahmood R et al, Impacts of landuse/landcover change on climate and future research priorities; American Meteorologist Society 91, 1, Jan 2010, 36-47.
149 Míchal, I, 1994, Ecologická stabilita. Veronika and Ministry of the Environment of the Czech Republic, Brno, p 217.
150 Pielke, Sr R, Adegoke J, Chase T, Marshall C, Matsui T, Niyopi D, 'A new paradigm for assessing the role of agriculture in the climate system and in climate change', *Agricultural and Forest Meteorology*, 234–54.
151 Derrick, Jim (1992), 'Alternate farming systems for the Riverina.' Conference Papers Bridging the gap between the philosophies of organic farming and conservation farming 21st Riverina Outlook Conference.
152 Vertessy, R et al, 'Independent assessment of the 2018-2019 fish deaths in the Darling River' Final Report 29 March 2019.
153 Kellet, Mark, *This Continent of Smoke: Fire and the Australian Bush*, Australian Heritage Autumn 2008 No 10, 63-70.
154 Pascoe, Bruce, Introduction Comments; Panel discussion: Bushfires, Indigenous land management and carbon farming, Part 2, Wednesday, 26 May 2021; Norton Rose, Fulbright, Brisbane, Australia.
155 Mariani, M et al 'Disruption of cultural burning promotes shrub encroachment and unprecedented wildfires' *Frontiers in Ecology & Environment* 2022; DOI;10, 1002/FEE.2395
156 Forest Fire Management Victoria, 'Past Bushfires: A chronology of major bushfires from 1851 to present.' Available from: https://www.ffm.vic.gov.au/history-and-incidents/past-bushfires [Accessed 01/07/2021].
157 ABC *Science Show*, Radio National, 'Smarter irrigation keeps Adelaide's parks greener and cooler' 15 May 2021
158 Bradshaw, Laura D, Padgette, S, Kimball, S, & Wells, Barbara H, (1997). 'Perspectives on Glyphosate Resistance', *Weed Technology, 11* (1), 189–98. Retrieved June 10, 2021, from http://www.jstor.org/stable/3988252
159 Shaner D, Lindenmeyer R, Ostlie M, 'What have the mechanisms of resistance to glyphosate taught us, surely?' *Pest Management Science* 2012, 68, 3-9; and Sammons R and Gaines T 2014 Pest Management Science 70:1367-1377.
160 Intergovernmental Panel on Climate Change (2019), *The Special Report on climate change, desertification, land degradation, sustainable land management, food security, and greenhouse gas fluxes in terrestrial ecosystems*, P R Shukla, J Skea & anor, p 53.
161 Burkitt L, et al, 2007 Comparing irrigated biodynamic and conventionally managed dairy farms;Soil and pasture properties; *Australian Journal of Experimental Agriculture*, 2007, 47, 479–488.
162 Savory, Allan, *Holistic Resource Management* 1988 Island Pr.
163 Jackson, Wes *Becoming Native to this Place*, University Press of Kentucky, 1993.
164 Salatin, Joe *Pastured Poultry Profits*, Polyface Farm, VA 1993.
165 Brown, Gabe *Dirt to Soil: One Family's Journey Into Regenerative Agriculture*, Chelsea Green Hartford VT, 2018. And Mark Shepard *Restoration Agriculture: Real-world permaculture for farmers,* Acres, Greely, CO.
166 Shepard, Mark, *Restoration Agriculture: Real-world permaculture for farmers,* Acres, Greely, CO.

167 Rebanks, James, *English Pastoral An inheritance,* Allen Lane, London, 2020.
168 Massy, Charles *Call of the Reed Warbler: A new agriculture, a new Earth,* University of Queensland Press, 2017.
169 Soils For Life Foundation, available at: https://soilsforlife.org.au/programs/case-studies/case-studies-round-1/ [Accessed 29/10/2020].
170 Hannah Gosnell, Nicholas Gill and Michelle Voyer, 'Transformational adaptation on the farm: processes of change and persistence in transitions to "climate-smart" regenerative agriculture', *Global Environmental Change*, Vol 59, November 2019. Available from: https://doi.org/10.1016/j.gloenvcha.2019.101965 [Accessed 29/10/2020]; and Stephen Burns, *Regenerative agriculture is an uncommon journey,* 11 December 2019, *The Land.* Available from: https://www.theland.com.au/story/6537134/regenerative-agriculture-is-an-uncommon-journey/ [Accessed 29/10/2020].
171 Melissa Pouliot, 'Prospect for a new agriculture', *VicNoTill*, 26 June 2019. Available from: https://www.vicnotill.com.au/2019/06/prospect-for-a-new-agriculture-natural-intelligence-farming Retreived October 29, 2020.
172 *Soils for Life 'Beetaloo Station*: first add water', Regenerative Agriculture Case Study. Available from: https://soilsforlife.org.au/beetaloo-station-first-add-water-2/ Retreived October 29, 2020.
173 Shan Goodwin, 'Microsoft buys carbon credits from NSW cattle operation' *The Land* 29 January 2021. Available online: https://www.theland.com.au/story/7106034/microsoft-buys-carbon-credits-from-nsw-cattle-operation/ [Accessed 05/07/2021].
174 Simmons, A *et al*, 'US scheme used by Australian Farmers reveal the dangers of trading soil carbon to tackle climate change', *The Conversation* 28 June 2021: https://theconversation.com/us-scheme-used-by-australian-farmers-reveals-the-dangers-of-trading-soil-carbon-to-tackle-climate-change-161358
175 Colodan: A Regenerative Agriculture Case Study Soils For Life, Soils for Life. https://soilsforlife.org.au/colodan/ [Accessed 7 July 2021].
176 United Nations Climate Change, Key Aspects of the Paris Agreement https://cop23.unfccc.int/process-and-meetings/the-paris-agreement/the-paris-agreement/key-aspects-of-the-paris-agreement [accessed 4 July 2021].
177 Section 22, 27 and Division 5 of the *Carbon Credits (Carbon Farming Initiative) Act 2011*.
178 Part 2 of the *Carbon Credits (Carbon Farming Initiative— Measurement of Soil Carbon Sequestration in Agricultural Systems) Methodology Determination 2018*.
179 Dooley, Kate 'Climate of stagnation: The EU seizes the green agenda' *Griffith Review* 69. Available online: https://www.griffithreview.com/articles/climate-of-stagnation/ [Accessed 01/11/2020].
180 Gammage, Bill, *The Biggest Estate on Earth: How Aborigines Made Australia* Allen and Unwin, Sydney, 2012
181 Respectively, *Soil Conservation Act 1938* (NSW), *Soil Conservation Act 1939* (SA) and the *Soil and Land Conservation Act 1945* (WA). The WA Act remains in force today.
182 Dumsday, Robert, and Anthony Chisholm, *Land Degradation: Problems and Policies,* Cambridge University Press 1987.
183 State Collaborative Soil Conservation Study 1978.
184 United Nations Treaty Collection https://treaties.un.org/Pages/ViewDetails.aspx?src=TREATY&mtdsg_no=XXVII-10&chapter=27&clang=_en [Accessed 06/07/21].
185 *The National Soil Research, Development and Extension Strategy, Securing Australia's Soil, For profitable industries and healthy landscapes* Commonwealth of Australia 2014.

186   Prime Minister Scott Morrison address, *Daily Telegraph* Bush Summit 18 July 2019 Dubbo. Available from: https://www.pm.gov.au/media/address-daily-telegraph-bush-summit [Accessed 29/10/2020].
187   NSW: https://www.environment.nsw.gov.au/topics/land-and-soil/information/soil-maps [Accessed 29/10/2020].
Qld: https://www.qld.gov.au/environment/land/management/soil/soil-testing/types [Accessed 29/10/2020].
Tas: Soil Maps of Tasmania and Modelled Land Capability Maps through Department of Primary Industries, Water and Environment (DPIWE): https://dpipwe.tas.gov.au/agriculture/land-management-and-soils/land-and-soil-resource-assessment/land-capability/modelled-land-capability-maps [Accessed 29/10/2020].
SA: https://www.environment.sa.gov.au/Knowledge_Bank/Information_data/soil-and-land/mapping-soil-and-land [Accessed 29/10/2020].
NT: https://denr.nt.gov.au/rangelands/information-and-requests/land-soil-vegetation-information [Accessed 29/10/2020].
188   Miles, Greg *The Flame of Convenience* 2020 ISBN: 978-1-922452-67-2
189   NSW Government 'State of the catchments 2010: Soil condition – Technical report series', 2011 State of NSW and Office of Environment and Heritage. Available from: https://www.environment.nsw.gov.au/-/media/OEH/Corporate-Site/Documents/Land-and-soil/assessing-condition-soils-nsw.pdf [Accessed 29/10/2020].
190   Western Australian Auditor General's Report, *Management of Pastoral Lands in Western Australia* October 2017. Available from: https://www.parliament.wa.gov.au/publications/tabledpapers.nsf/displaypaper/4010833a47ac7e4cc25e5b46482581b600166282/$file/833.pdf [accessed 13 November 2020].
191   Professor Will Steffen and Dr Annika Dean, *Land Clearing & Climate Change: Risks & opportunities in the Sunshine State* 2018 Climate Council of Australia Limited. Available from: https://www.climatecouncil.org.au/uploads/c1e786d5d0fe4c4bc1b91fc200cbaec8.pdf. [Accessed 05/12/2020].
192   NSW Environment, Energy and Science Department of Planning, Industry and Environment, Woody vegetation change, Statewide Landcover and Tree Study 2021, Figure 1. Available from: https://www.environment.nsw.gov.au/research-and-publications/publications-search/woody-vegetation-change-statewide-landcover-tree-study-summary-report-2019 [Accessed 01/07/2021].
193   Dooley, Kate 'Climate of stagnation: The EU seizes the green agenda' *Griffith Review* 69. Available online: https://www.griffithreview.com/articles/climate-of-stagnation/ [Accessed 01/11/2020].
194   EPBC Act Section 522A (2).
195   Australian Bureau of Statistics, Australian Environmental Economic Accounts No. 4655.0, Canberra, 2014.
196   Australian Bureau of Statistics, Land Management and Farming in Australia No. 4627.0, Canberra, 2016.
197   Australian Bureau of Statistics, Australian System of National Accounts No. 5204.0, Canberra, 2016.
198   Craik, W, Review of interactions between the EPBC Act and the agriculture sector. Independent report prepared for the Commonwealth Department of the Environment and Energy Aither Pty Ltd, 2018: https://www.environment.gov.au/epbc/ publications/review-interactions-epbc-act-agriculture-final-report [Accessed 29/10/20].

199 Craik, W, Review of interactions between the EPBC Act and the agriculture sector. Independent report prepared for the Commonwealth Department of the Environment and Energy Aither Pty Ltd, 2018: https://www.environment.gov.au/epbc/ publications/ review-interactions-epbc-act-agriculture-final-report [Accessed 29/10/20].
200 Craik, W, Review of interactions between the EPBC Act and the agriculture sector. Independent report prepared for the Commonwealth Department of the Environment and Energy Aither Pty Ltd, 2018: https://www.environment.gov.au/epbc/ publications/ review-interactions-epbc-act-agriculture-final-report [Accessed 29/10/20].
201 Section 68 EPBC Act.
202 [2019] NTSC 69.
203 Hannam, Peter, 'Proposed environment standards fall far short of recommendations', *Sydney Morning Herald*, 11 February 2021: https://www.smh.com.au/ environment/ conservation/proposed-environment-standards-fall-far-short-of-recommendations-20210211-p571k5.html [Accessed 20 February 2021].
204 Final Report page 204.
205 Tarkine National Coalition Incorporated v Minister for the Environment and Others [2015] FCAFC 89
206 Department of Agriculture, Water and the Environment, 'Proposed timeline for EPBC Act reform': https://www.environment.gov.au/epbc/publications/ proposed-timeline-for-epbc-act-reforms
207 PM Scott Morrison, Address, National Press Club, Canberra, 29 January 2020: https:// www.pm.gov.au/media/address-national-press-club [Accessed 29/10/2020].
208 Intergovernmental Panel on Climate Change 2019: *The Special Report on climate change, desertification, land degradation, sustainable land management, food security, and greenhouse gas fluxes in terrestrial ecosystems*, P.R. Shukla, J Skea & anor, page 51.
209 John McLean Bennett et al, 'Soil Security for Australia', *Sustainability* 2019, 3416.
210 mirrigation.com.au/ArticleDocuments/213/MI_ANNUAL%20REPORT_DOCUMENT_2020.pdf.aspx?embed=Y
211 Final report p 143, quoting Ward A Lassen M (2018) Scoping Paper: Expanding Finance Opportunities to Support Private Land Conservation in Australia, Australian Land Conservation Alliance, Trust For Nature.
212 EPBC Final Report quoting Ward A Lassen M (2018) Scoping Paper: Expanding Finance Opportunities to Support Private Land Conservation in Australia, Australian Land Conservation Alliance, Trust For Nature.
213 Commonwealth Government Agriculture Stewardship Package https://www.agriculture. gov.au/ag-farm-food/natural-resources/landcare/sustaining-future-australian-farming [Accessed 2/12/2020]
214 Mike Foley 'World-first biodiversity scheme could help farmers cash in' *Sydney Morning Herald* 24 May 2020. Available online: https://www.smh.com.au/politics/federal/world-first-biodiversity-scheme-could-help-farmers-cash-in-20200522-p54vla.html [Accessed 2/12/2020]
215 Nick O'Malley 'Farming and conservation groups call for $4b post-pandemic jobs boost' *Sydney Morning Herald* 3 April 2020. Available from: https://www.smh.com.au/ environment/conservation/farming-and-conservation-groups-call-for-4b-post-pandemic-jobs-boost-20200402-p54gjc.html [Accessed on 6 December 2020].
216 Ernst & Young Report to Conservation Council of South Australia *Delivering economic stimulus through the conservation and land management sector* 25 June 2020 http://

nrmregionsaustralia.com.au/wp-content/uploads/2020/07/Economic_impact_of_the_conservation_and_land_management_stimulus_proposal_EY_Report_25_June_2_.pdf [Accessed 6/12/2020]

217 National Farmers Federation *2030 Roadmap: Australian Agriculture's Plan for a $100 Billion Industry* 2020. Available from: https://nff.org.au/wp-content/uploads/2020/02/NFF_Roadmap_2030_FINAL.pdf [Accessed 20/12/2020].
Australian Government, Department of Agriculture, Water and the Environment, *Delivering Ag2030* October 2020. Available from: https://www.agriculture.gov.au/sites/default/files/documents/delivering-ag2030.pdf [Accessed 20/12/2020].

218 National Farmers Federation *2030 Roadmap: Australian Agriculture's Plan for a $100 Billion Industry* 2020, page 43. Available from: https://nff.org.au/wp-content/uploads/2020/02/NFF_Roadmap_2030_FINAL.pdf [Accessed 20/12/2020].

219 National Farmers Federation *2030 Roadmap: Australian Agriculture's Plan for a $100 Billion Industry* 2020, p 27. Available from: https://nff.org.au/wp-content/uploads/2020/02/NFF_Roadmap_2030_FINAL.pdf [Accessed 20/12/2020].

220 Hughes-d'Aeth, Friday Essay: 'Dark Emu and the blindness of Australian Agriculture', *The Conversation*, 14 June 2018.

221 Fitzpatrick R W, Powell B & Marvanek S, 'Coastal Acid Sulfate Soils: National Atlas and Future Scenarios', *Coast to Coast* 2006: Australia's National Coastal Conference, May 22-25 2006, Melbourne, viewed 23 October 2007.

222 Bennett, John McLean et al, 'Soil Security for Australia', Sustainability 2019, 3416, 2.

223 Alemu 2016; Altieri and Nicholls 2017.

224 White Paper on Developing Northern Australia – Our North, Our Future Commonwealth of Australia 2015. Available from: https://www.industry.gov.au/data-and-publica tions/our-north-our-future-white-paper-on-developing-northern-australia [Accessed 29/10/2020].

225 Hannam, Peter, 'Proposed environment standards fall far short of recommendations' Sydney Morning Herald, 11 February 2021. Available from: https://www.smh.com.au/environment/conservation/proposed-environment-standards-fall-far-short-of-recommendations-20210211-p571k5.html [Accessed 26/01/2021].

226 Gardening Australia Series 30 Episode 1, Published: Fri 1 Feb 2019, 8:00pm: Food Scrap Friday – Fact Sheets – Gardening Australia – GARDENING AUSTRALIA (abc.net.au)

227 The Land 6 April 2021.

228 Australian Farm Institute Recognising On-farm Biodiversity Management, July 2020, p 1. Available from: https://nff.org.au/wp-content/uploads/2020/11/Recognising-on farm-biodiversity management_AFI_Aug2020.pdf [Accessed 06/12/2020]. Derrick J, (1992) Alternative farm systems for the Riverina http://www.regional.org.au/au/roc/1992/roc1992005.htm; Burkitt 1, Small D, McDonald J, Wales W and Jenkin M, 2007, 'Comparing irrigated biodynamic and conventional dairy farms 1: Soil and Pasture prop erties'. Australian Journal of Experimental Agriculture 47(5) 479–488.

229 David Bauman et al, *Tropical tree mortality has increased with rising atmospheric water stress*, Nature (2022); https://doi.org/10.1038/s41586-022-04737-7 [Accessed 03/06/22]

230 English translation by David McLean and Jonathan Gresty. Available from: http://www.waterparadigm.org/download/Water_for_the_Recovery_of_the_Climate_A_New_Water_Paradigm.pdf [Accessed 08/06/2021].

231 Indian Ocean Climate Initiative (2002) 'Climate variability and change in south west Western Australia', Dept Environment Water and Catchment Protection WA State Govt.
232 Willis, Paul T; Frank Marks; John Gottschalck (2006). 'Rain Drop Size Distributions and Radar Rain Measurements in South Florida'. Available from: https://www.aoml.noaa.gov/hrd/FlBay/florida_bay_99.html [Accessed 29/11/2020].
233 Willis, Paul T; Frank Marks; John Gottschalck (2006) 'Rain Drop Size Distributions and Radar Rain Measurements in South Florida'. Available from: https://www.aoml.noaa.gov/hrd/FlBay/florida_bay_99.html [Accessed 29/11/2020]
234 Bureau of Meteorology, *State of Climate* 2020. Available from: http://www.bom.gov.au/state-of-the-climate/2020/State-of-the-Climate-2020.pdf .
235 Elseveir Publishing:2002 Climate variability and change in south west Western Australia, Dept of Environment Water and Catchment Protection, Western Australia
236 Steffen, Will and Annika Dean, *Land Clearing & Climate Change: Risks & opportunities in the Sunshine State,* 2018 Climate Council of Australia Limited, On p 4, Available at: c1e786d5d0fe4c4bc1b91fc200cbaec8.pdf (climatecouncil.org.au) Accessed 08/05/2021
237 Bob Berwyn, 'Many Scientists now say global warming could stop relatively quickly as emissions go to zero', *Inside Climate News* 03012021, 2021 https://insideclimatenews.org/news/03012021/five-aspects-climate-change-2020/

Acronyms and Abbreviations

AAS	Acid Sulfate Soils
ACCU	Australian Carbon Credit Unit
BCE	Before the Common Era
BOOT	Better Off Overall Test
C/N/P/S	Carbon/nitrogen/phosphorous/sulfur
Carbon Credits Act	*Carbon Credits Act Carbon Credits (Carbon Farming Initiative) Act 2011*
CO_2	carbon dioxide
COAG	Council of Australian Governments
CoP21	Conference of the Parties
CSIRO	Commonwealth Scientific, Industrial & Research Org
Cth	Commonwealth (law)
EPBC	Environmental Protection & Biodiversity Conservation Act
ESD	Ecologically Sustainable Development
Excess Till	crop sown in soil disturbed by plow, scarifier etc
GED	General Environmental Duty
GHG	Greenhouse Gas
GIS	Geographical Information System
GRDC	Grains Research & Development Corporation
Ha/ha	hectare = 0.01 km2 = 2.47 acres
IGAE	Inter-governmental Agreement on the Environment
IOCI	Indian Ocean Climate Initiative
IPCC	Intergovernmental Panel on Climate Change
LCC	Land Cover Change
M&LA	Meat and Livestock Australia Ltd
MAP	Mono-Ammonium Phosphate
MER	Monitoring, Evaluation & Reporting

MIA	Murrumbidgee Irrigation Area
MNES	Matter of National Environmental Significance
NASA	National Aeronautical and Space Administration
NDC	Nationally Determined Contribution
No Till	crop sown directly in undisturbed soil
NOAA	National Oceanic and Atmospheric Administration
NSW	New South Wales
NT	Northern Territory
NZ	New Zealand
PASS	Potential Acid Sulfate Soils
PAW	Plant Available Water
Pg	petagram = 1000 million tonnes = 10^{12} kg
Qld	Queensland
SA	South Australia
SLCF	Short-Lived Climate Forcer
SLM	Sustainable Land Management
Soil Carbon Methodology Determination	*Carbon Credits (Carbon Farming Initiative – Measurement of Soil Carbon Sequestration in Agricultural Systems) Methodology Determination 2018*
SRCCL	IPCC Special Report on Climate Change and Land
SWWA	South west Western Australia
Tas	Tasmania
UN	United Nations
UNCCD	UN Convention to Combat Desertification
UNFCCC	UN Framework Convention on Climate Change
Vic	Victoria
WA	Western Australia
WALFA	West Arnhem Land Fire Abatement
WANTFA	WA No Till Farming Association